IN THE AGE OF PROSE

IN THE AGE OF PROSE

Literary and philosophical essays

ERICH HELLER

CAMBRIDGE UNIVERSITY PRESS

Cambridge

London   New York   New Rochelle
Melbourne   Sydney

Published by the Press Syndicate of the University of Cambridge
The Pitt Building, Trumpington Street, Cambridge CB2 IRP
32 East 57th Street, New York, NY 10022, USA
296 Beaconsfield Parade, Middle Park, Melbourne 3206, Australia

© Cambridge University Press 1984

First published 1984

Printed in Great Britain by Redwood Burn Ltd., Trowbridge
Library of Congress catalogue card number: 83–7680

British Library Cataloguing in Publication Data
Heller, Erich
In the age of prose
1. German literature – 18th century – History and
criticism 2. German literature – 19th century
– History and criticism 3. German literature
– 20th century – History and criticism
I. Title
830'.9   PT236
ISBN 0 521 25493 0 hard covers
ISBN 0 521 27495 8 paperback

FOR PAUL AND LIESE HELLER

CONTENTS

Acknowledgments ix

Preface xi

1 The poet in the age of prose: reflections on Hegel's
 Aesthetics and Rilke's *Duino Elegies* 1

2 The broken tradition: an address 21

3 Nietzsche's last words about art and truth 43

4 Thinking about poetry, Hölderlin and Heidegger 63

5 Karl Kraus 85

6 Literature and political responsibility: apropos the
 letters of Thomas Mann 105

7 The taking back of the Ninth Symphony: reflections
 on Thomas Mann's *Doctor Faustus* 127

8 Thomas Mann's diaries and the search for identity 149

9 Knut Hamsun 163

10 Observations on psychoanalysis and modern
 literature 177

11 The dismantling of a marionette theatre; or,
 psychology and the misinterpretation of literature 193

12 Man ashamed 215

13 Theodor Fontane: the extraordinary education of a
 Prussian apothecary 233

14 The little world of Wilhelm Busch 251

ACKNOWLEDGMENTS

The author and publisher would like to thank the following for their permission to reprint material in this volume: the editor of *The Monist*, for 'The poet in the age of prose: reflections on Hegel's *Aesthetics* and Rilke's *Duino Elegies*', from *The Monist*, vol. 63, no. 4, October 1980; Max Niemeyer Verlag for 'Thinking about poetry, Hölderlin and Heidegger' from *Herkommen und Erneuerung: Festschrift für Oskar Seidlin*, ed. G. Gillespie and E. Lohner, Tübingen 1976, pp. 168–84; the editor of *The New York Review of Books* for 'Karl Kraus' from *NYRB*, vol. 20, no. 7, 3 May 1973, copyright © 1973 Nyrev, Inc.; the editor of *Commentary* for 'Literature and political responsibility' from *Commentary*, vol. 52, no. 1, July 1971: the editor of *The New Republic*, for 'Knut Hamsun' from *The New Republic*, 2 and 9 August 1980 and 'Thomas Mann's diaries and the search for identity' from *The New Republic*, 21 February 1983; Yale University Press for 'Observations on psychoanalysis and modern literature' from *Psychiatry and the Humanities*, vol. 1, 1976; The University of Chicago Press for 'The dismantling of a Marionette Theatre; or, psychology and misinterpretation of literature' from *Critical Inquiry*, vol. 4, no. 3, Spring 1978; the editor of *Psychiatry* for 'Man ashamed' from *Psychiatry*, vol. 34, no. 2, May 1974; the editor of *The Times Literary Supplement* for 'Theodor Fontane: the extraordinary education of a Prussian apothecary' from *TLS*, 20 October 1978, and for 'The little world of Wilhelm Busch' from *TLS*, 7 October 1977; Michael Hamburger for his translation of 'Hälfte des Lebens' by Hölderlin which appears on p. 70; and the Württembergische Landesbibliothek for the illustration which appears on p. 72.

'The broken tradition', in a shortened version, was delivered as a lecture at the 1981 autumn assembly of the German Academy for Language and Literature in Darmstadt. 'Nietzsche's last words about art and truth' have been printed privately by The Enigma Press, Mt. Pleasant, Michigan 1981.

PREFACE

I would, of course, like to think that the friends, listeners and readers were right in urging me over the years to gather the following essays and lectures into a book. Here, then, it is, more conveniently accessible than the various journals or anthologies where these pieces – some of them enlarged now or otherwise edited – originally appeared.

I have called the volume 'In the Age of Prose' – 'The poet in the age of prose' is the title of one of the essays – because all its chapters are concerned, in one way or another, with the fate of art, literature and thought in an epoch that is dominated by prose; and prose, as the title essay puts it, 'implies not merely a manner of writing, but a style of comprehension'. This means that the poetic (the word denoting more than simply poetry) has been assigned a kind of Cinderella role – with the fairy tale's happy ending unhappily in suspense.

It is, perhaps, unfortunate that it was Hegel, in his *Lectures on Aesthetics*, who allotted to this development a most important place in his panorama of history – unfortunate for me who is not only no Hegelian but highly critical of the philosopher's notion of historical inevitability. Yet it is, I think, impossible not to make perfect sense of Hegel's diagnosis and brilliant description of the 'age of prose' – his age and in this respect still ours – when 'poetry finds itself involved everywhere in manifold difficulties' to the point of having to struggle for its survival by melting down and then pouring the prosaic matter that constitutes our reality into very different moulds. Indeed, it has to do so even with the very stuff on which it lives: language. If poetry was still to win victories in the age of prose, it had to discover, and take possession of, new lands of the verbal imagination that had not been frozen over yet by the chills of the prosaic. This is what the poet of the *Four Quartets* meant when in the fifth section of 'East Coker' he spoke of the poet's difficult task to recover what has been lost; to assert poetry in unpropitious and 'always deteriorating' linguistic conditions. It would amount to special pleading if I said that this is the theme that all the essays here have in common, but its reverberations are, I am sure, discernible throughout the volume and give it the unity it may modestly claim to possess. I have grown so allergic to words like 'Rilke-Forschung' or 'Kafka scholarship' that I was rather negligent in providing references, a rather tiresome way of proving one's 'scholarliness'; but partly also because of my – possibly overambitious – wish that these essays should be read as essays rather than be looked upon as sources of learned information.

If I were to list all the providers of assistance I have had in publishing these essays – that most enlivening help that is given by intelligent response and criticism – I would have to produce a long register of names. Although I cannot do that, I beg them to be sure of my gratitude. But I must mention my student Gregory Maertz without whose energetic initiative this collection would never have been assembled, and David Relkin whose alert and witty intelligence transformed the tedious business of proof-reading into sheer pleasure (which unfortunately is no insurance against persistent errors). The book owes its final form to the perceptive advice of Michael Tanner, Fellow of Corpus Christi College at Cambridge, and to my thoughtful editors at the Cambridge University Press, Jonathan Sinclair-Wilson and Penny Souster.

Spring 1983   E.H.
Northwestern University
Evanston, Illinois

I
The poet in the age of prose

reflections on Hegel's *Aesthetics* and
Rilke's *Duino Elegies*

WITH Hegel's observations in his *Lectures on Aesthetics*, on the difference between the *epic* poetry of the ancients and the *novel* as the dominant literary form of the present, we are at the centre of these meditations. The great epic poems of antiquity, Homer's *Iliad* and *Odyssey*, for instance, or Virgil's *Aeneid*, not only reflect the minds of certain poets; they are, at the same time, as are all great literary works, recognizable as the product of an age; and the age of Homer, the age of epic poetry, Hegel characterizes as a 'fundamentally poetic state of the world', that is, a world in which poetry is not merely written, but, as it were, lived. The active intervention and participation of gods in the lives of mortals; groves and springs and hills as the habitats of nymphs and fauns; the poetic comprehension of life was at that time not a matter of the poetic imagination at work in the minds of a few chosen individuals, of artists whose successors, much later in history, more often that not lamented their separation from their contemporary surroundings, but was 'natural', a matter of fact, of ways of thinking and feeling shared by the whole community. It is not absurd to say that in such a world *our* distinctions between imagination and fact were of little importance, if not unknown. It is this that led the young Nietzsche to accuse the first great analytical rationalist of Greece, Socrates, the indefatigable questioner, of having destroyed mythology (or what now goes by that name), of having helped to bring about the end of tragedy, indeed, of Greek art.

But back to Hegel: of his own epoch he said that it was the age of prose, and in this respect it certainly is still ours. The age of prose: this meant for him that prose had become the ruling mode of perception. Understanding is prosaic understanding. Our science is, or course, written in prose, and this implies not merely a manner of writing, but a style of comprehension, and prose is our psychology, our economics, our sociology — all our efforts intelligently to grasp the nature of the world.

For Hegel all articulate religious beliefs of the past, Greek mythology, for instance, are part and parcel of a poetic understanding of the world although the purified religion of the future would be, he asserted, beyond any kind of truth that can manifest itself entirely in images, or in works of art. Still, with regard to the past and the present he distinguishes between 'two spheres of human consciousness: Poetry and Prose'. Yes, of course, he was what Jacob Burckhardt called him, a *'terrible simplificateur'* of history: the world of the ancients was 'poetic', the modern world is 'prosaic'. Clearly, it would be pointless even to try to prove that there was a great deal of prose in the 'age of poetry' and that there is a great deal of poetry in the 'age of prose'. For Hegel's distinction is not a technical one: it is concerned with modes of perception, universes of understanding. It is not a question of more or better poetry being written in an age of poetry; what Hegel means are different coinages of the mind, different currencies by which we pay for our attempts to understand the world. It is, therefore, an understatement within his incomparably more comprehensive historical statement when he says of poetry as an art that, in the poetic age, it has 'an easier life' than in the age of prose. An easier life? Only because Hegel speaks at this point of poetry in a technical sense. Obviously, the poems of Archilochus or Sappho differed from the talk of ordinary Greek people as they conversed on the agora, the market-place; and yet the poetry of the poets was, according to Hegel, merely a more glorious flower of the common soil, related to it as the sunflower is mysteriously related to what looks prosaic enough: the seeds, the roots, the ground from which it grows. An easier life? It is the least that can be said when it comes to distinguishing the nature of Homeric poetry from literature written at a time when, in Hegel's words, 'prose has appropriated to itself everything that is of the mind, and has impressed the stamp of prose upon it'. Once this has happened, poetry, if it survives at all, 'must melt and pour into a fundamentally other mould' the material supplied by reality, in the end even language itself. No wonder that, with such resistance of the prosaic, 'poetry finds itself involved everywhere in manifold difficulties'.

Never mind the intelligently informed or pedantic arguments that can be raised against any such grand historical categorizing: there is no doubt – to choose an activity of the mind other than poetry – that the philosophy of Anaxagoras or Heraclitus is closer to the poetic mode than to the philosophizing of Kant or Locke; and no doubt whatever that the novels of Stendhal are not only written in prose, but are, *therefore*, representative of the nineteenth century just as the epic poetry of Homer stands for a form of writing irrevocably of an age long past.

After the mythological crystallizations of ancient art – or, for that matter, the art of the Middle Ages – the modern novel is abundantly more 'interesting' because it has discovered the 'interestingness' of things that apparently were of no interest to the ancient poet or, it is to be assumed, his public: the nuances of love or love-making, the shades of greed or jealousy or envy that determine human relationships, the subtle subterfuges and self-deceptions, the infinite variety of objects with which man has surrounded himself. It is, then, in radical opposition to the Homeric epic that Hegel judges the modern novel: it is often superbly successful in revealing an entire world through many details of individual characters and their interactions, through their varied responses to the events they bring about or to which they become victims, through the fine delineations of things and the manifold impressions they make on different kinds of people. Yet, because the novel presupposes, as Hegel puts it, a 'prosaic world order', it unavoidably lacks the poetic condition that could only be supplied by a world that is, or that is felt to be, poetic at its very core. And if the novel, nonetheless, is successful in occasionally creating *poetic* effects, this is due, as Hegel says, above all to the collisions between 'the poetry of the heart' and the inexorable prose of the external sphere. No doubt, in saying this, Hegel, like the early German Romantics, for instance Novalis, thought of Goethe's great prose works, his novels, above all his *Wilhelm Meister*. Still, it is amazing how far this conflict between 'the heart' and 'the circumstances', between 'within' and 'without' will take us – as far as Rilke's radical withdrawal, in the *Duino Elegies*, from the external sphere: 'Nowhere will world exist but within.' Rilke did not know Hegel's *Lectures on Aesthetics* but he knew or divined the character of the world in which he lived and in which, sometimes desperately, his poetry strove to assert itself as a valid aspect of truth.

The sense of having been born into a wrong age – a sense that, in one form or another, has been uttered by poets writing in the high season of what Hegel called Romanticism, the mode of poetry trying to survive, to assert itself even in the age of prose – has been most succinctly conveyed by Goethe. During his second sojourn in Rome in September 1787, beholding works of Greek sculpture, he wrote: 'Those superlative works of art are superlative works of nature, brought forth by human beings in accordance with true and natural laws. Chance and fancy are gone. What is there, is there of necessity: God wanted it to be like this.' It was, at that time, Goethe's ambition to pursue as an *ideal* what he saw as *nature* in those human creations; and when he denounced most of the artistic productions of his own age as lawless, forced, 'unnatural', he appeared to have done so because they defied what in that passage he called, with rare directness, the will of God. And indeed it would take up more time than we can afford to spend if we were to cite, from the Goethean and post-Goethean epoch, only a select few of the poets' sublime lamentations about the pathology of their spiritual existences in the age of prose. We might begin, perhaps, with Schiller's poem 'The Gods of Greece' that views anything beautiful in the poet's own time as nothing but the dead monument to what was once a *living* truth; or Hölderlin's elegy 'Bread and Wine' that mourns the absence of the gods from the poets' lives – 'But we, my friend, are too late', the gods 'are far above ourselves, away in a different world'; or Keats's 'Sylvan historian' who records a time of poetic beauty that is irremediably lost; or Yeats's forms created by 'Grecian gold-smiths', forms in whose company he desired to be once he was 'out of nature', or what was looked upon as nature in the age of prose; or Rilke's 'Who, if I cried, would hear me among the orders of Angels?'

This is the beginning of the First of the *Duino Elegies*, the cry – in the conditional – of one who indeed felt that he was a native of the age of the novel, that literary form that Hegel had defined as being the representative genre of the prosaic epoch; the cry of a poet who had himself just essayed his only major prose work, *The Notebooks of Malte Laurids Brigge*; the cry that seemed to fall in with Hölderlin's lament, much later than Hölderlin and, there-fore, more timidly and insecurely. Never before has so ambitious, so successful and partly even so great a series of poems about the spiritual condition of man so openly revealed its tentativeness, the helplessness that its author carried into his most audacious assertions by such an abundance of conditionals and subjunctives:

'Who would, if I cried',

... And even if one of the Angels suddenly
pressed me against his heart, I should fade in the strength of his
stronger existence ...

We shall be staying for a while with Rilke's Angel, but not
without first briefly recapitulating the strange history of those
Rilkean lines, and not only because they are a kind of climax to
the long history of the increasing spiritual uncertainty of the arts.
In the years 1907 and 1908 Rilke had published the two volumes
of what he called *New Poems*. They were new, new in substance
and tone and manner, much different from what he had written
before, *The Book of Hours*, for instance, or that *Song of Love and
Death* of the legendary cornet Christoph Rilke, who was a kind
of lyrically and heroically exalted matinee idol of the belated muses
of Romanticism. What, then, was new in the *New Poems*? That
the poet, judging the poetry of individual emotion, of what went
by the name of Neo-Romanticism, exhausted, determined to sing
no longer the songs of his subjective experiences and feelings,
but to try to express the essence of the things themselves, just
as if the things themselves opened their mouths to say what they
were: a panther in its cage, the wind of the nocturnal sea, a fig
tree on a rocky height on Capri, a blue or pink hydrangea, Venice
on a late autumn day. With extraordinary intensity and virtuosity
he sought to carry out a poetic programme that, in 1908, he laid
down in his 'Requiem for a Young Poet', a young man who had
killed himself because of unhappy love. That desperate young poet
had acted so desperately because he was not yet poet enough to
have learned how to survive poetically what humanly had become
unbearable: namely, as that 'Requiem' pronounced with the typi-
cally Rilkean mixture of humility and hubris, by no longer using
words in order to say, like a sick man, where it hurts, but to
build from them, as if from stone, an edifice, much as medieval
stone-masons did, who sank their private selves into 'the equanimity of stone'. That 'Requiem' is, perhaps, too impressive a
poem simply to say of it that it anticipated by nine years the anti-
Romantic dogma of T. S. Eliot's most influential essay 'Tradition
and the Individual Talent'; yet this is exactly what it did.

If Hegel had been as subtle a critic of individual poems as he
was a grand metaphysical historian of the arts, he might have said

of Rilke's *New Poems* that they abound in those paradoxical and superlative qualities that poetry can still achieve against the unrelenting defiance of the prosaic age: they are vigorously rarefied, energetically subtle, vitally decadent. If they were music, they would have to be intoned in sustained *forte dolce*. Achievements of such paradoxical kind, and only such achievements, are still possible after the 'death of art', that is, after it had passed the historical phase in which it had, according to Hegel, fulfilled its 'highest destiny'. The poet, in such a period, has to produce out of his own inner self, not only the poetry, but also, as it were, the climate, the temperature in which it can breathe. No wonder there is something febrile about such works, something terribly exhausting about the labour of producing them. Indeed, these were the conditions of his own self that Rilke, through his double, the young poet Malte Laurids Brigge, poignantly describes in Malte's *Notebooks*. Rilke transcended this situation by the 'violent' deeds, as he himself said, that he had perpetrated with his *New Poems*. He indulged the illusion that fresh poetic enterprises would *easily* succeed now that he had purged his soul and mind by making Malte Laurids Brigge suffer what he himself suffered. But his anxiety continued after the *Notebooks* were published in 1910. It lasted and certainly returned again during the years of the First World War and during the years that, with horrible explosions, followed upon the horrible explosion of 1914.

Yet there came that *dies mirabilis* in January 1912 when inspiration returned and 'the Voice' spoke to him out of the storm that blew from the Adriatic as he walked along the ramparts of Castle Duino, the Voice that, as was revealed ten years later, intended to teach him the great lesson of why such a violent effort had been needed to wrest, in the age of prose, from the 'things' of *New Poems*, from those blue or pink hydrangeas, or those rocks in the moonlight, their poetic essences. It was because the world outside was being progressively deprived of any meaning it had for the inner soul. Not even the apples – though Cézanne could still paint them strenuously with dedicated love – were lovable any more: they now looked and tasted as if they had been produced by machines. Where once there had been houses built to survive centuries, some flimsy structures were run up that seemed to be the embodiments of transience; excogitations of mechanical brains

8

formed avenues of soullessness, and silos, brimful of spiritual emptiness, rose into the sky. The Seventh of the *Duino Elegies*, written in 1922, deplores in this manner the state of the world: 'Und immer geringer schwindet das Aussen', ever more diminishes the substance of the external world, thus justifying to him the momentous insight: 'Nowhere will world exist but within.'

This is what 'the Voice' finally intended to say when on that January day in 1912 it first spoke to the poet, who had spent many months of aridity and barely hopeful waiting. Only ten years after that extraordinary epiphany at Duino the cycle of the ten *Elegies* reached its conclusion. It was in that mysterious, lonely, little castle of Muzot in Switzerland, in the valley of the Rhône. Nothing like the immense productivity of those few February days in 1922 is known in literary history. Their result is not only the complete sequence of the Elegies that have retained the name of Duino, but also the *Sonnets to Orpheus*, with which he believed he celebrated the long-awaited rebirth of the god of song. (Although as the god of *music* he had been the only divinity who, in the age of prose, had not only remained alive but attained to unprecedented glory in the resounding articulations of pure human inwardness.) Nonetheless, the protagonist of the drama of Duino and Muzot is the Angel.

Who is the Angel? If I may paraphrase Rilke's epistolary statements – his letters, more often than not, are the bad prose side of his good poetry – the Angel has to be thought of as the being in whom is *realized* that which emerges from the Elegies as the *task* of man: to transform the doomed external world – doomed not merely through present technologies and future wars, but through the diminution of its spiritual status – into pure inwardness. And this is why the Angel is so terrifying to us: he deprives us of the hope of ever recovering what mistakenly we most desire: happiness within the sphere of the visible, and points to the kind of salvation that we most fear: the salvation that depends on an inner metamorphosis, 'Herzwerk', as Rilke called it in a poem he wrote between the time of Duino and the time of Muzot, 'work of the heart' that aims at the most radical renunciation, a more active renunciation than any monk had ever imposed upon himself.

Rilke's Angel, then, is the last consistent poetic creation – if

9

it can still be called by that term – through which he sought recklessly to transcend the conditions of the age of prose, or even to
resurrect the true spirit of poetry after its demise threatened by
the end of mythology. There can hardly be a more irrelevant or
more trivial response to the *Duino Elegies* than: never mind their
philosophy, or their theology, or their religion; what matters is
their poetry. No. It would do more justice to their grand purpose
to say, in the words of T. S. Eliot's *Four Quartets*: 'The poetry
does not matter.'

Of course, this would be an exaggeration. For the poetry
matters, and matters much: but it matters, above all, as a kind
of vindication of the *Elegies*' ultimate purpose, as proof of the
authenticity of their ambition. If the poetry were less successful,
the ambition would be badly discredited. Yet there is an important
connection between Rilke's *Elegies* and historico-philosophical
beliefs or insights that were, a considerable time before Rilke (but
without Rilke's knowing them), written in prose, and not even
in the best prose imaginable. To be sure, I am thinking again of
Hegel, the nineteenth-century diagnostician of the end of poetry,
indeed of art; Hegel who, mind you, lived at a time when the
German arts flourished as hardly ever before: suffice it to name
only Goethe and Beethoven. Hegel did not ignore them; but like
a prophet's or madman's, his intuition went beyond them; and
his intuition went beyond them because history would; and history
for him – modern historians may, please, turn their deafest ear
to this – history for him had definite and recognizable intentions.

In the sphere of art, what he called Romantic Art had succeeded
Classical Art of which he said, as a true representative of his Greece-
enamoured age, that nothing more beautiful would or could ever
exist. For the World-Spirit, in whom Hegel believed – just as his
Protestant ancestors believed in God – had for an eternal moment
been incarnate in the art of Greece. Yet its predestined voyaging
compelled the Spirit to leave this unique incarnation again. All
Romantic Art – and Hegel called Romantic all the arts that
followed upon Classical Art – shows the striving of the Spirit to
dissolve its classical oneness with the material in obedience to
its true destiny: its ultimate self-realization through which the
world, as it was known hitherto, would either end (as it would
end on the Day of Judgment) or be relegated to spiritual irrele-

vance. Think of the Gothic cathedrals, of Chartres, for instance, the cathedral invoked in the *Duino Elegies*, where the stone itself seems impatiently to want to free itself of its own heavy materiality in order to set free the heaven-bound Spirit; remember Shakespeare's *Hamlet* where the poetry of heart and mind most formidably clash with the state of the external world, the corruption of the state of Denmark. What, according to Hegel, is bound to win, not only the day but the age, is *'absolute inwardness'*, that *inner* Spirit that all the time had been 'the true nature', that is, the ultimate aim of the Romantic: its victory over the material world. At this point Hegel sounds like Rilke's prompter: for this victory will do away with all gods and all their temples, 'the fire of inwardness has destroyed them'; only one god remains and he dwells within the ideal subjectivity of man. Thus Hegel. And Rilke: 'Nowhere will world exist but within.'

And the Angel? There is no reason *entirely* to doubt Rilke's own interpretation that the Angel has achieved what finally man will have to achieve in a meaningless external world: to kindle the fire of subjectivity, as Hegel puts it, that has to consume the Without. To the Angel 'externals' mean so little that he no loger even distinguishes between life and death while human beings still

> make the mistake of drawing too sharp distinctions.
> Angels, it is said, are often unable to tell
> whether they move among living or dead . . .

This is what Rilke means when he says 'Angel'. Yet while his explanation need not be rejected, there is no necessity either why it should be accepted in its entirety. For is it not paradoxical that he gives an outward name to him, or endows him, in the Second Elegy, with most striking metaphors of appearance? And how not, after the poet's having chosen the name Angel, a name that the mind cannot help but associate with numberless images from religious memories, stories, pictures, and dreams? Whatever else the Angel may be, he is also the being with whom, for the last time with such persistent energy, a poet has striven to create a mythology, analogous, though by no means identical, with the great mythologies of the past, these condensations of the Spirit that pass from epoch to epoch: gods, devils, saviours, and, yes, angels. They are all certainly much superior to man and, although much superior, yet related to him: for how else should his mind be able to comprehend them, or his soul have the strength to bear their manifesting themselves? Rilke's Angel holds a unique place among known mythologies in that he has been created by a mind that was at the same time convinced of its inability to bear his presence.

'A castle immensely towering into sky and sea: it is like a promontory of human existence' – this is how in October 1911 Rilke, a few months before the Voice spoke to him from out of the storm, described Duino. A castle that is like a promontory of human existence – the very phrase reveals what at that time and during the preceding years – the years after *New Poems* – was Rilke's most urgent poetical concern: to find among the things of the external world a concrete equivalent – ten years later T. S. Eliot would call it the 'objective correlative' – of his inner state. *The Notebooks of Malte Laurids Brigge* tell the story of this quest. The survival of poetry, indeed of art, seemed to depend on its success: to find the object, or the configuration of objects, that would naturally, spontaneously, express, or rather contain and convey, the poet's inner vision, the mode of his feelings, thoughts, passions, affections or dislikes. What Rilke had observed in Paris of the emergence of an 'object-less' art, an 'abstract' art (to use a convenient misnomer), or an art that distorts, disorders and sensationally rearranges the forms of the world as it is habitually perceived – well, what Rilke saw in the shops of the art-dealers, be it even the most recent experiments of a painter he dearly loved, Picasso, filled him with deep anxiety; indeed, with unrestrained anger. 'Mischief and senseless caprice', he said of those works, or even 'poison, sheer poison'. They struck him as excesses of human hubris, the arrogant betrayal of a world given to man so that it should provide him with his bread and his wine and with the occasions of his art. And he saw even more, namely that this art, by 'transcending' the common human reality, announced future catastrophes: wars and destructions and deformations of the real world. Was it really impossible to save the inner and outer life of the creations of nature and man, to rescue our inheritance from senseless waste and neglect? Had the world, as it is, finally become a hindrance rather than an inspiration to human creativity? Such were the questions Rilke asked in 1906, long before the full meaning of such acts of desertion were revealed to him at Duino and Muzot.

The world as it is . . . No, at no time was Rilke naive enough to believe that a work of art is, can, or ought to be a dutiful 'imitation' of nature. But although there was clearly, throughout history, a great variety of perspectives and insights offered to art in comprehending the world, they had been the manifold gifts of truth. In this belief he was, like his contemporary Proust, close to Plato. This is why he could say, seeing some products of modernity, that they reflected 'that anarchy of vision driven to extremes through having become corrupted by microscopes and the increasing invisibility of so many experiences'. 'Invisibility', at that time, had not yet established itself as the domain of the Angel. Rilke was still engaged in the kind of work of which his mouthpiece, Malte Laurids Brigge, said that it perpetrated 'unexampled acts of violence' by 'more and more impatiently, more and more despairingly, seeking among visible things (that turned out to be prosaic things) equivalents of the inner truth'. A dramatist whom Malte much admired – he obviously meant Ibsen – had preceded him in this search with brilliant and yet, to Malte, not quite satisfactory results. It seemed to the young poet that Ibsen reached out for tragic depths that could not possibly be contained within the prosaic bourgeois dwellings which he chose as their visible scenes. There was a little girl's wild duck imprisoned in its cage; there was a man, meant for a different life, restlessly pacing up and down within the narrow walls of his room; there was a fire outside the window that burnt to the ground the edifice of mendacious respectability; there was the sun which a young artist, collapsing into madness, begged of his mother. 'But that was not enough', is Malte's conclusion. Why not? Because what was needed, was not 'the unexampled acts of violence' that forced the vision within on to a stage cluttered up with stuff the symbolic power of which was shop-worn if not altogether spent and exhausted; what was needed was, as emerged in the end, the unexampled act of liberation that is prefigured in the Angel, the transformation of the visible world, its melting in the 'fire of subjectivity'; its resurrection in the pure and ideal spaces within – 'Weltinnenraum', as Rilke called it – and all this for the sake of truth, the true relationship, so badly upset, between the world of human inwardness and – the world. Truth. Although Rilke hardly uses the solemn word, it would be misleading to avoid it. For Hegel, the philosopher who had anticipated Rilke's problem, indeed many of the problems of modern art – and had anticipated them with surprising exactitude – certainly never ceased speaking of truth. It is a common misunderstanding that, in proclaiming the end of art, Hegel played the part of Cassandra, obsessed with a dismal prophecy. Art, he believed, was doomed because History itself had deprived it of its function as the epoch's arbiter of truth. This is what, for Hegel, art used to be in the age of poetry, and this is what it had ceased to be in the age of prose. Even Nietzsche, whom nobody would suspect of a secret alliance with Hegel, once said that we are in need of the lies and illusions of art – mind you, lies and illusions – so that we should not perish of truth. Hegel had no such fears. It was the birthright of man to live in the truth. In his often awkward language he said that poetry would cancel itself out because human consciousness would claim, with historical necessity, higher forms than art can offer for the recognition of truth. Rational thought, religion and philosophy, Mind's highest activities, would supersede the creations of art as messengers of truth; and art would show its decline by becoming more and more anarchic. Indeed, Hegel, in his *Aesthetics*, is at his most inspired and convincing when he describes the course art has taken from its single-minded dedication to a few grand subjects toward its ever more arbitrary and promiscuous dealings with things and themes.

Is it not correct to say that a history of the arts, including poetry and literature, could be written with the title 'Background into Foreground'? To tell its story, such a history need not even cover larger portions of time than those that lie between Giotto and Carpaccio and the Dutch still-life painters of the seventeenth century in order to show how the holy or heroic scenes and figures of the centre were gradually pushed back by what, with merely decorative intent, used to fill in the background: trees and flowers; castles, houses and bridges; people meeting and conversing, leading horses, playing with poodles and cats; not to mention the aesthetic arrangements, in the Netherlands, of apples, grapes, lemons, glasses, bees, butterflies, knives and softboiled eggs. A priceless enrichment of interest taken in our world? Yes, perhaps. Certainly it seems so, particularly if, going back in time even beyond Giotto, we are given as objects of our contemplation only God or God-appointed delegates of the divine, placed against the plain infinities of blue or gold. No doubt, the arts, since then, have become incomparably livelier. Who would be prepared to sacrifice to any kind of holy monotony the crowded exuberance and precision of Carpaccio, the all but sacred cembalos or milk jugs of Vermeer, the sanctification of 'things' performed by Chardin? Livelier, yes, but only to a point. To which point? To the point where this formidable increase of 'significances' was felt to be inflationary, where the riotously proliferating printing-presses of the prosaic managed to devalue the currencies of the poetic, and Rilke, speaking of the anarchy of the modern vision, created, compelled by inner necessity, a majestic foreground figure once more: the Angel. Needless to say that he could not succeed entirely. If history appeared to urge him on, it worked at the same time against him. There was no future any more for the mythological in art.

I am saying this without recommending that we should accept Hegel's mundane theology of history. But is Hegel not right, with the force of self-evidence, when he says of modern poetry, of – in his sense – Romantic poetry, that of necessity it lacks any 'pre-established objectivity', any mythology or definite images and constellations which only wait to be taken up by the poet? No, he answers, the imagination is now wholly unfettered, there is no matter that matters more to it than any other matter happening to arouse the interest of the artist who behaves as if he were absolutely free to create anything he pleases. But this is, alas, the kind of freedom that spells chaos, and is the most important moment in Hegel's history of the decline and fall of art.

There are many poets and writers of the early twentieth century who, without having read a line of Hegel's *Aesthetics*, echo this from their own experience, often speaking of it as a predicament or at least as something exceedingly perplexing. Rilke's Angel may well owe his 'monotheistic' existence to the teeming confusion of, as it were, 'polytheistic' intimations. The clouds over the age of prose release their occasional poetic thunderbolts quite arbitrarily, let the lightning strike where it will. Suddenly and unpredictably, this or that experience, quite trivial in itself, is set on fire by the memory. It rises, who knows why, above the dull routine of the day, as if magically illuminated, mysteriously transfigured. Proust is the finest recorder of such moments. There is, of course, the episode of 'the little crumb of madeleine', as ordinary and everyday a piece of pastry as is displayed on the trays in French bakery windows. Yet its taste brings back to the author the precise sensation of childhood bliss, the summers in Combray, a story, in which the madeleine and the tea acquire sacramental qualities, almost of the bread and the wine, and aunt Leonie, dipping the madeleine into her cup of tea and letting the child taste it, the power of a priestess initiating him into religious mysteries: 'And at once', we read, 'the vicissitudes of life had become indifferent to me, its disasters innocuous, its brevity illusory – this new sensation having had on me the effect which love has of filling me with a precious essence ... I had ceased to feel mediocre, accidental, mortal.' Why, Proust asks, should this childhood memory, rising from the depths of oblivion, evoked by the spontaneous recollection of that taste, have such power, in his description indeed sacramental powers? And he is, of course, at a loss for an answer. It is a Hegelian or Rilkean scene, as Hegelian and Rilkean as Proust's description of his early poetic experiences, when, during a walk, and without, in the common order of things, any definite or obvious importance attaching to the object in question, 'suddenly a roof, a gleam of sunlight reflected from a stone, the smell of a road would make me stop still, to enjoy the special pleasure that each of them gave me'. It was more than a 'special pleasure'; it was as if such chance objects, and only just these – but why just these? – were about to yield to him, in his words, 'the secret treasure of which they were themselves no more than the outer coverings'.

T. S. Eliot, when he wrote prose, was more prosaic than Proust, but he means the same (insofar as meanings can remain unaffected by differences of style) when, in *The Use of Poetry and the Use of Criticism*, he asks, more impatiently than Proust, why the poetic imagination should every so often be at the mercy of 'a few meagre arbitrarily chosen sets of snapshots' of the memory, 'the faded poor souvenirs of passionate moments'? The derog-

atory tone of 'meagre snapshops' as well as of 'faded poor souvenirs' would show the direction of a mind set on overcoming
such haphazard spiritual dispersal through ecclesiastical discipline.
Nonetheless, how Hegelian is that passage in Eliot's discourse!
For it is Hegel's diagnosis that to the Romantic mind of poetry
– so different in that from the Classical – it is all the same 'to
which circumstances it applies itself or which it encounters'. In
the poem 'Lebenslied', Hugo von Hofmannsthal says

> Ihm bietet jede Stelle
> Geheimnisvoll die Schwelle,

meaning that for the latecomer in the tradition of poetry it may
be any point in the outward crust of the world that unexpectedly
breaks and becomes for the poet the threshold of the mystery.
For W. B. Yeats this may be 'The rattle of pebbles on the shore/
Under the receding wave' ('Though the great song returns no
more/There's been delight in what we have'); or for T. S. Eliot
it may be 'the song of one bird, the leap of one fish, at a particular place and time, the scent of one flower, an old woman
on a German mountain path, six ruffians seen through an open
window playing cards at night at a small French railway junction
where there was a watermill: such memories have symbolic value,
but of what we cannot tell . . .' Hegel thought he could tell: symbolic of that pure human inwardness, the final abode of the
Spirit, that, opposed by the spirit-forsaken world of circumstance,
would appoint at random 'the leap of one fish' or 'an old woman
on a German mountain path' its emissary, yet without entrusting
him with any easily decipherable messages. How to decode them?

Rilke, throughout the *Duino Elegies*, interprets them as the few
moments in our 'disconnected' life which intimate, but only intimate, that, perhaps, we are after all 'related', as he puts it, to
the Being whose full revelation in the Angel we would not be
able, or not yet be able, to bear. (And what Heidegger means
by 'Being' – in his chief philosophical work *Being and Time*
– is beyond any doubt a close relation of Rilke's Angel.) Eliot's
'meagre snapshots' and 'faded souvenirs' also momentarily hint
at a world to which we truly belong: the world that is prey to
our inwardness. As it is now, we cannot, isolated as we are, 'make
use', as Rilke's First Elegy puts it, of either Angels or human

beings – and even the animals are already informed by their
instincts 'that we are not very securely at home' within the varying interpretations into which, throughout the epochs, human
beings have pressed their existence. In the First of the *Elegies*
such hints may be given by 'a tree on the slope' (Van Gogh,
it seems, has painted it in its almost mystical presence), or by
'the road we travelled yesterday' (when unexpectedly, at a bend
of it, a little group of birch trees, their foliage yellowing,
silently said the unsayable), or by a certain starlit night, brought
back to us 'on a wave of the past', or by the sound of a fiddle
coming out of 'an open window along our way'. All this was
like an annunciation and demanded a response but helplessly we
did not know what it should be; was like morsels of eternity
in a universe of stubborn transience; was like meteors of unknown
origin rushing across a dark sky where the stars have been
extinguished.

Before the *Elegies* encircled such moments with an endless
number of question marks – or made them issue into the one,
yet ever-repeated, exclamation that invoked *and* warded off the
Angel – Rilke, writing about Cézanne in 1907, spoke of them
as occasions for the artist to transfigure the most ordinary things,
and through them in the end, perhaps, the whole of life. Of
Cézanne's apples he said that they were, in actual fact, the
commonest stewing apples, and of his wine-bottles, in their
reddish black, that they came out of a peasant's bulging coat
pockets; and these apples the painter arranged on bedcovers
(which his housekeeper was bound to miss one day) and added
those bottles or whatever else lay about in the house. And then:
'Like Van Gogh he makes these things into his "saints", and forces
them, *forces* them, to be beautiful, to draw into them the meaning
of the whole world and all its bliss and glory ...' This was in
1907. But in 1912, on that January day at Duino, he saw this
metamorphosis – if only for a moment, but how momentous was
that moment! – with the eyes of his Malte Laurids Brigge as
the product of unexampled 'acts of violence' (after all, he had,
even in 1907, underlined 'forced' in that passage about Cézanne)
and was sure that, like Ibsen's symbolism, it was 'not enough'.
The Angel had to intercede to bestow upon a world that appeared
to have become spiritually useless in its grey, unyielding prose,

the blessing of a resurrection in the invisibility of the inner spirit. How seriously should we take this? As seriously as we are still capable of taking art and poetry and religion. True, at the same time as Rilke, after years of waiting, concluded the *Elegies*, he wrote the *Sonnets to Orpheus* in praise of the son of a king and a muse, the patron of song, who descended into the dark underworld, lost to it what he loved most, and revived it in his poetry. And during the four years that were left of Rilke's life he continued to write poems. Some of these belong to his most beautiful. Yet even those that impress us first as most 'visible' and even serene are bathed in a radiance that seems to come from the Beyond where there is light after the suns of the Here and Now have set. No matter whether the Hegel–Rilkean findings will be proven true or be refuted by what is to come (I think I have reason to doubt the latter alternative), they will remain as most remarkable documents of a historical hour even if it was not the last one of poetry. But in the poetic world of Rilke, which with possibly equal right we may call the world of Yeats, George, Hofmannsthal, Benn, Valéry, or, going back a little in time, of Mallarmé and Rimbaud, the poets created 'absolute' poetry, 'pure' poetry, the kind of poetry that flourished in the chasms and gulfs that the poets themselves felt were fixed between their poetic dedication and 'life', the prosaic life of the epoch. After such extremes it is not surprising that language itself, the coherent speech of the race, should be suspected of having been drawn into the conspiracy of the prosaic against the mind of poetry. To yield poetry again, it had to be taken apart and made incomprehensible, untouchable, as it were, by the prosaic understanding. For what can be comprehended does not seem to be worthy of poetic attention. Of course, there are remarkable exceptions: Walt Whitman instantly comes to mind, Yeats, Robert Frost, Bertolt Brecht, Wilhelm Lehmann and some that have settled down somewhere in between. But the main stream has, I think, been traced by Hegel and by Rilke's *Duino Elegies*. The river's estuary is still uncharted; but the spirit of poetry, and of what hitherto has been called humanity, is bound to face hard times in the age of prose. Let us meet, as an intellectual and moral challenge, what Hegel – perhaps mistakenly – deemed to be historical inevitability.

2
The broken tradition
an address

for Dolf Sternberger

THE DIFFICULTY OF DEFINITION

As soon as I utter the word 'tradition', I am disconcerted by an almost paralysing self-consciousness. Ought I not to define first what is meant by tradition? Perhaps I might take my cue from the celebrated *Querelle des Anciens et Modernes* because of the important role played in it by the opposition between the traditional and the spirit of modernity. Nonetheless, our quarrels differ from the quarrelsome ways of seventeenth-century France where, for instance, Nicolas Boileau-Despréaux, the friend of 'the traditional' and of Racine and Molière, feuded with Charles Perrault who had acquired the reputation of being 'modern', progressive, because − or in spite − of his having written the song of praise *Le siècle de Louis le Grand*. The age of Augustus had, he believed, returned with this king, a civilization as splendid as the Augustean, even heightened and ennobled by the subtleties of the nation's language, the superb use made of it by its poets, the increase of knowledge and science, and the refinement of morals and manners.

If it was objected that, in spite of it all, poetry had not produced anything that equalled the glories of Homer or Virgil, a picture of progress was evoked, reminiscent of the pleasure taken by children in the visit of a playful uncle, a picture in which the ancient giants had to put up with the youngsters' climbing on to their shoulders so that the little ones in all their smallness were yet able to see more than those who carried them. Yet it remained puzzling that the embodiment of absolutism, the ruler who said 'L'état, c'est moi!', was acclaimed by Charles Perrault as modern and progressive. And indeed some Marxist historians interpret, not unconvincingly, the literary *rencontre* that so agitated seventeenth-century France in their own manner: it may well have been the concern of Boileau-Despréaux and his followers, the advocates of the *anciens*, to save the honour and goodness of a tradition, truly preferable to the 'progress' of the *modernes*, favoured by Perrault and his friends. At first glance this is certainly a surprising position to be taken up by Marxists. It becomes less startling as soon as the question 'progress whither' is asked. The kind of progress, perhaps, that sped in the direction of unrestrained and monstrously selective financial gains and wars of expansion? This is, without question, what emerges from those Marxist analyses, without the analysts being disquieted by the simultaneity of the utmost social inequality (accumulated riches in the hands of a few and wretched poverty of the many) with a glorious efflorescence of cultural vitality: name only, among very many more, Racine, Molière, La Fontaine, Bossuet, La Rochefoucauld, Poussin, Claude Lorrain, and the inescapable question arises whether the misery of the poor or, going back in time, even slavery, may not be the price to be paid for the most exquisite monuments of human creativity. For the disciples of Marx this is nothing to worry about. Like their master they superstitiously believe that a truly egalitarian (and therefore, as William Blake or Nietzsche would tell them, profoundly unjust) society would set free all the resources of the maltreated human spirit. Be this as it may, the 'modernist' glorifyer of Louis XIV, Perrault, willy-nilly supported, or so these historians opined, what later was given ugly names: the ruthlessness of high finance and capitalism. In praising the enterprises of the great king, he was, even without knowing it, preparing to sacrifice the private and public virtues of the older tradition to the – ultimately destructive – merits of acquisitiveness.

And Boileau-Despréaux? This advocate of the *anciens* was, in this perspective, the 'conservative' revolutionary. His attitude was partially determined by the suspicion that the designs of Louis XIV were bound to bring about a reconciliation between the aristocracy and the *successful* members of the bourgeoisie who were ready to abandon their traditional ways if only they gained financial power through their good relations with the aristocracy (which not infrequently were initiated and fostered in the boudoirs of sought-after ladies: hence the feminism that is almost always allied with 'progress'). These bourgeois supported with greedy expectations the financial and foreign policies of the king – at the 'economic base', to use here, appropriately, the idiom of Marxism – while the 'ideological superstructure' was looked after by Perrault's hymnic praise of Louis XIV. Boileau, in contrast, sensed that the 'modern times', so generously and royally sub-sidized, boded ill for the human spirit. With his love of the *anciens* his mind was, surprisingly, a mild, very mild, anticipation of Robespierre's, fearing the consequences of 'progress' of the powerful. The conservative opponent of the progressive Perrault appointed the early period of classical Greece, the – as yet uncorrupted – ways of republican Rome, the history of the – as yet straightforward – political rhetoric from Demosthenes to Cicero, *his* tradition and opposed the modern faith in progress with a cultural pessimism not quite unlike that of the later Burke, Schopenhauer, or Burckhardt, a scepticism distantly related to an anti-mundane theology that reaches from St Augustine to the puritanical Jansenism of Port Royal.

To avert for a while our glance from the history of the *anciens* and *modernes* and consider instead the activities of the Perrault family: has one ever looked attentively at the colonnade of the Louvre? It was partly designed by Claude Perrault, the brother of the 'modernist' Charles. If one wishes to discover family likenesses, one cannot help noticing that they are as little straight-forward, unadorned and classically austere as the brother's poem. Classicistic, certainly; but this is the kind of classicism that is nothing if not manneristic, full of signals sent out by the approaching Baroque. Therefore, it called forth the displeasure of Perrault's rigidly classicistic contemporaries, above all Nicolas-François Blondel. This led to a polemic very much after the model of that between Charles Perrault and Boileau-Despréaux. If, from the Louvre, one allows the historical memory to go back as far as the emperors of Rome, one finds oneself in the midst of a pugnacious dispute about the rules of rhetoric, and thus also of literature, a dispute that at the time of the Roman Empire became known as 'Atticism contra Asianism', a designation pointing to the contrast between the pure classical style that the Romans had inherited from the Greeks and the 'Baroque', indigenous to the Asian colonies of Rome. Thus the affinities between the mind's configurations reach from here to the *Querelle* and, maybe, as far as Nietzsche's inspired Apollo–Dionysus intuitions. That much can be said about the insurmountable oppositions *within* the idea of 'tradition', indeed, the impossible test that he who in-sists on defining 'tradition' would have to pass – unless he is prepared to regard all the instances of 'anti-traditionalism' as mere aspects of the tradition itself. Whosoever, ignoring these warnings, speaks without 'Well, yes – but' of 'tradition', is bound to become hopelessly entangled in history's impenetrable thickets.

2

PAGANISM AND CHRISTIANITY

Our tradition, it is said, has been formed by the confluence of classical antiquity and Christianity. There is little doubt that it has. Yet in Goethe's *Faust* the marriage between the pagan woman Helena and Faust, the – not all *that* Christian – would-be translator of the Bible, is not concluded in front of an altar. Still, nobody will deny that our humanity, as long as it has not transcended itself in obedience to Nietzsche-Zarathustra's vision, would surely be very much poorer without the sermon that Jesus preached on that mount – *how* much poorer we can see whenever those who know of no gentleness and no meakness rule over the lands. And yet, and yet ... No straight route of the mind leads to the place where the Christian message met the pagan ways of thought and feeling, or where exceedingly visible churches and cathedrals were built to celebrate the invisible domain of inwardness. How was it possible that Plato's notion of the Beautiful, the only emanation of the transcendent Ideas that is accessible to the human eye, associated itself with that Truth that shines only in the soul, or that the unwritten law of Love that defies any words attempting to define it, let itself in with legal codes and paragraphs, or, finally, that the deputy of Christ competed in worldliness, splendour, and power with the emperors of this world?

Such questions point towards the persistent discomfort the Christian sensibility is bound to suffer in any mundane civilization. There exists an unresolvable inner tension within the body of spiritual, ethical, and aesthetic principles that nevertheless make for our only tradition. Uncounted books have been written about this problem. The footnotes alone would fill libraries. Why, then, speak of it once more? Because we are concerned with the future of this tradition that may well be doomed; and that may have no future because the coincidence of opposites that is its very essence can no longer be sustained. For it was from the beginning a highly precarious conciliation that, over an astonishingly long period, has been achieved by this tradition -- not only in learned and philosophical treatises but in lives actually lived: the conciliation between the necessities of social order and the disorderly, anarchic promptings of the spirit within, between the majestic sensuousness of Greek art and the pervasive suspicion cast by Christianity upon the joys of the senses, a suspicion that from time to time erupted in iconoclastic violence. Or is there not a striking similarity – a damnable similarity, as some of the pious would and did say – between Botticelli's bewitching images of the goddess of love and other dispensers of sensual delights, and his madonnas? Indeed, such aesthetic concord could not last. Much later, Hölderlin strained to the point of madness to serve with the Bread and Wine of the 'Only one' also the other god, the intoxicated Dionysus.* – Tradition?

The feud starts with the very beginnings of Christianity. Does our imagination suffice truly to understand the calamitous role played by the slandered Pharisees – slandered, I believe, unjustly? Imagine you are appointed to watch over a community's faithful observance of the laws; and along comes one who, although he says that not one iota must be changed or neglected in the canon of the mosaic tradition, yet asserts that justice, as understood by him and his disciples, is more just than that of the scribes. No doubt Cain, who killed Abel, was condemned by the Lord's judgement; but according to the new teaching he would have offended God's will almost as badly even if he had not actually committed the crime but only harboured hatred in his heart against his brother. And what about adultery? When the people, obedient to the accustomed rule, insisted upon taking the life of the woman who was caught in the act, he said ... Well, we know what he said about the right to throw the first stone. He who is free of sin ... And whosoever has, in his thoughts, desired a woman has broken the marriage vows. And as the people, suddenly conscious of their own moral imperfections, dropped the stones that were meant to kill the adulteress, and stole away, he told the frightened woman that he himself

* This, of course, refers to Hölderlin's great poems 'Brod und Wein' and 'Der Einzige'.

would not pass judgment on her either: 'Go and sin no more!' Was there really no iota crossed out in the legal text? Was the external law not all but superseded by the invisible and incalculable promptings of the purified soul?

Or imagine what the guardians of the law must have felt when they reproached him because, as he walked through the fields with his disciples on a Sabbath, they plucked and ate the ripened corn for they were hungry; and he countered the accusation by asking the Pharisees to remember that even David and his companions ate of the shewbreads of the Temple and thereby violated a privilege of the priests? Or when, still more disturbingly, he said: 'The Son of Man is lord over the Sabbath.' Alarming indeed to the servants of the established law, the 'outward' and yet holy law that, incomprehensibly, was reduced to insignificance, outshone by the light from within. It would not have been their calling to see this light even if they had had the eyes to perceive it. What they did see and were sure about was that there could be no human society that would not fall into anarchy if the voices of inwardness, so difficult to make out, were thus to render inaudible the commandments of the law.

This, it seems, was the real cause of the wrath of those who firmly believed that they had to watch over the integrity of divine ordinances. They could not but be irreconcilably inimical to him who called himself the Son of Man but conducted himself as the Son of God, claiming to know what pleased his Father in Heaven: the untainted inwardness, the love, humility, and mercy which were above all the commandments of the Thora, sometimes even above the ten, if they were not acknowledged from the depth of love or, from the depth of love, now and then disregarded. This conflict between legal order and the annunciation of the inner truth makes for the strain at the very centre of our tradition. Whenever the strain becomes unbearable, there are crucifixions, torture chambers, bloodsheds, conflagrations; and when for the last time death will be suffered on the last stake of history, the victim may well be one whose conscience rose against what he felt was an unscrupulous law. It need not always be Golgothas where the tension is dramatized, and not always Thirty Year Wars that result from it. Yet in one way or another the conflict is fought out every day.

This incompatibility of the external order with the inner truth is, in its most radical forms, the great danger of our tradition, whatever this tradition may be: something faithfully accepted, consciously or unconsciously followed, or only an assemblage of amiable conventions. That tension has come into the open in manifold forms. It characterized, for instance, the whole Romantic epoch of Europe as the painfully suffered incongruity between within and without. It soon produced two extreme opposites.

One extreme shows in every anti-traditional, revolutionary ideology that aims at a transformation of the external world, a transformation so radical that all human beings would live without their humanity being damaged by the social organization. The other extremists, no matter whether they call on Buddhism or Tao or Christian Pietism or only Herman Hesse for support, turn, on the contrary, radically away from a world that offends their souls, practising a kind of conscientious objection with regard to reality, a creative negation which has found its ultimate poetry in Rilke's *Duino Elegies*: all that is 'without', all 'things' are bound to fall away from the inner spirit, give notice to the soul which is no longer nourished by them. Only in pure inwardness will true existence be possible. 'Nowhere will world exist but within', says the Seventh of the *Elegies*.

Either pole of the tension attracts the abominable. Incessantly bombs explode (will it be long before they are nuclear? This, not the ugly hithering and thithering of the great powers, is the most acute danger), people are abducted and murdered, and the ideologized criminals, in broad daylight, rob banks to obtain the money for their monstrous misdeeds. As is only to be expected, life is quieter among the 'inner' circles: there the upsurges and ecstasies of the soul are produced pharmacologically because the addicted psyches are incapable of rising to those heights on their own natural strength. – Tradition?

3
THE GREAT DISCREPANCY

As bombs were mentioned, some attention may be paid in passing to a development that is the greatest danger to the humane tradition, and even to any form of civilized life, indeed to the whole world – not only of human beings; in passing, for the immense theme would demand a long stay. It is about the terrifying discrepancy between the intellectual tradition, the devotion to great enterprises of the mind, the sacrifices of comfort and even of life which the passion of scientific discovery has exacted throughout the centuries, and the ease with which the technical products of those labours can be managed (or exploited). The alarming contrast which might teach the world what sin is, if it were still capable of learning such lessons, is between the immense subtlety of the sciences that have resulted in the historically unique means for the extinction of life on earth, and the tough simple-mindedness of many who, after a few days of instruction, can learn how to handle them. If the humane arts still exist – *Bildung* is the German word that can hardly be used any more without a sense of embarrassment – then they differ from the scientific-mathematical disciplines in one crucial point: Homer, Plato, Dante, Goethe, cannot be 'applied', unless we mean by that the delights and efforts of the mind's immersion in their works. But he who has learned competently to manoeuvre an aeroplane, need not even know the name of Newton, although without him he would have nothing to manoeuvre; and if, by pulling a lever, he devastates a big city and, in addition, poisons the piece of nature on which it was built, we have to be grateful that, in doing so, he gives no thought to Einstein, Niels Bohr, or Heisenberg. Why should he? For he is unlikely to comprehend any of their theories if for no other reason than because of their being incommunicable in language; and if they were, he would probably understand them even less.

4
CONVERSATION WITH A PHYSICIST ABOUT LANGUAGE

Which brings us to language, and here reflection is endless. One question can only be touched upon although it is of great importance. Surely, it is true to say that the humanistic–literary–philological tradition betrays its increasing decline through the indisputable fact that an ever greater proportion of the epoch's intellectual activities is dedicated to those spheres of abstractions that are unreachable by words, and are satisfactorily communicable only in an idiom that, utterly un-Goethean as it is, defeats the concrete imagination by no longer being *anschaulich*, to use a Goethean word. Not to mention the perverse attraction that this type of scientific approach had for the so-called humanities, inspiring there the ambition to do as the sciences do, without these 'humanists' realizing the futility of this undertaking or recognizing that it would get in the way of their essential task, namely to cultivate human faculties other than the faculty of abstract thought.

When one day in a conversation with Werner Heisenberg I heard the renowned mathematician–physicist say that one of the criteria of scientific correctness was the aesthetic satisfaction afforded by a mathematical formula that was conclusive, simple, elegant – in one word, beautiful – I assumed (rightly, as it turned out) that he wished to modify something he had said several years earlier, during the last year of the war. He lived at that time, together with other nuclear physicists from Germany, as a prisoner-of-war of the English in a country house near Cambridge, enjoyed considerable privileges and was, for instance, free to accept the invitation of a small discussion group formed by research students of my college, Peterhouse. On that evening he told us what he thought about the difference between humanistic studies and scientific pursuits. What afterwards attracted the attention of the man, who was also a remarkable musician, was not so much the discussion as a grand piano that stood in the room. Soon he had settled down at it and, having been for a long time deprived of such an instrument, began to improvise. Then he played very beautifully a Beethoven sonata. Afterwards he said that now he could, better than in his talk, explain that difference: 'If I had never lived, someone else would have discovered the Uncertainty Principle. For this was the solution of a problem that had emerged from the logical development of physics and had to be solved in this and no other way. But if there had never been a Beethoven, this sonata would not have been composed. The two different scholarly pursuits, science and humanities, should reflect this fundamental difference.'

But now, much later, it seemed to me that, extolling the aesthetic aspect of mathematics, he no longer thought too highly of the claim of aesthetic exclusiveness that art raises. To be sure, it remained undisputed that the 'substance' informing the aesthetic appearance of an equation differs from the substance of art. Still, this did not much diminish the disquieting effect the conversation had upon me, although the message involved was by no means new. It might have been received from Leonardo da Vinci, or even from the Pythagoreans, and, quite apart from nature, it is obvious that beauty is no prerogative of works of art. Beauty can also be experienced, by minds thus gifted, in abstract-mathematical reflections and calculations. Still more: before the Age of Absurdity dawned on the worlds of science, philosophy, and art, many thinkers derived from such meditations the most pleasing assurance of the harmony between the human mind and the universe, a harmony that has been the fundamental chord of the humanistic faith. It is announced by the very title of Kepler's *De Harmonice Mundi* (1619) with equal confidence as by the 'Forest and Cave' monologue of Goethe's Faust: 'Erhabner Geist, du gabst mir, gabst mir alles,/Worum ich bat' – Lofty spirit of Nature, you have granted me everything that I desired – namely the sublime gift to feel at one with Nature as much as with a beloved human being. This, even if less ecstatically uttered, is no more; and with its disappearance an essential element of our tradition has disappeared.

In that scientific-aesthetic conversation, Heisenberg continued: 'The possibility of expressing the Uncertainty Principle in a manner that is mathematically so concise, if not beautiful, should perhaps cast doubt on the Principle's correctness. For is there not a contradiction in speaking so 'harmoniously' of the discordant relationship between our ability to perceive, know, make sure, and the *natura rerum*, the inmost nature of the world? If there were really such a falling-off, it could not, one might suspect, be said so logically, so "beautifully".' Heisenberg underscored this incongruity by recalling a conversation with Niels Bohr about the newest insights of physics; after which, on his way back to his Copenhagen hotel, he asked himself if it was conceivable that nature should behave so crazily? This was in 1926. But now I asked him: 'You were surprised that such "crazy" discoveries should be expressible in such "beautiful" language? – In the manner, perhaps, of the shattering paradox pronounced in *King Lear*: "The worst is not so long as we can say: This is the worst"?' 'Not quite', answered Heisenberg, 'I mean the language of mathematics.'

'There', I replied, '"speech" can go on when it has been silenced anywhere else? There it is possible to use speech, a certain kind of speech, in order to say that the world has become unspeakable? Where language has to shut up, the mathematician, like Goethe's Tasso at the end of the drama, proclaims that he, so different in that from other men, was divinely endowed with "speech"?' The question-mark, at that time having remained suspended in mid-air, obstructs to this day the breathing of language. What Heisenberg recounted in the end was a meeting with Einstein. He too was disquieted and puzzled by the newest developments in mathematical physics – despite the part he himself had played in bringing them about. Still, he said: 'What you and your colleagues try to prove, cannot, must not, be correct. God does not play a game of dice with the world.' And, as Heisenberg put it, 'his unruly white hair looked at that moment like the halo of *sancta simplicitas*'.

These reminiscences may show that more is at stake than a 'disturbance' within our tradition. It is this tradition itself that is in jeopardy when the most important and – heaven knows – most risky discoveries about our world can no longer be conveyed in the traditional language but *only* in the thinnest air, poor in oxygen, of mathematical abstraction. Let it not be said that it has always been like that. No, certainly not in this shocking and ever-increasing measure. It took a long time before the World Spirit had its revenge on that brute of a soldier who killed Archimedes and no doubt destroyed the circles and mathematical symbols the sage had sketched in the sand. Only in the seventeenth century were these figures restored and even began to shine with the bright light of the mind's spectacular conquests. Isaac Newton, hit on the head by that legendary apple dropping from a tree (these trees, these apples!) took no interest whatever in it as a concrete object, its form, colour, or taste, but only as something that was falling, as an occasion for ingeniously abstracting from its concreteness. By a strange accident, Newton was born in the same year as Louis XIV under whose rule France went through the intellectual agitations of the *Querelle*, while in Newton's own country Jonathan Swift wrote *The Battle of the Books*, the satire on the combat between the innovators and the 'ancients' where the latter still easily won,

Aristotle got the better of Descartes and, of course, Homer of Perrault. The ancient warriors routed, in the roundness of their poetic and philosophical powers, the 'moderns' whose imaginations, Swift believed, had been flattened by the scientific currents of the time. It was a Pyrrhic victory. With the death of Goethe there ended the last determined campaign, brilliant and not a little quixotic, to prevent the complete alienation of the natural scientists from the spirit of poetry by purging them of their Newtonian passion for abstraction. The attempt was doomed to failure. After the nineteenth century, the high season of the realistic novel, language and its works lived, compared to the sciences, in reduced circumstances. If they did not want to accept them, they, proudly transmogrifying their misfortune, became symbolistically obscure, experimentally eccentric, or realistically gloomy. We seem to have arrived, after Kafka, at Samuel Beckett, and have to deem ourselves lucky if this is a terminus. It seems probable that still darker darknesses are in the making.

5

EARTHQUAKES OF LANGUAGE

It is undeniable that we are passing through a crisis of language. To assess its extent and depth, one need only listen to the speech of young students (America is particularly suited to the purpose), and then spend a great deal of time labouring to initiate them into the literature of the past, and finally try not to fall too far behind in following the debates of modern theoreticians of language and critics of literature. In these three employments the teacher has perpetually to cross abysses, the deepest having opened between, say, a poem by Goethe or a novel of Stendhal and, at the other extreme, these advanced critical activities that, intent upon splitting hairs with pseudo-scientific earnestness, regard all poetry and literature as an ultimately inexplicable and incommunicable phenomenon, or else as being written in a secret code that demands to be broken before the text can be understood. The times when the *beaux-arts* were sought after for their beauty and the pleasure they gave to mind and imagination – those times seem irretrievably past. The belief that a poem can be comprehended and intelligently enjoyed by a reader equipped with a secure knowledge of the language in question, linguistic and historical sensitivity, patience and goodwill has been looked upon as superstitious peasant lore ever since promising words (that never keep their promises), words like 'deconstruction' or 'Lacan', spread like unilluminating wildfire throughout the schools of literature, and even in the circles of poets themselves, of whom many appear exclusively engaged in supplying the market of interpretation.

Indeed, it is a rugged terrain on which moves the education of the young. It is a landscape of chasms, and bridge-building appears to be unfeasible when a guileless undergraduate calls upon his teacher, who is just trying to puzzle out what a certain 'postmodernist' critic wishes to tell him, and proceeds to talk about his intellectual worries which he finds as hard to articulate as the rock musicians to whom he listens day after day would find it to play pianissimo. 'What I mean to say', he pronounces, 'between the Hegels and the Schlegels, what are they after with all that mythology and stuff . . . Well, you know what I mean.' If the teacher regretfully replies that he cannot possibly know what the student means unless he tells him, the questing young man looks sad and helpless. Or another who knows this particular teacher as amiable and accessible approaches him in the library, in the section of the ancient Greeks, asking him for assistance. He has to write a paper on a Greek poet, but unfortunately has forgotten which one. The teacher names a few of the most famous. The young man sadly shakes his head at each name. Finally, Euripides is mentioned and the light of recognition brightens the young face. '*That's* the guy!' he says and, anxiously seeking knowledge, disappears among the shelves.

No, these are no caricatures. I merely report from experiences that I have had in reputable colleges and not in the lowest strata of ignorance. And then one goes to read with one's class Schiller's *Robbers* with its countless biblical references; and has to explain every single one. For, so different in this from their church-going ancestors who were well up in Scripture, the Bible is to these youngsters a book with seven seals, the whole of it and not only that episode of the Apocalypse. The teacher's life is not easier when it comes to Goethe's *Iphigenie*. There one cannot possibly do without 'mythology and stuff'; and only a few have ever heard of old Tantalus although the word 'tantalizing' is familiar to them. (They probably think it applies to the chore of reading the literature of German classicism.) Would they be more responsive to the 'moderns', to T. S. Eliot, for instance, or Wallace Stevens, or James Joyce? By no means. For there one gets even more deeply into the mysteries of mythology, meets the Fisher King, the symbolism of the tarot cards, the topos of the knight errant and of the homecoming of the lost seafarer, or the inexhaustible resources of Irish folklore. Between '*that's* the guy' and, for instance, the question why Goethe would not rest content with his prose *Iphigenie* and resolved to make it into a poetic drama, one of those gulfs is fixed. Another opens if one asks how, in the logical course of literary history, T. S. Eliot, in a poem, came to say that 'the poetry does not matter'; or again, why James Joyce had to invent the architecture of those pedantically designed labyrinths of language. Asking such questions, one finds oneself standing on the verge of the deepest abyss, the one that lies between the inarticulate naiveté of those appealing youngsters and the sophistries of the interpreters who approach the through-and-through mundane words of mundane literature in the attitude of initiates expecting from it disclosures of mysteries just as if it was made up of the oracular utterances of a *deus absconditus*, a veiled divinity that dispenses salvations or damnations.

Certainly, there always have been great differences between the intellectual manners of those who formed the high culture of an epoch and the *profanum vulgus* which to call by its Latin name strikes us in these egalitarian days as an elitarian offence, so that nobody feels quite comfortable talking about it. Yet at no time has the division been greater than now. It is not snobbish, though it may seem so, to take cognizance of it but, as one diffidently hopes, helps a little to recover a measure of sanity. Also, speaking of it means drawing attention to yet another phenomenon that badly disturbs the idea of tradition. Primitivity (it hardly exists any more as innocent spontaneity but almost exclusively as corrupt taste) has never before been in possession of such limitless means to dominate, and this not only through the vehement promulgation of the cheapest platitudes and idiocies – if this were not so, we might have been spared Hitler and other charismatic poisoners – but through the all but magical authority of the mechanisms of diffusion. It is an error to believe that these could be made to serve better things. Yes, now and then, in this or that corner of public life, self-consciously set aside for the 'higher' concerns. The title at least of a notorious book hits the ferocious bull's eye: the Medium is the Message; and the 'message' is unpropitious even for those who are determined to resist. They invariably become outsiders, capricious and esoteric, and untiringly busy to widen those gulfs with still more complex patterns of words, sounds, and figures. An intelligent, experienced, and hardened critic said of a recent big exhibition of 'Modern Western Art' that most of the works shown would be incomprehensible without the commentaries of the voluminous catalogue (which makes no smooth reading either), and the director of a respectable museum confessed that, looking at a half-hundred of the exhibits, he could only say: 'I have no idea what they mean.'

Tremors, more or less tremendous, within language consciousness and, therefore, tremors within the tradition – to use again the word that defies defining, and to add that, if there could be a definition, there would be no tradition – such tremors have often occurred. One might, for instance, pursue young Nietzsche's intuition that the death of the Greek gods who died of the 'progress' of thought, the Socratic philosophical sensibility, caused deep spiritual unrest, not unlike our own, to the Greek world. The demise of the gods not only destroyed the faithful belief in the literal truth of the Homeric epics and the Attic tragedies, transforming their religion into pure art, but also had momentous effects upon language. A new agility of expression gained, owing to the rhetoric of the Sophists, almost universal respect at the expense of what integer minds and souls, the pre-Socratic philosophers according to Nietzsche, had known and felt to be true. The virtuosities of mere talent took the place of a people's genius that had its roots in the substance of truth. Probably less open to question than Nietzsche's and, in his succession, Heidegger's conjectures is a much later connection that can be made between modes of philosophical and linguistic thought. When Machiavelli and Hobbes abandoned the Aristotelian doctrines of classical politology, the thoughtful 'users' of language became exceedingly conscious of linguistic problems and began to speculate about them in ways that led straight to the language philosophies and sophistries of modern times.

What is meant here is, of course, not the incessant, unavoidable, gradual changes in the life of language, but the earthquakes and volcanic eruptions. But even less dramatic deviations from the traditional linguistic order have at all times given rise to opposition and resistance, and not only among the cliques of narrow-minded and obstinate purists. No, there were also, in German, Schopenhauer and Karl Kraus and the courageous early diagnosticians, foremost among them Dolf Sternberger, of the corrupting use the leaders and leader-writers of the national revolution made of the native idiom. Their concern was by no means some aesthetic cleanliness of the language; no, they were imbued with the convictions that the 'innovative' speech reflected the mind, or rather the mindlessness, of the speakers. For Schopenhauer, still more was at stake when he indignantly flew at the innovators, above all the journalists, asking them to take their hands off the German language: we have inherited it and must hand it on to those who will come after us; and just as there are engraved in it the greatest poetry and the noblest thought of the nation, the corruption of language is bound to corrupt the writing and thinking of the future. It was in this Schopenhauerian sense that Karl Kraus, boastful in the guise of modesty and in defiance of all the 'Neugetön', the literary 'modernism' of his contemporaries, wrote:

> Ich bin nur einer von den Epigonen,
> die in dem alten Haus der Sprache wohnen.

I am only one of the epigones living in the old house of language.

Yet the earthquakes of language are still different. They overtake a people and its traditions not only when, as happened once upon a time, the gods of antiquity die – 'dead is the great Pan!' – but also when radically new constellations of power arise or dissolve. Such a time was the epoch of the Renaissance in which the word 'modern', coined at the end of the Middle Ages, truly came into its own. We shall not pause where pausing can hardly be profitable any more: at the scientific, the astronomical revolution. But with the vast three-dimensional spaces it opened, it also brought about the emergence of perspectivism that reached much further than the art of painting. It shook many seemingly unshakable certainties of faith. It widened and colonized the world without and also what Rilke in later days would call 'Weltinnenraum', the inner world of subjectivity. With its ever subtler shadings it began to render problematical the communication from person to person. Also, it bestowed honours upon the vernacular, the 'dialects of the tribes', honours that had hitherto been reserved for the formalities of Latin. Words became more spacious, resonant and powerful, just as if they armed themselves against the onrush of the mathematical sciences and their abstractions. All this should at least be hinted at before we turn for a concluding moment to Shakespeare, the richest among those who, at that time, had acquired new riches of language, but who was also the most perspicacious when it came to doubting the dependability of words – as did, in a much more infirm and grief-ridden future, many writers who arrived long after him.

Never before did language possess such freedom. Shakespeare's art appeared to have shaken off all the orthodoxies and limitations of the flat Ptolemaic cosmos. But this was also why he opposed the threat of relativism, the loss of 'degree', the incipient confusions of unbelief, with an emphasis on order and the moral verities of tradition, a conservatism that wholly and fascinatingly contrasts with the liberties he took with words. And then, in the midst of it, Hamlet's scruples about language, worries that would not be Hamlet's if his author had not known them himself.

Among the works of the dramatist this drama of language makes its conspicuous appearance. It is most surprising. For from the beginning of his making poetry Shakespeare moves through the world of things as well as the stirrings of mind and heart like one who was born to command; and what he commanded was that all those things, thoughts and feelings should turn to words. If ever a poet seemed to live by certain naive notions the Middle Ages had about language, it was, anachronistically, Shakespeare: namely the sense that the verbal sign does not differ in any relevant degrees of reality from that which it signifies. For when Adam named all things, he named them in accordance with the will of God; and thus things and names became one. What appears inseparably to merge in all sublime moments of poetry, the peace above the mountain tops, in Goethe's poem, with the word 'Ruh', or the brightly burning 'tyger', happens again and again in Shakespeare's poetic dramas. But then there appears

Hamlet who seems to extend invitations to translators through his tormenting conviction that all words are inadequate designations of the real things or the real inner states. It is not merely Polonius who, foolishly and timidly, at Hamlet's teasing, accepts a sequence of incompatible names for the form of a cloud; it is Hamlet himself who, declaring implicitly the names of all things to be arbitrary, has 'that within that passes show'. Or worse: there are times when he suspects that everything he does or says is an actor's pose, full of falseness and deception, evasions of a weakling who is incapable of living and acting in the truth: 'Words, words, words'.

With the great monologue of self-indictment and self-humiliation in the second scene of the second act, Hamlet, at the same time, is denigrating language itself and thereby brings into question the tradition of humanistic certainties insofar as they are founded upon language. Moreover, he slanders the very genre of poetic drama – one of which, a very famous one, is being performed at that moment:

> ... This is most brave,
> That I, the son of a dear father murdered,
> Prompted to my revenge by heaven and hell,
> Must, like a whore, unpack my heart with words ...

Although it is doubtful whether whores have ever been in the habit of doing this, the 'must' is extraordinary. For it is the 'must' of every hero of every tragedy even if his resolution to act is less inhibited than Hamlet's. Could there be poetic dramas at all if their leading actors simply 'acted' and not, before the act, unpacked their hearts with words put together in long and moving speeches? And indeed, Hamlet's very hesitancy to act is inseparable from his misgivings, intense and oppressive, that his inner condition is inexpressible, be it in words or deeds, in love or murder; and when finally the deed is done, it kills one who was not meant. The false death of Polonius illuminates, like a giant will-o'-the-wisp, the meaning of the dramatic plot. All that is rotten in the state of Denmark, which means, in the human estate, in the constitution of humanity and its tradition, results from the falsities of language. *Hamlet* is the first great drama in which the acting of the actor plays itself a main part. Small wonder that Nietzsche made man as an actor, man wearing masks, one of the recurrent themes in his analysis of European decadence. Yet what, with Shakespeare, comes uniquely to the fore in *Hamlet* – unless punning itself is regarded as a playful symptom heralding a weightier crisis of language consciousness and self-consciousness – spreads like a literary epidemic at the end of the nineteenth century.

It was a much more recent poet who devoted a long essay in the form of an imaginary letter (as well as his best comedy, *Der Schwierige*) to this calamity: the disproportion between the word uttered and the awareness within, a commotion that tends to render uninhabitable every shelter that the mind could hope to find in the tradition of language. Hugo von Hofmannsthal's essay-letter, known as the Chandos Letter, was written in 1902. By a strange intuition, Hofmannsthal appointed a young poet from an epoch that was as mighty in its commands of words as that of Shakespeare, to write this epistle: a Lord Chandos addressing himself to his old friend Francis Bacon, explaining to him why he so badly disappointed the later Lord Chancellor's expectations by ceasing to write poetry. (It is, of course, what happened to Hofmannsthal himself after he had produced astonishingly mature poems in early youth.) The letter is about language and its falling silent, about saying and the unsayable, about tradition and its dissolution.

How did it come to pass? Because, Hofmannsthal-Lord Chandos writes, the words which literature has habitually used in dealing with its traditional subjects, no longer make any impression on his mind. All these words now strike him as mendacious because they simulate coherence, myths of significances, to which he cannot respond. For, he says, he has 'lost the ability to think and speak about anything in tidy sequences'. It is left to seemingly quite unimportant occasions to evoke strong, even powerful emotions – a kind of mystical enthusiasm, unsayable, incommunicable because the intensity of feeling is utterly out of keeping with the banality of the apparent cause. It is not the beauty of Helena, or the founding of Rome, or the assassination of a king that is the 'givenness' which T. S. Eliot would later call the 'objective correlative' of a great emotion. It is, on the contrary, nothing but 'nothings' that have never had a place in the canon of great poetry: 'A watering can, a harrow left behind in a field,

41

a dog lying in the sun, a neglected churchyard, a little farmstead – all this may become the vessel of my revelation', and may 'assume a sublime or moving quality which to describe words seem to me not rich enough.' Such a letter could never have been sent by an Elizabethan nobleman but was certainly written, in one variation or another, by many, who, like Hofmannsthal, have made a name for themselves in modern literature. It would be possible to fill a volume with strikingly similar quotations, identical in meaning, and the contributors would be Proust, Rilke, Kafka, T. S. Eliot.

Kafka had learned the lesson of young Lord Chandos early in his life as a writer, as early as his *Description of a Struggle*. There someone says to a stranger to whom he feels attracted: 'Your eyes have comforted me for a long time. And I hope you will teach me what really is the matter with these things that swirl around me and vanish like snowflakes, while for others even a little liquor glass stands firmly on the table like a monument.' Whereupon the man, thus addressed, diagnoses the affliction of the questioner as 'seasickness on land'. He also recognizes instantly that this seasickness is, in fact, the sickness of language: 'You have forgotten the true names of things and now hastily pour arbitrary names over them ... The poplar tree in the field that you used to call the "Throne of Babel" sways again namelessly and you must call it: "Noah, when he was drunk!".' – If one compares this desperate reaching for words with the quarrels about tradition that went on between the defenders of the *anciens* and the advocates of the *modernes* in seventeenth-century France, the *Querelle* looks like a reportage on minor intellectual skirmishes.

Will the poplar tree, which has lost its name in the confusion caused by the divine intervention in Babel, ever take root again in the ground of the true word? This might save at least a measure of that tradition which is evoked a hundred times in this year of remembering the 'Father of the Occident'.* Strange that Virgil as well as Kafka should have asked their heirs to burn their unpublished manuscripts. They refused to do it. Perhaps it is not always ashes that the mythic bird needs for new flights. Language itself will show whether such hope is justified or in vain.

---

* This was written in 1981, two thousand years after Virgil's death.

3
Nietzsche's last words
about art and truth

for David Relkin

'FOR a philosopher to say "the good and the beautiful are one" is infamy; if he goes on to add, "also the true", one ought to thrash him. Truth is ugly. We possess *art* lest we *perish of the truth*.' This utterance, at once crystalline and tumultuous, brilliant and violent, was written by Nietzsche in 1888, the year preceding his mental collapse. It is contained in one of the posthumous notes that have been collected in *The Will to Power* (M.A. XIX, 229 and W.822)* and has the resonance of last words, words spoken or cried out with that assured despair or hope that allows for no debate; and perhaps it was really meant as Nietzsche's last word concerning a problem of which – apropos his rereading, in the same year, of his youthful *Birth of Tragedy* – he said that it was the earliest which compellingly demanded his serious attention; and even today, he added, this dilemma filled him with 'holy terror' (M.A. XIV, 326).

The problem, so terrifying to Nietzsche from beginning to end, is the relationship between art and truth. Even in the context of *The Birth of Tragedy* it is exceedingly difficult to grasp. For whatever meaning is given to the word 'truth', no common denominator can possibly be found among the endless varieties of 'art': a sculpture of ancient Egypt, an archaic Apollo, *Antigone*, *King Lear*, Michelangelo, Bach, Mozart, Beethoven, Bizet or Offenbach, not to mention a short poem of Goethe's or Mallarmé's. Even if we equate art with ancient tragedy, as *The Birth of Tragedy* might suggest, just as it proclaims tragedy's rebirth in Wagner's music drama, the question is whether the dilemma, whatever its 'true' nature, was resolved and the terror diminished by the terrifying 'We possess *art* lest we *perish of the truth*'. Has the ugliness of the ugly truth increased so drastically since Plato's time that now anyone associating it with beauty commits a

* Abbreviations: W, followed by the numeral indicating the numbered section = *The Will to Power*, translated by Walter Kaufmann and R. J. Hollingdale, New York 1967. M.A., followed by a Roman numeral indicating the volume and the Arabic numeral the page = Musarionausgabe of Nietzsche's works, 23 volumes, Munich 1920–9. In this case the translations are my own.

philosophical felony? Has truth become so militantly aggressive that art must serve as a fortification against its invading our lives? That we should not be able to live with the truth, the whole truth, has surely been said before, and by no one more memorably than by Plato in the cave parable; and it has been repeated again and again, by Lessing, for instance, who, had God given him the choice between the truth and the infinite search for it, would have asked him for the endless striving because the truth, he wrote, was only for God Himself; or by the story of the veiled image of Sais, the mysterious image of 'the truth', whose unveiled sight would have been deadly. In all these instances, and many, many more, it is a matter of the whole truth being unattainable or not meant for the treasury of man. But that truth would kill us *because of its devastating ugliness* has never been said – surely not with Nietzsche's aphoristic vehemence. As the 'truth' in Nietzsche's saying obviously means the true character of existence, and not merely this or that experience in our individual lives that may shock us to death, what, once more, can 'art' mean as its radical contrast and 'remedy'? There are many reasons for our reluctance to answer this question.

There is above everything else the indisputable fact that, since the generation of Rilke, George, Mann, the idea of art as the quasi-religious opposite of 'life' has run its course. Who among the young can understand Stefan George's imperial pronouncement that 'kein Ding sei, wo das Wort gebricht' – there ought to be no thing where language fails in naming it – which in the end meant the same as Karl Kraus's celebrated and notorious declaration that where the task was to find the right words for the domination of Hitler language had to abdicate: 'Mir fällt zu Hitler nichts ein.' Certainly, there is no longer an artist who would look upon his art as an all but ecclesiastical, indeed monastic, devotion. 'I have many brothers in cassocks', Rilke wrote, and the young Thomas Mann's Tonio Kröger even thought of having to sacrifice 'life' in the service to his art: Not one leaf from the laurel tree of art, he said, may be plucked without the artist's paying for it with his life. Meanwhile, art has come to be as 'ungodly' as life itself, and the evergreen laurel tree, for Tonio Kröger so dangerously in foliage, has been badly damaged by an autumn in which more has withered than the

leaves of trees. 'O trees of life, when will your winter come?'
Rilke asked at the beginning of the darkest of the *Duino Elegies*,
the fourth, written entirely in the deep shadow of the First World
War. 'Now', is the unison answer of modern literature. It is not
for its practitioners to dedicate themselves to literature with that
idolatrous religiosity that was Flaubert's, Thomas Mann's, Rilke's,
and – amid the endless curses he uttered against the idol – Franz
Kafka's. Indeed, art is no longer as 'heiter', as serene, as Schiller
believed it should be; yet it has ceased to be as serious as to
demand the sacrifice of 'life'.

Then, there is the unsettling fact that during Nietzsche's lifetime, and even before, a species of literature emerged that hardly
earned his praise but that, for the sake of his consistency and our
intellectual comfort, he ought to have judged even more harshly.
Sometimes he did, but only selectively (although when he did
so, he discriminated with his unfailing artistic instinct). What I
have in mind, is realism and of course naturalism; and the
naturalists pride themselves upon forcing 'the truth of life', as
they see it, not 'art', as Nietzsche understands it, upon the attention
of the public. Nietzsche would have approved of our using the
word 'forcing'; for he once, and more than once, characterized
'modern art', above all naturalism, as 'the art of tyrannizing'.
Those 'artists', he wrote, were in the habit of employing an
'overwhelming mass' – an ugly mass, it is to be presumed –
'before which the senses become confused', and 'brutality in
colour, material, desires' (W.827). One wonders, with regard to
both the tyranny and the brutality, what his vocabulary would have
been if he had lived to witness the productions of the cinema (a
form of presentation that is, quite apart from any content, by its
very nature incomparably more 'tyrannical' than any art that preceded it: the very darkness in which it is being watched opens the
spectators' eyes and minds to the vision of the film's maker with
a hypnotic exclusiveness that is unique in the history of the arts)
or of Eugene O'Neil or Tennessee Williams or Thomas Bernhard.

Or did he anticipate all this when in 1888 he wrote: 'The ugly,
i.e. the contradiction to art, that which is outside the scope of
art, its No; every time decline, impoverishment of life, impotence,
disintegration, degeneration are suggested even faintly, the aesthetic man reacts with his No' (W.809). Or when he said in the

same year of the increase in civilization 'that it necessarily brings with it an increase in the morbid elements, in the neurotic-psychiatric and criminal' (W.864) all of which is as 'depressing' as it is 'the symptom of a depression', and 'takes away strength, impoverishes, weighs down...' (W.809) It is exceedingly doubtful whether history is bent upon teaching lessons; but if it does, it proves right the grand gesture with which Nietzsche dismisses the revolutionary claim of 'naturalism'. A critique of social ills? By no means, a pathological fascination with them and a fore-boding of ever more pathology: '... the artist, restrained from crime by weakness of will and timidity, and not yet ripe for the *madhouse*' makes himself the bearer of the message 'of the Revolu-tion, the establishment of equal rights', and becomes the paragon 'of the instincts of decline (of *ressentiment*, discontent, the drive to destroy, anarchism and nihilism), including the slave instincts ... that have long been kept down' (W.864).

As examples of the massive tyranny of the arts, Nietzsche quotes the creations of Zola and Wagner. Zola and Wagner may seem a surprising pair of brothers in the art of hypnotic brutality, yet their features do display a family resemblance (of which Thomas Mann, in his most important essay on Wagner* made a great deal and thus provoked some guardians of the 'German genius', intellectual warriors that, under the rule of Hitler, happened to live in 1933 in the 'Wagner City' Munich, to that notorious 'Protest' that certainly helped to keep the author of *Buddenbrooks* outside the frontiers of Germany for the rest of his life).

In the order of aphorisms collected in *The Will to Power* the succinct proclamation of the function of art – to make the unbearable bearable – is preceded by an observation that, of course, denies the possibility of pessimism in art: 'There is no such thing as pessimistic art. – Art affirms. Job affirms' (W.821). True, true, although one may not without some scruples accept the abrupt inclusion of the Book of Job in the category of Art. But had we not been prepared for such manoeuvres by Nietzsche's persistently speaking of Art as the power that raises us above the wretchedness of life? It was for this very reason that he denied the possibility

* Thomas Mann, *Gesammelte Werke*, IX, Frankfurt 1960.

of such a thing as pessimistic art; and there is no mistaking the religious resonance of the voice that pronounces: 'What is essential in art remains its being bent upon perfecting existence, its creating perfection and plenitude. Art is essentially *affirmation, blessing, deification* of existence ... Schopenhauer is *wrong* when he says that certain works of art (what is meant is once more Attic tragedy) serve pessimism.' And in case his *Birth of Tragedy* was not yet understood – as late as 1888 – he emphasizes again that tragedy does *not* teach resignation, as Schopenhauer believed. No, for an artist 'to represent terrible and questionable things shows in itself his instinct for power and magnificence: he does not fear them' (W.821), but affirms even evil in its transfiguration through art. He affirms like Job.

To descend from such heights into the lowlands of grammar, looks like seeking shelter in banality. Yet is it really banal to enquire whether the verb 'affirm', a transitive verb, does not stand in need of an object? My Latin teacher, a kindly Cistercian monk, rigorously insisted on his pupils' asking 'whom or what?' to find out whether a verb was transitive. If it responded positively to the question, it was. 'Affirm?' he would have said: 'whom or what?' and might have failed Rilke on the famous opening line of the Orphic sonnet 'Rühmen, das ist's!', 'Praising, that's it!' 'Whom or what?' he would have asked and waited for a considerably more particular answer than 'life as such'. 'Life is not "as such".' And indeed, it is probably due to Nietzsche and Rilke that the language of poets has become accustomed to the – as it were – intransitive use of such verbs as 'affirm' or 'praise'. This is more than a matter of grammar: grammar, as often it does, mirrors here the grammar of consciousness itself. It is impossible to make articulate sense, and not merely an ecstatic-intoxicated dithyramb, of the praiseworthiness of praise itself; or simply to affirm affirmation. 'Ein Gott vermags', 'A God may do it', Rilke's third sonnet says; but, before Rilke took charge of him, Orpheus was no god. Rilke raised him to the status of a god by merging him with Nietzsche's Dionysus; and he, the god, surely succeeds where a mere human being is bound to fail: in the lavishing of unconditional yea-saying upon an existence in which the No of disaster, sickness, mass murder, cruelty and senseless death is as inescapable as the Yes of love and happiness. With Job the object

49

is easily supplied – in as un-Nietzschean a manner as can be: Job affirms God. Even so, the story of Job is never easy to take, and had Job received and in the end believed Nietzsche's message of the death of God, it would be a downright unbearable tale.

He who is not inclined to dwell on such questions, may meditate for a while the song of the Watchman on the Tower in the fifth act of *Faust II*. The first verses of it are one of Goethe's most beautiful lyrical poems, a song of praise intoned by one who is at that moment in the state of pure, will-less contemplation, the ineluctable condition of what Schopenhauer calls aesthetic experience – the experience that is untouched by any self-interest. Lynceus sees, *sees*, and only the happiness of seeing matters to him. *What* he sees, is almost irrelevant. It is beautiful, because he sees it with eyes that are undistracted by anything that is not pure seeing; nearby the wood and the deer, and high above it the moon and the stars; and beside himself with ecstatic yea-saying, he speaks the words that are always quoted as proof of Goethe's affirmation of life. Yet they lose sight of any definable or even particular grammatical object; for

> Es sei, wie es wolle,
> Es war doch so schön.

Be it as it may (in the sight of those blissful and blessing eyes – 'Ihr glücklichen Augen//was je ihr gesehn ...') it has been nothing but beautiful.

In the whole range of literature there is no purer lyrical expression of the jubilant yea-saying affirming the world as 'aesthetic phenomenon' as young Nietzsche, in *The Birth of Tragedy*, renames what for Schopenhauer was the artist's intuition of the Platonic idea beyond the mere appearance of a thing, an intuitive vision that is undimmed by any self-will. But because Nietzsche, as early as the otherwise faithful Schopenhauerian *Birth of Tragedy* robs this vision of its transcendental object, the Platonic idea, it is bereft of any object whatever. This is a philosophical act of surgery the consequences of which proved fatal to his philosophy of art.

What in the monologue of the Watchman on the Tower breaks, with catastrophic suddenness, into the celebration of the 'ewige Zier' ('kosmos' in Greek), of the 'aesthetic phenomenon', is hardly ever quoted. Indeed, it is no longer a song and differs from what precedes it by the changed rhythm: Goethe has separated it from the celebration by the stage instruction 'pause'. And what a pause is this!

For abruptly the Watchman's aesthetic contemplation finishes when he is reminded of his task as an active human being, placed upon the tower not to celebrate life as an aesthetic phenomenon, but to guard Faust's estate against threatening dangers. And what he sees now is the smoke rising from the little house of the dear old couple Philemon and Baucis. It is on fire, as a consequence of Faust's megalomaniac orders to Mephistopheles: to remove the two ancient people from the smallholding on Faust's empire; and the fire may spread, destroy not only the two but cause more disasters. Thus the Watchman's glorious yea-saying ends. He now reminds himself of his duty as a Watchman: he was up on his tower not merely in order to delight in the view. 'Nicht allein mich zu ergetzen, bin ich hier so hochgestellt', and is now terrified by the horrible threat from out of the dark world:

> Welch ein greuliches Entsetzen
> Droht mir aus der finstern Welt.

The indiscriminate object of praise has changed to the accusative of terror. Only a few verse lines before, the Watchman's eyes were happy to see *whatever* it was; but now he deplores that his sight reaches even as far as the burning hut:

> Sollt ihr Augen dies erkennen!
> Muss ich so weitsichtig sein!

The exact transitiveness of transitive verbs cannot easily be circumvented.

Is this, then, the way in which art affirms even the ugliness of life, 'art understood as the potent incentive to living, as the eternal urge to live, to live eternally' (M.A. XIV, 328)? We only just heard such yea-saying, heard of an art that deifies life and blesses it as Lynceus does before he espies the flames, an art that refutes Schopenhauer's belief that tragedy teaches resignation; and immediately upon the yea-saying Job there follows, with a question mark, Zola, this time not in the company of Wagner but in that of the equally questionable Goncourts. What is wrong with those Frenchmen? 'The things they display are ugly: but

that they display them comes from their pleasure in the ugly.'
One is tempted to interject: 'from the pleasure taken in the truth?'
And how does this 'pleasure in the ugly' differ from the artist's
fearlessness in 'representing terrible and questionable things', a
courage that shows 'his instinct for power and magnificence'?
No doubt, this instinct differs from that pleasure. But how? Yet
Nietzsche continues: 'It's no good! If you think otherwise, you're
deceiving yourselves. – How liberating is Dostoevsky!' (W.821)

This is a psychological coup and shows Nietzsche's superb
literary instinct: praise for Dostoevsky (and Stendhal) despite
their practising 'realism' and even 'naturalism' in literature. We
do not know for certain how much of Dostoevsky Nietzsche had
read, but it must have been more than *Notes from Underground* (a
book that undoubtedly had prompted him to call himself in the
preface to *Dawn* – 1881, preface of 1886 – an 'underground man';
it is certain that he knew *Crime and Punishment*, too. When he
chanced upon Dostoevsky late in his life, he said of him not only
that finding him was one of the most welcome strokes of good
luck (even more so than his 'discovery of Stendhal') but also that
he was 'the only psychologist from whom I had something to
learn' (M.A. XVII, 145). The question 'What?', although it lures
us into the unknowable, is irresistible. Dostoevsky is 'liberating'
and different in that from the Goncourts and Zola, the 'naturalists',
who took pleasure in showing the ugly; non-artists who did not
know that just because the truth of life was its spiritually killing
ugliness, we have art, the beautiful illusion, the redeeming untruth, the bewitching lie. Indeed, Zarathustra calls himself a liar
insofar as he is an artist (M.A. XIII, 166).

The beautiful illusion versus the ugly truth: surely, it cannot
be in this aesthetic sense that Dostoevsky could possibly have
proved 'liberating'. His world can be as ugly as any naturalist's,
and is as inelegant as his style. Well then, how is the sentence
'We possess *art* lest we *perish of truth*', a dictum that is the extreme
formula of the mature Nietzsche's philosophy of art, to be reconciled to his praise of Dostoevsky? The answer is 'Not at all.'
And the same applies to every passage in the *young* Nietzsche's
Birth of Tragedy that celebrates the Greek redemption of suffering
through the 'aesthetic phenomenon' of tragedy. What, then, is it
that Nietzsche could have learned from Dostoevsky, the *psycho-*

logist, that he might not have learned from, say, Shakespeare, or indeed – from himself, incomparable psychologist of crime and criminal that he was, and the tireless, even if sometimes tiresome, explorer of the psychological roots of religion, asceticism and saintliness; the Ivan Karamazov, as he inhabits Dostoevsky' book? At this point we need only mention the names of Zossima or Alyosha – despite the improbability of Nietzsche's having read *The Brothers Karamazov* – not to feel too insolent in our insolent venture. We venture then, hesitantly, timidly, the answer to our question how the philosopher who called himself 'the first psychologist of Europe', had profited from Dostoevsky's 'psychological novels' and what, perhaps, might even have 'liberated' him. Liberated from what? From the fetters of his own psychology? For reading again and again what Nietzsche, again and again, and in a voice that sounds shriller and shriller as the years go by, says about the origins of 'ascetic ideals' and the Christian religion, we sense that this immensely intelligent thinker had sometimes to deafen the gentle voice which within himself kept insinuating that all was not well with the monotony of his psychologizing. Monotony? True, there are moments when the drumming subsides and that voice makes itself heard, for instance in *The Genealogy of Morals* when the 'torture' of the psychologist's compulsion to guess 'the true nature' – and that is, of course, the ugly nature – 'of great men' (M.A. XV, 243) suddenly relents and quite a different tone comes into its own, namely the psychologist's confession that he, who in his determination to disclose the ugliness beneath the masque of greatness, violates the rule of respect and discretion and, revealing the 'truth' about others, only reveals his own character. For greatness and 'finer humanity', he says, is also in a man's respect for the masque (M.A. XV, 246) and in his unwillingness to pursue his psychological curiosity 'in the wrong places'. It is as if Nietzsche had just read another great psychologist's psychological observation about psychology, the German Romantic Novalis's saying that psychology, or what goes by that name, is one of 'the ghosts ... that have usurped the place in the temple where genuine images of the divine ought to be'.*

*Novalis, *Fragmente*, ed. Ernst Kamnitzer, Dresden 1929, p. 381.

What then – to continue for a little while along the precarious path – could Nietzsche have learned from Dostoevsky? First, that psychology may indeed affect – disastrously or beneficially – a man's pieties but most certainly cannot *establish* the worth or unworth, the beauty or ugliness, the truth or untruth of what has grown from roots sunk deeply into the psyche; as little as botany or soil analysis or meteorology or geology can prove or disprove the justification of the sense of autumnal glory one may have in the sight of that yellowing birch tree before the window or of the play of sunlight on the rugged faces of the mountains that rise beyond it.

That a man may be too weak to endure the tribulations of his existence – its 'truth' – without faith in God (would Job have endured them?); or that the strongest sensual impulses may have led to Dante's divine love of Beatrice; or that Nietzsche might be right as, no doubt, Freud would have it, even where he is least convincing: in assuming, for instance, that 'without a certain overheating of the sexual system a Raphael is unthinkable' or that 'making music is another way of making children' (W.800) – all this does not in the slightest touch upon the question of the validity or falseness of the faith; or upon the true nature of Dante's love or the beauty of the poetry celebrating that love; or on Raphael's artistic integrity in painting his chaste madonnas; or on the greatness of Bach's B minor Mass (was he really in need of making music in addition to making twenty children?). If a believer, in the agony of his dying, is comforted by the thought of a Beyond, or a pagan hero, deadly wounded, by the promise of national glory, both the believer and the hero may consolingly deceive themselves with illusions. Yet what is certainly *not* proved by the torments that bring forth such consolations, is the absence of a Beyond or the emptiness of posthumous glory.

And Nietzsche's work itself? Would we grasp *anything* of his intellectual passion or of the quality and style of his thought if we merely remembered that he was the son of a mentally endangered Protestant pastor and a mother as ordinary as anyone can be (child of the same parents that a little later produced the notorious, rather than famous, Elisabeth)? Deplorable that it is still necessary to insist upon the obvious: the utter inconclusiveness of all conclusions drawn from origins when we wish to assess the true nature and the moral or aesthetic worth of that which has come from them; particularly when the origins are sought in the physiological, as Nietzsche increasingly did towards the end of his intellectually responsible life. 'Countertranscendental reductionism' would be too polite a word for this process. No, this method that defines the value of the pearl by referring to the grain of sand that had pathologically irritated the oyster's mucous membrane does not 'reduce' the level of the phenomenon in question; it passes it by, it misses it.

'It is exceptional states that condition the artist – all of them profoundly related to ... morbid phenomena – so it seems impossible to be an artist and not to be sick', Nietzsche noted in 1888 (W.811), but at the same time he maintained that 'artists if they are worth their salt ... must be – also physically – of strong disposition, excelling in vigour, powerful animals ...' (W.800) This appears to be a tremendous contradiction, yet it is one with which he began to live even two or three years earlier when he knew how to be at his most 'healthily' Dionysian. He would at that time ask 'in regard to all aesthetic values: "Has hunger or super-abundance become creative here"?' (W.846) The question was undoubtedly meant to establish a difference in artistic ranks: Homer, Hafiz, Rubens, Goethe, are given as examples of artists who, in the fullness of their creative powers, 'eternalize', 'apotheosize' existence while the others, the 'hunger artists', are Nietzsche's unloved romantics. Profoundly conscious as he was of the ambiguities that prevail in the relationship between origins and outcomes – unavoidable morbidity and sickness as the source of all art, but then again inexhaustible riches of health and strength – Nietzsche should not have been in need of Dostoevsky's instructions; yet again and again he tempts us to find that he was.

It may have been Dostoevsky, the liberating teacher, whom Nietzsche had in mind, when in the later part of the above note in *The Will to Power* (he used it almost verbatim in the *Joyous Wisdom*, section 370) he acknowledges, as if to make ambiguity still more ambiguous, an art whose abundant sources of energy spring, as it were, from hunger, expressing themselves in 'the tyrannic will of one who suffers deeply, who struggles and is tormented' (M.A. XII, 311). Dostoevsky might indeed have taught him this. But he could have taught him still more, something that audaciously one might call an ontology of human being. It was the psychologist in Nietzsche that was averse to learning it. The lesson is this: it is impossible for the human mind to overcome the compulsion to make fundamental discriminations. No amount of psychology, of *tout comprendre*, can possibly lead to *tout pardonner*: whatever is felt to be scandalous will keep scandalizing us, whatever the historically changeable occasions of the scandal are; whatever has been experienced as truly outrageous will for ever call forth the response of outrage. Surely, the psychological diagnostician Nietzsche, in distinguishing between the soul's plenitude or its starvation as the begetter of different kinds of art, does certainly judge their value. To discriminate in this manner is not simply a bad habit instilled in us by upbringing or language; on the contrary, our discriminating language is merely the expression of an elemental need that will persist as long as the mind is a human mind.

There is no 'beyond good and evil' for us. If we miraculously ever reached that terminus, he who deems it desirable that we should, would exclaim: 'How good it is to have reached the state beyond good and evil!' And what applies to good and evil, does in equal measure apply to the distinction between true and false. *The Twilight of the Idols* (1888), one of the last of the extraordinary books Nietzsche wrote shortly before his mental breakdown, contains an astonishing and astonishingly condensed 'narration', entitled 'How the "true world" (once again we have returned to "truth") finally became a fable' and claims to trace 'the history of an error'. It ends thus: 'We have abolished the true world' – and when he speaks here of the 'true world', he means the 'world of ideas', the only really real world that ever since Plato has dominated most of our philosophies and religions, the 'true world' as distinct from the world of our ordinary experience – well then, this true world 'we have abolished: which world is left? Perhaps the apparent one? Certainly not! *Together with the true world we have also abolished the apparent one!*' (M.A. XVII, 76) Are we to respond by saying: 'How true! The distinction between a true world and an apparent world, and thereby between true and false, is false!'?

Once more, Nietzsche appears to be determined to refute himself and to embrace the very nihilism which he desired to conquer.

For if one has even the slightest feeling for the communications of language that, to spite the credulous semioticist, is capable of 'meaning' incomparably more than it actually says, then one cannot but doubt that Nietzsche, in his 'fable', announced only what is logically self-evident; and the logically self-evident does not need the rhetorical support of the accents of prophecy. As soon as we deny the reality of that ideal world – and Nietzsche is by no means the first to do so – we are clearly left with nothing but the world of our immediate experience, the world that for Plato was merely the world of shadow appearances. If that dualism collapses, there exists only *one* world. Who would doubt that? Every highschool boy who has ever heard of the doctrine of positivism is able to comprehend it. Whereupon one ought to listen a second time to the conclusion of Nietzsche's 'fable': 'We have abolished the true world: which world is left? Perhaps the apparent one? Certainly not! Together with the *true world we have also abolished the apparent one!*' What is the appropriate response to these hammer blows of language? Should we say, 'This is clear enough! What is the agitation about?' No, but rather to share the deep spiritual apprehension which is conveyed by the voice that says what the opinion it utters does not say: namely not merely that from now onwards we shall have to make ourselves at home in *one* world, but much more: that now we must be prepared to exist in *not even one*, at least in no world which would allow us truly to exist. Two or three years before this, Nietzsche drew up a sketch of a preface – it was replaced by that of 1886 – for the new edition of *The Birth of Tragedy*. It says: '... there is only one world, and this is false, cruel, contradictory, seductive, without meaning. – A world thus constituted, is the real world' (W.835). And, therefore, one is led to ask: a world – false, he calls it – that Nietzsche's *Übermensch* would experience as beyond good and evil? Not likely, unless he succeeded in what not even he could succeed in, namely in ecstatically 'transvaluing' that world which, in Nietzsche's description, teaches us that *horror vacui*, the horror of nothingness, of nihilism, that determines the *style* of the 'fable'; and to succeed although he *knows* that it is in the depth of its nature an evil world?

Can anyone accept such a world which is, decidedly, not a human world? Even if we achieved the impossible and found the appropriate language for it, a language that would be able to renounce what Nietzsche's language cannot do without: namely such words as 'true' or 'false', 'good' or 'evil', would then our inner nature be so radically changed as to enable us to discard those distinctions? Perhaps we might; but only if they no longer corresponded to anything within ourselves – and so we never shall, unless our nature ceased to be human nature.

Yet if this ever happened, we would no longer know what, for instance, could possibly be tragic in Sophocles' *Antigone*. It would seem absolutely senseless to us that a woman should risk her life by obeying the divinely ordained law which demands the burial of her slain brother because she deems it superior to the contrary decree issued by the king. And the tragic metamorphosis that, according to Nietzsche, is the 'true' and 'good' effect of tragedy: the transformation of terror into bliss, the ecstatic yea-saying that triumphantly resists the most forceful temptation to negate, would inevitably be lost on us. Or we would, reading *King Lear*, no longer perceive any moral difference between Cordelia and her sisters, or between Gloucester's sons, and thus judge the whole course of action, the grand sublimity of the poetry and the ending a tiresome futility; or we would be unable to grasp the extreme brilliance of Nietzsche's paradox: 'Truth is the kind of error without which a certain species of life cannot live' (W.493), or indeed of 'We possess *art* lest we *perish of the truth*.'

With this we are back at our beginning and forced to ask whether Nietzsche himself, at that time of his life, allows us to make sense of this sentence. Of course, to ask thus goes against the grain. The sentence instantly *shocks* us into understanding it. But do we really? It may appear to us that we know 'what he means' and may even marvel at the marvellous power with which 'truth' is here endowed: it kills through the force of its ugliness; and by thus cutting short our lives, brings Nietzsche's philosophy of art to its climax. For until Nietzsche arrived on the philosophical scene, it had – at least on that scene – always been regarded as a blessing to live 'in the truth'. Plato may have looked upon it as a dangerous, even a blinding blessing, but a blessing nonetheless. Has it now transpired that we have to make a living of absurdity? For we appear to be so absurdly constituted that one of our deepest, most honourable and most human desires, the desire for truth, would lead to our perdition, if there was no art. But this is an echo from that 'once upon a time' which has been mentioned before. Once upon a time – or once in the past – it may have seemed that art could save us from the fatal attacks of truth. In the meantime, it would appear, art has often joined the perpetrators of the ugly, thus becoming the kind of art which could never have inspired him to say what the young author of *The Birth of Tragedy* might have confessed (as he later did): that he was 'passionately in love with art' and finally 'saw art in everything that is' (M.A. XXI, 68).

Long before Nietzsche wrote that philosophically breath-taking reflection on 'How the true world became a fable', this consummation was well-prepared by the very logic of the aesthetics at work in *The Birth of Tragedy*, the book that could not have been written without Schopenhauer, whether it is obedient to him or whether it flagrantly violates his teachings; whether it splendidly supplements it (as, for instance, 'rescuing' lyrical poetry for Schopenhauer's code of art by revealing the 'objectivity' behind its semblance of 'I-saying', its subjectivity: for '... we cannot imagine the smallest genuine work of art lacking objectivity and disinterested contemplation', Nietzsche says in the perfect Schopenhauer idiom), or whether he brings about the collapse of Schopenhauer's aesthetics by undermining the foundation on which it rests, namely the thesis that the work of art is a *revelation of the truth*, truth in the metaphysical sense of Plato's ideas (M.A. III, 40f.). Without as yet declaring war on Schopenhauer, he quietly topples the 'aesthetic phenomenon', the work of art, from its Platonic base, from 'truth', letting it bring about '*redemption in illusion*'.

The German word is *Schein*. It is an uneasy compromise with philosophical respectability: Appearance (*Erscheinung*) would be the word that traditionally goes, as its contrast, with the Platonic Reality, the ultimate reality of the Ideas – or, as Christianity would have it, of that God whose reality is not the reality of 'this world'. To show the way that leads from Appearance to appearance, *Schein*, illusion and finally to the 'fable' that 'the true world', that ruinous invention of Plato and the Christian religion, was to become, we could quote endlessly from Nietzsche's later writing. We won't. A few passages will have to suffice to make the dramatic point: 'Assuming the true world, it could still be a world less valuable for us; precisely the quantum of illusion might be of a higher rank on account of its value for our preservation.' And then Nietzsche adds in brackets: 'Unless appearance (*Schein*) were ground for condemnation?' (W.583 b). Does one dare to counter the question with a question of one's own and ask: Who speaks of condemnation? Or, perhaps more damaging: Who would be able to believe in the higher rank of the illusion, whatever its quantum, once he *knows* that it is an illusion?

No, this reversal of Platonism will not work. 'Assuming', on the contrary, that the empirical world is only apparent, an assemblage of shadows cast by the ideal Truth, who will hinder those who are hungry for initiation into the ultimate knowledge to set out on the Platonic quest? They will be unlikely to heed Nietzsche's instructions that the 'true' antithesis is 'the apparent world and the world invented by a lie', even if 'hitherto' this mendaciously invented world has been called the 'real world', 'truth', 'God', all the notions 'we have to abolish' (W.461). Would this not be also the abolition of art? And once we have succeeded in abolishing that world? Then we would have reduced the antithesis of the apparent world and the true world to its 'true' meaning, namely 'the antithesis "world" and "nothing"' (W.567). This is Nietzsche's most succinct equation between the 'true world' of Platonism or Christianity, and Nihilism. It is an equation as forceful as that between the *one* world, that 'false, cruel, contradictory world', with which we are left after the toppling of Plato's 'true world', and the Nihilism of this one world's meaninglessness. Either way leads, it appears, to spiritual Nothingness, at least according to that unpublished preface to the second edition of *The Birth of Tragedy*. Even more than the published one, it would have insisted on the 'gloom' and 'unpleasantness' of the book's basic conception: the disappearance of the Platonic distinction between a true and an apparent world; and because the *one* 'real world' is false, cruel, contradictory, meaningless, '*we have need of lies*, in order to conquer this reality, this "truth" ... in order to live'. 'The terrifying and questionable character of existence' is borne out by this abysmal necessity. But there is worse to come. Remembering that art is an illusion, a lie, and the artist an illusionist, a liar, we shall be struck by the enormity of this sentence: 'The will to appearance, to illusion, to deception ... counts as more profound, primeval, "metaphysical" than the will to truth, to reality ...', because 'art is worth more than truth' (W.853).

Where the truth is as intolerably ugly as this, a ceaseless offence to the spirit, and the lie as beautiful as the beauty of art (surprising how consistently Nietzsche clings to beauty as the foremost criterion of art); where the 'real' is man's worst enemy, and illusion, therefore, becomes the redeeming deceiver, there the human world has been torn asunder. A vast gap has opened, attracting – irresistibly, it would seem – swarms of demons. Some of them – these need not be failed artists, bad painters – would noisily claim that it is their mission to fuse the severed worlds again by appropriating the real as if it were the raw material for the making of a work of art, a pseudo-aesthetic phenomenon, an unblemished body politic, a perfect society. This is the connection, if any, between the philosopher of art and the devastating usurpers of the human estate. But it is of course only one of modernity's many elements that disastrously connect.

4
Thinking about poetry, Hölderlin and Heidegger

for Oskar Seidlin

THINKING about poetry is not the same as poetic thought, but such 'thinking about' would certainly busy itself in a void if it cut itself loose entirely from its subject matter's imaginative intellection; and it is the alpha and omega of Heidegger's philosophy that poetry *is* thought, just as true thought – that is, thought concerned with the meaning of Being – partakes of the essence of poetry. Yes, the alpha too, although it is only in his writings after *Being and Time* that poetry, above all Hölderlin's, assumes the role of Being's authentic and most 'thoughtful' messenger: 'In a work' (in a work of art, that is) 'truth is at work', truth and hence Being (if only together with its simultaneous concealment, and this not only through the inescapable 'seeming' of art) – truth and hence thought; although 'at this moment in the world's history we have to learn again', Heidegger says in the essay 'Why be a Poet?', 'that the making of poetry ... is a matter of thinking'. For the domain of poetry is language, and even in *Being and Time* it is said of discourse in language that it is 'existentially equi-primordial with understanding': 'If we have not heard "aright",' Heidegger writes – characteristically taking an idiomatic expression at its word: 'Ich höre wohl nicht recht' – 'if we have not heard aright, it is not by accident that we say we have not "understood"', and understanding involves thinking even if it is of a vestigial kind in our daily routines of comprehension. But quite apart from such explicit statements about the near-identity of language and understanding, it is the burden of *Being and Time* – in every respect the burden – that its philosophical idiom is fashioned by the desire, or even the felt necessity, to say something that has not been said (in German, or in any other 'modern' language) since the time some Greek poetic philosophers, or philosophical poets, Anaximander or Parmenides or Heraclitus, said it more than a century before Socrates. Through them, Heidegger believes, Being itself opened its eyes to inspect itself, opened its mouth to ask what it was. 'What we call Greek, is not a

national or cultural or anthropological character; Greek is that
early historical dispensation by which Being itself lights up in
all beings and determines the nature of man', Heidegger writes
in his reflection on 'A Saying of Anaximander'. No such
immediate disclosure occurred afterwards. Indeed, language itself
was all but divested by Time of its power to reveal Truth, except through the poetry of the rarest of poets, through the art
of the most 'gifted' artists. For the rest, language became a foreign
tongue with regard to Being, estranged from its true nature
through the service into which it has been taken by meta-
physicians, not to mention empiricists, positivists, or idle talkers
in their *Seinsvergessenheit*, their forgetful remoteness from Being.

Heidegger, then, has attempted ontologically to reinstate the
language of poetry as the language of *true* thought, the poetic
language of the homecoming to that Origin of which Hölderlin
said:

... Schwer verlässt
Was nahe dem Ursprung wohnet, den Ort.

Not easily leaves its place that which dwells near the Origin.

To have tried to restore the language of poetry (by which is
meant not merely the language of 'poesy', or poetry in the narrow
sense) to its rightful dwelling in the house of truth (or, in the
words of Heidegger's own deliberately circular way of speaking:
in the truly real) is likely to be remembered as his heroic adventure in the history of philosophy, but not, I believe, the use he
himself has made in his own writing of 'poetic' language, often
strained and awkward in his employment, and again and again
guided, it would seem, by the principle of *obscurum per obscurius*.
And this, perhaps, cannot be otherwise if Heidegger is right in
believing that the *true* disclosures of thought and language are
like the unfolding of blossoms in their own season, or like the
growing of the old oak tree by the pathway of Heidegger's Mess-
kirch childhood, the tree that, in growing, has opened itself up
'to the breadth of heaven' and sunk its roots 'into the darkness
of earth'. Heidegger's philosophical language has nothing of the
solid simplicity of that oak tree; and, to judge by his own account
of the history of Being, his *Befindlichkeit*, the mode of his thinking and speaking, must have some of the qualities that character-

ize all things grown out of season. In his time and his time's distance from Being, a distance of which he has been the tireless land-surveyor, the idiom of Being, and be it the idiom of Being's withdrawnness, must necessarily – once more: on the grounds of Heidegger's own ontology – be dimmed by the haze of remoteness. But ironically – if this word is not instantly stifled by a philosophical atmosphere so utterly lacking the element of irony – this unseasonable language does not have the appearance of the frailty customarily shown by forced organisms. Its demeanour does create the impression of great force, even if this force is not the power of that deeply rooted oak tree. And the fascination Heidegger has held, a few decades ago in his homeland, then, for a while, in France, and now in some American philosophical enclaves, has been, I think, partly due to the quasi-mythological, centaur-like shape of his intellectual character: a human head sometimes thinking truly profound thoughts, sometimes merely thoughts of profound inaccessibility, yielding illuminations that not always justify the burning up of so much energy, yet a head placed upon an intellectual body that seems to possess the muscular vigour of a horse.

One who is unable to forget the Heidegger of 1932 and 1933 and 1934, a picture above all that shows him, moustachioed like Hitler, sitting at a platform table in the company of other committed academic personalities and surrounded by an ecstasy of swastikas and S.A. men – one who is plagued by such memories is tempted to ask whether it was not the ambiguities resulting from such twin-nature and such a strained relationship to his time that made this interpreter of Hölderlin for quite an extended moment deaf to the resonance of hell conveyed by the voice and the language – yes, the *language* – of the *Führer* and his companions, creatures in whom abysmal inferiority uniquely mingled with the demonic. Be this as it may, it should not be forgotten because it was not the private person Martin Heidegger but unmistakably the author of *Being and Time* who accepted in 1933 the office of Rector of Freiburg University, prematurely vacated by a scholar thought to be less fit to lead the academic revolution, the *Gleichschaltung*, that the new rulers demanded. Unmistakably the author of *Being and Time*, for again and again, in speeches, pronouncements, and official letters he verbally behaved as if, with the arrival of Hitler, Being had unexpectedly and triumphantly returned to Time, choosing as its vessel the German nation in the manner of Jehovah's once electing the Jews.

Heidegger's was not merely the indiscretion or weakness or betrayal of a person who six years before had dedicated, 'in friendship and admiration', *some* book he happened to have written to *some* Jewish teacher of his. No, the teacher was Edmund Husserl, and the book was *Being and Time*, and what Heidegger did in 1933 came close to announcing the bankruptcy of a philosopher and a philosophy, a total failure of the intuition of Being without which his philosophy would be as nothing. And if one of the expositors of Heidegger's philosophy in English, Father Richardson, squeezes into a footnote the observation that 'no one denies that after the stern lessons of the intervening years' the pages that Heidegger wrote in 1933 'make unpleasant reading', he misjudges the situation. 'Unpleasant reading' is of course an Anglo-Saxon understatement of a great and loud scandal; but that he believes it needed 'the intervening years', the years of the Second World War and its extermination camps, to teach 'the stern lesson', can only be due to ignorance. It is impossible that anyone living in Germany in 1933 had not heard on countless occasions the voice of Hitler or even the song in which there occur the words

Wenn's Judenblut vom Messer spritzt
Geht's uns nochmal so gut,

meaning that slaughtering Jews makes us feel better and better. And Heidegger never publicly regretted the fact that in 1934 he himself handed over for publication a photograph taken of him with the insignia of the National-Socialist *leadership* pinned to his jacket. But not only did he never regret the part he assumed in that degradation of 'Being', he even referred contemptuously to suggestions that since 1947 his thinking had undergone an 'in-version', or even, since 1945, a 'conversion'. Yet it was indisputably his *thinking* that he had dedicated to what he took to be the regeneration of the German people, and did so despite the depraved *language* and published programme of those who promised to do the 'regenerating'.

This, I am sure, has to be remembered and should never be forgotten, if only to inject a measure of scepticism into the reception of what is often taken to be a series of infallible revelations of the Ultimate Ground by one upon whom has been bestowed the privilege of access to the sphere of Being – a privilege that would not seem to be quite consistent with his own philosophy of Time, and Being's historical inaccessibility. No, there are and remain riddles; and not the least riddle – one that is certainly not exclusive to the contemplation of Heidegger's work and life – is the nature of human integrity; or the incredible possibility (which is yet a common event) that great profundity and abysmal foolishness, authenticity and its scandalous betrayals, may occur side by side in one mind and character, or as Karl Kraus once put it: 'I cannot get over the fact that half a man may write a whole sentence.' In the politics of the mind, that is, in the attempt to tidy up one's intellectual household, it would certainly be permissible to use blatant instances of foolishness in order to bring into doubt what is offered with the inherent claim of being authentic wisdom. On this occasion, however, I shall simply acknowledge that the riddle of such coexistence is insoluble and, explicitly or by implication, avail myself of some of Heidegger's illuminating intuitions concerning the nature of poetry or, to be more precise, Hölderlin's poetry. For just as Kierkegaard meant *Don Giovanni* when he wrote of music, or as most of Thomas Mann's observations about music fit Richard Wagner but not Bach or Mozart, so Heidegger's meditations upon poetry are determined by Hölderlin (although sometimes poems by C. F. Meyer or Georg Trakl or, of course, Rilke, are called in as witnesses). And, indeed, these meditations would meet with considerable resistance from the poetic works of other undoubtedly 'poetic' poets such as Virgil, Dante, Shakespeare or Goethe.

2

HÄLFTE DES LEBENS	THE MIDDLE OF LIFE
Mit gelben Birnen hänget	With yellow pears the land
Und voll mit wilden Rosen	And full of wild roses
Das Land in den See,	Hangs down into the lake,
Ihr holden Schwäne,	You lovely swans,
Und trunken von Küssen	And drunk with kisses
Tunkt ihr das Haupt	You dip your heads
Ins heilignüchterne Wasser.	Into the hallowed, the sober water.

Weh mir, wo nehm' ich, wenn   But oh, where shall I find
Es Winter ist, die Blumen, und wo When winter comes, the flowers,
Den Sonnenschein,   The sunshine   [and where
Und Schatten der Erde?   And shade of the earth?
Die Mauern stehn   The walls loom
Sprachlos und kalt, im Winde   Speechless and cold, in the wind
Klirren die Fahnen.   Weathercocks clatter.

Friedrich Hölderlin   Translated by Michael Hamburger

I wish to speak about Hölderlin's poem 'The Middle of Life'. Michael Hamburger has translated it almost as well as the untranslatable will ever be rendered in another language. (It is only in parenthesis that I should like to touch upon yet another insoluble problem besetting all philosophies of language, be it Heidegger's or that of Wittgenstein's *Tractatus*, which base themselves upon an ultimate equation of Being, or World, and Language; upon the power of Language to reveal, or at least intimate, the nature of Being or World. With regard to the problem I have in mind, the Wittgenstein of the *Tractatus* fares a little better than Heidegger, for Wittgenstein calls upon the *logic* of language to provide the ontological revelation, but the later Heidegger upon poetry in the widest and yet essential sense. And with regard to poetry the question is: if in the poetic work of art 'truth is at work', as Heidegger believes and states and exemplifies in the case of Hölderlin's late hymns, is it also working in a Japanese translation? Or must we go for such disclosures to the original? And if it can be said only of the original that it shows 'truth at work', may this come to pass in the poetry of *any* language? In Swahili poetry as well as in

Hölderlin's German? In the Greek of the pre-Socratic philosophies as well as in Heidegger's translation – and thus interpretation – of them, an interpretative translation often as much
inspired as it is extravagant, as 'poetic' as it is, at times, etymologically extremely hazardous? Are all languages equidistant
from the centre of the sphere of Being? These questions may
well be too weighty for a parenthesis and too damaging to my
own intention to support Heidegger's doctrine insofar as it gives
the highest possible status to language and poetry – to some
poetry, namely to the kind of poetry that may be defined as
having, according to his philosophy, the highest possible ontological status. Once again the argument is as circular as circles
can be and the questioning as inconclusive as are all questions
that allow for no answers – except perhaps for those given by
the faith in one's own language and the love of its poetry.)

Hölderlin's poem 'The Middle of Life' is one of the greatest
ever written in the German language. I shall try to say why. Its
title is part of the poem, and this title's logical place is, as it
were, in the empty space that separates the first verse of seven
short lines from the second comprising the same number. We
do not know when Hölderlin gave the poem this name; when
he first essayed it, he seems to have intended to call it 'Die
letzte Stunde' – 'The Last Hour'. *This* title he probably wrote
down as the poem began to emerge, in 1800, on the extraordinarily crowded manuscript page that in the Stuttgart Hölderlin
Archive's 16th folio volume carries the number 17 verso (see
reproduction overleaf). It appeared first in print, in 1804, in the
Taschenbuch für das Jahr 1805, a Poetic Manual for the year
1805, and did so already with the title 'The Middle of Life'.
Hölderlin had used the phrase, or very similar ones, before. At
the beginning of 1796 – he was 26 at the time – he wrote to
his brother of the need to rejuvenate himself, if he was not to
become an old man 'in the middle of my life'; again, on 12
November 1798, he said to Neuffer: '... I fear that the warm
life within me will be chilled by the icy coldness of the times';
and four years later, in the year the poem was written, he confessed in a letter to his sister the fear that, in order to conquer the
'deafening turmoil' within, he would have to become, in the
second half of his life, 'cold and all-too sober and withdrawn'.

Hölderlin, draft manuscript, 1800. Hölderlin Archive, 16th folio volume, fol. 17ᵛ. Württenbergisches Landesmuseum, Stuttgart.

Even earlier, in September 1795, he anticipated the imagery of the poem's second verse in a letter to Schiller: 'I am freezing and stare into the winter that surrounds me. The sky is made of iron and I of stone.' It is instructive to mention this; it allows us to observe the metamorphosis of a deeply depressed mind's momentary lamentations into the durable firmness of poetry.

Yet, if the poem had been called 'The Last Hour', the first verse – of which only the last four lines are rehearsed on that manuscript page – would have given the lie to the title. For what is evoked in that verse is not even the last hour of summer, let alone the last hour of life. True, autumn announces itself with the yellow pears and altogether with a ripeness so ripe that the earth can hardly contain it. She almost gives under its weight, and, as if taking her cue from the branches of the pear tree, 'hangs down into the lake'. Or was it the water that, over the years, has hollowed the bank, making the top layers of soil almost cave in under the burden they carry? (A whole lesson, by the way, of poetry's fragility could be taught by pointing to a mistake an early editor of Hölderlin's *Collected Works*, Christoph Theodor Schwab, made in 1846 when he copied the poem from the original page in the Manual: 'Blumen' he put where there was 'Birnen', yellow flowers in the place of yellow pears. Perhaps he believed that flowers were more poetical than pears, or he was so nearsighted as to misread the small print of the Manual; whatever the cause, the effect was catastrophic: the beginning of a marvellous poem was destroyed; for what this first line demanded, was a fruit heavy with maturity and radiant with a long summer's sunlight. Yellow flowers would never do.)

The first three lines are like a picture without the painter's presence being as much as hinted at. Common usage suggests the designation 'objective'. But in the fourth line the person of the artist makes a sudden if unobtrusive appearance by addressing the swans with the exclamation: 'Ihr holden Schwäne.' Although I would be unable to propose a much better translation than 'You lovely swans', the English line is indeed affected by the plight that is the lot of any translator of poetry. The words 'lovely swans' seem simple and unproblematic enough, and yet 'hold' is what these German swans are; and the adjective *hold* comes from the noun *Huld*, and *Huld* suggests the particular benevolence and even love a powerful man feels, an emperor or a king, for a courtier or citizen of his realm, indeed the affection of a god for his servant. *Huld* borders on grace, perhaps Apollo's grace that Socrates means when in his last hour he speaks, according to Plato's *Phaedo*, of the god's birds, the swans, and their legendary song, explaining why he was not afraid of death.

Do you really think, Socrates asks Simmias, that I have less insight into the future than a swan? For swans, when they feel that their time has come to die, sing more sweetly and powerfully than ever before, and they do so for joy that they are going away into the presence of the god whose servants they are. Did you perhaps believe that their song expresses their grief at their approaching end? You are misled by the common fear of death. Has any bird ever been heard beautifully to sing when it was in distress, hungry or cold or fearful? No, the swans, dedicated as they are to Apollo, have prophetic powers and sing because they know that only good things await them in the unseen world and therefore are happier in their last hour than they have ever been before. I too, Socrates continues in this Dialogue, am a servant of Apollo, and he has endowed me, not less than his swans, with prophetic powers; therefore, I am not more disconsolate than they are at leaving this world. – A faint emanation of such grace is in 'hold'. It is not in 'lovely', and yet 'lovely' is a more acceptable translation than would be 'graceful' or 'gracious'. Such are the idiosyncrasies of language, the miseries of the translator's labour, and the doubts inevitably raised by an ontology of language, let alone by its translation into another one.

Of course, I do not suggest that Hölderlin thought of Socrates-Plato's swans when he ecstatically greeted those birds in the poem that on the manuscript page appears together with the title 'The Last Hour', under which are written other titles he apparently considered earlier, or perhaps only motifs: 'The Rose', 'The Swans' and 'The Stag'. The stag disappeared from the several texts on the page, texts hurriedly and in parts almost illegibly written, with later lines scribbled in between and in the margin of previous ones, but the rose remained (if only in the ensemble of 'wilde Rosen'), and certainly the swans that put me in mind of the swans of Socrates' last hour. This was not much more than a free association, yet one not entirely free from the thought of Hölderlin's devotion to the thinkers and poets of ancient Greece. Nonetheless, my sole purpose in introducing the Socratic swan song was to draw attention to an element in poetry that is of its essence: the refusal of poetic language to pinpoint a thing or an idea or a concept, isolating it from the soil from which it has grown or from the air which it breathes. The very 'impurity' of language which 'linguistic analysis' wishes to clean up, makes for the richness of words in poetry. The meaning of words in poetry is certainly not definable by quasi-logical procedures; on the contrary, their lives are identical with their history in the minds and souls of men; and their history is what they have gathered into themselves in the course of cen turies and during the years of a reader's life. It was the young Hofmannsthal who wrote the line of verse: 'Und dennoch sagt der viel, der "Abend" sagt', meaning that much is said by one who says 'Evening', and more than the evening hours registered by the clock: young love may be in it, the first walk together through the garden at nightfall, or the colours of the sunset flooding sky and sea, or the chirping of a late bird, or the white mist and aroma that rises from the meadows, or 'Über allen Gip-feln ist Ruh', the peace that is above the mountains during the hour between daylight and darkness. And swans, the 'holden Schwäne', gracefully gliding on this particular lake, may have assimilated into their poetic being even the memory of Socrates' bidding farewell to his disciples and thus become more 'hold' and dearer than before to the genius of poetry.

The swans glide into sight as the poet himself, through his exclamation, appears on the scene of the landscape to which, were it a painting, Van Gogh might have contributed the pear tree. Heidegger, in his essay on 'The Origin of the Work of Art' has chosen Van Gogh as one of those who show in their art 'truth at work', letting us know through a painting of them what, for instance, peasant shoes 'in truth' *are*; and he might have named, in the place of shoes, Van Gogh's sunflowers or chairs or poplar trees. Speaking of Van Gogh's painting of the peasant shoes, Heidegger claims that these come 'to stand in the light of their being'. It is as if for the first time we truly knew the 'being' of peasant shoes, for 'true art' does not concern itself with beauty as aesthetics means beauty (peasant shoes are not 'beautiful') but with things that *become* beautiful when they appear in the shining-forth of their being as it is revealed by the work of art. Rilke, in the first of the *Duino Elegies*, long before Heidegger's essay, knew this when he spoke of beauty as merely the beginning of that terror which is lodged in what to him is the Angel, the being that we do not greatly misinterpret by calling it the being of Being;

> ... Denn das Schöne ist nichts
> als des Schrecklichen Anfang, den wir noch grade ertragen,
> und wir bewundern es so, weil es gelassen verschmäht,
> uns zu zerstören ...

... For Beauty is nothing but the beginning of Terror, the Terror of Being, that we are still able to bear, and we admire it so because it serenely disdains to destroy us in our feeble condition, in our estrangement from Being, indeed our *Seinsvergessenheit*, a condition Heidegger once defined very concisely and with emphasis: it lies in our forgetting the difference between Being and beings.

I did say that through the exclamation 'Ihr holden Schwäne' we become aware of the poet's presence. But this presence is contained entirely in the exclamation. We learn nothing else of the person. All that there is of a person is in the utterance of wonder, carrying something of that wonder which is the main-spring of all philosophical thought, the wonder of wonders, the astonishment at anything being at all, let alone anything as 'hold' as swans. Does not the poet, marvelling at the unexpected and joyful sight, have to catch his breath with the 'And' that opens the fifth line against all rules of syntax, an absolute 'Und', syntactically unrelated to what was said before, the greatest 'Und' in German poetry? Or *is* it the poet who is breathless with wonder? Is there a person at all and not rather poetry itself, the soul of poetry, the same soul that voices in the second part of the poem the lament at the wintry withering of all the flowers. *Voices* the lament? No, *is* the lament. But we have not yet reached the 'Weh mir', the cry of woe that deplores a deplorable fate, a cry as simple as it is untranslatable, at least during the present phase in the history of the English language.

We are still with the swans and accept as a matter of course, as a matter of truth, what only the truth of poetry can persuade us to accept without question: the swans' Dionysian rapture which is at one with the enraptured poet's state of mind, an ecstasy that has been evoked by the sight of the swans in the rose-bordered lake at this rich harvest hour of the summer. At one with? ... Evoked by ... ? The truth is that the state of mind is one and the same as the swans that are drunk with kisses; that the swans, here the servants not of Apollo, but of Dionysus, are the creation, irrefutable in its poetic reality, of a state of mind; but not more than the state of mind is created by the pear tree, the roses, the lake and the swans. Creator and creature have merged in one incarnation, and this incarnation is a poem.

'Where sobriety leaves you', Hölderlin wrote in contemplating his poetic powers, 'there is also the limit of your inspiration. The great poet is never beside himself.' Yet we spoke of the poet's ecstasy, and ecstasy means exactly what, according to this saying, the great poet never indulges: being beside himself. How is this? We seem to be trapped in a contradiction. But the seeming contradiction is caused by the ambiguity of words. For the self that Hölderlin has in mind is not just any self; it is not even the self that, as a long historical sequence of meditations on poetry will have it, a sequence marked by the names of Schopenhauer, Nietzsche, Thomas Mann, Rilke, Valéry, T. S. Eliot, Heidegger, has to be left behind or transcended or conquered if the *work* of the poet is to come into being: 'In great art the artist remains inconsequential in relation to the work, almost like a passageway that destroys itself in the process of creation', says Heidegger, and it could have been said, and *has* been said, by Schopenhauer or Nietzsche or Thomas Mann or Rilke or Valéry or T. S. Eliot. But it is clearly not this self that Hölderlin has in mind when he says that the poet must never be beside *himself*, never be deserted by sobriety; clearly not the self which with its 'self-willed' purposes stands in the way of poetic creation, not the self of common experience, but the *poetic* self, the self of the 'great poet'. *This*, he believes, must never be abandoned by the poet if inspiration is not to fail him. For it is this poetic self that possesses the eyes which see what truly is; and the vision of what

truly is may well seem a drunken extravagance to a world forgetful of the truth of Being, indeed deserted by it. Yet the inspired
poet knows in his inspiration the sober truth. There is no other
poet who at the turn of that century, in 1800, was as tormented
as Hölderlin by this ambiguity and reversal: that the withdrawnness of Being – to him it meant the absence of the gods – was
regarded by the citizens of the deserted world as the only true state
of affairs, the affairs they conducted in *their* sobriety, while *his* sober
vision comprehended both the gods and, in anguish, the void
they left behind when they absented themselves as the poet laments
in the great elegy 'Bread and Wine':

> But we, my friend, are too late. The gods, it is true, are living
> Yet far above ourselves, away in a different world.
> There they are endlessly active and seem but little regardful
> Whether we live or not, such is their tender concern,
> Knowing that fragile vessels like us cannot always contain them.
> Only at times can man endure the abundance of gods . . .
> . . . Meanwhile, it seems to me often
> Better to slumber than live without companions, like this,
> So to linger, and know not what to begin or to utter,
> Or, in such times of want, why to be poet at all?

'Why to be poet at all?' The answer may well be: because there is no
other choice as long as there still are those moments of 'hallowed
sobriety' that are given to a few as tokens of Being, as proof that
'the gods are living', even if their abode now is a sphere very
different from this world of want – the moments of the vision
true, holy, and sober. *This* is why the water in the last line of
the first stanza of 'The Middle of Life' is called – once again
untranslatably – 'heilignüchtern', the cool water into which the
swans dip their heads inflamed by Dionysus, the wine god, to
regain the sobriety they need in the service of *their* god, the
clearsighted Apollo. Hölderlin used the two adjectives, 'holy' and
'sober', in another poem, his ode 'Gesang des Deutschen', 'The
Song of a German', but there they stand merely next to one
another. It is only in 'The Middle of Life' that they are conjoined
to form one word, Hölderlin's very own word. It cannot be rendered in English. Nonetheless, the unavoidable separation of the
two need not be as overdone as it is in Hamburger's version
through the repetition of the article: 'the hallowed, the sober'.

Another translator, the late J. B. Leishman, did better with the hyphenated 'sacredly-sober'. Yet both translators have missed the etymological chance that Heidegger would of course have grasped hold of had he written about this poem; he did so on other occasions by pointing to the relatedness of 'heilig', sacred, to 'heil', integer, unhurt, undiminished. It is an etymology that is even more apparent in English: 'holy' is a relation of 'wholeness', pointing perhaps to the sacred wholeness of Eden where, before the rift of the Fall, all beings were at one with God, or to 'the Holy' that would manifest itself in the entirety of all beings shining with the light of Being itself. It may well be that a reflection of this light is spread over the lake, and that the flow from that 'Source', the origin, ripples the water in its sober holiness, and may do so even without our remembering that Thales of Miletus, one of the seven wise men of Greece, taught that water is the common ground of everything that is. Yet this is probably going too far. But then, who can measure the light of memories, clear or faint, by which the words of poetry are irradiated?

Upon the splendour of this late summer there follows abruptly, with the second verse, the exclamation of woe. It is winter and the 'Heilignüchtern' is frozen over. Once again the 'I' of the poem, the voice of the poet – which is like the voice of poetry itself – is heard, this time not in wonder but in desolation. Where, in this wintry desert, are flowers to be found, flowers and the light and shade of the earth? Yes, the shade too, and so much so that, like the sunshine of line four, it has the whole line five to itself. For such is the nature of life that, to give its best, it needs not only the light and warmth of the sun, but also the cool of the shade. How true is this combination of sunshine and shade! Indeed, it would be sentimentally untrue if the poem's yearning were for the sun alone. (Sentimentality results from such a distillation of a chemically cleansed sentiment out of the complex nature of all true and real feeling.)

This is why the light and the shadow appear together in the poem's lamenting the passing of summer. Only the passing of summer? Is it not the essence of great poetry that it *means* more then it *says*, more even than the poet may be conscious of? Would the voicing of woe not strike us as exaggerated if the sorrow were entirely about the arrival of winter? May the summer not stand for the shining-forth of Being itself, its 'Lichten' in 'beings', in the roses, the lake, the swans? It is in Heidegger's essay on Fragment 16 of Heraclitus that he insists more emphatically and more concisely than elsewhere upon the inescapable simultaneity of the truth of Being with its negativity, of its shining through beings with its awful concealment, of the light with the shadow, the shadow that light needs because the shadow enables the light to disclose what it truly is. Whether or not we are prepared to make that much room in the poem for Heidegger's thought, it cannot be doubted that we owe the poem's light and shadow, and thus its summer, to a poetic intuition that, in its celebration of the summer as well as in its mourning of loss, comprehends – no, not the 'symbolic significance' of summer and winter (at least not in the sense or nonsense of the 'symbol' in our daily literary criticism), but their true being; and this poetic intuition *knows* that, for the sake of the poetry, the explicit statement of 'meaning' and the 'significance' of the symbols had to be concealed.

On that folio page 17 (that contains a profounder lesson concerning the making of poetry than many a learned book on the subject) the 'Weh mir' that was to be the beginning of the second verse of 'The Middle of Life', was originally followed up by the fragmentary and desperate close of the hymn 'As when upon a day of rest'. Heidegger has devoted an essay to it without acknowledging its broken ending. This runs as follows:

> Und sag ich gleich,
> And even if I say

Then comes an empty space, and then this:

> Ich sei genaht, die Himmlischen zu schauen;
> Sie selbst, sie werfen mich tief unter die Lebenden alle,
> Den falschen Priester ins Dunkel, daß ich
> Das warnende Lied den Gelehrigen singe.

> That I approached to see the dwellers in Heaven,
> But they themselves cast me down, deep down
> Below the living, into the dark they cast me,
> The false priest that I am, to sing
> For those who have ears to hear the warning song.

And with 'Dort', 'There', that was to be the beginning of a new line, the fragment on this manuscript page breaks off, as if choked by despair. But then, obviously later, other lines were written around and underneath that 'Weh mir', the poet making use of the distance he had previously left between it and the line 'And even if I say'. And what he wrote is the beginning of the second verse of 'The Middle of Life': '... where shall I find/When winter comes, the flowers ...' Yet upon this 'there' does not follow the sunshine and the shade of the earth, but the poet's explicitly stating what purpose the flowers were to serve, namely 'that I may bind them into wreaths/Then it will be as if I had never heard of the gods/For the spirit of life has deserted me/ When I search for the signs that would show the heavenly powers that I love them, and find no flowers in the barren field/and find you not.' 'You' is perhaps the rose that appeared at the same time as those lines as one of the three quasi-titles I have mentioned before. Perhaps the rose, but who will want to be quite sure that it is not a god, not even Christ, the – after Dionysus – uniquely divine to whom Hölderlin's hymn 'Der Einzige', 'The Only One', is devoted? Astonishing, is it not, this profound obedience of one who has suspected himself of being 'a false priest' and is terrified at the thought of having been cast off by the gods – astonishing, this obedience to their verdict. For now he will not even dare to speak of 'the dwellers in Heaven' or of his not finding the flowers with which to woo or to reconcile them. It must be enough that, in the terrible second half of life, there are no flowers, no light and no shade. 'Then it will be as if I had never heard of the gods/For the spirit of life has deserted me.' Hölderlin was right in dismissing this. It 'talks' too much, and talks too much of the poet himself and the inaccessible heavenly powers. Compare it to the flowers that have died, simply to the death of flowers, and to the lost light and shade of the earth, and you will know what is merely lofty discursiveness and what great poetry.

On the same page – what abundance on one page of a manuscript! – there are also three stanzas of the ode 'To the Germans'. The first of these – not the first of the completed ode, but the first on that page – reads:

In the age of prose

For too long now, too long, I have roamed
In the workshop . . . of the Spirit that forms.
Only his blossoms I recognize,
His thought I cannot make out.

The very thought of the 'bildender Geist', the Spirit that forms
and shapes and reveals itself in the beings of his making – his
very thought Hölderlin wanted to come to know. But his poetry
is greatest when he entrusts himself to the 'blossoms', that is,
to the forms and shapes from the workshop of that Spirit, the
Spirit's disclosures in things that at the same time are the veils
enveloping the Spirit's thought. The 'speechless walls' of that
city of winter say as much as poetic speech can say about the
absence of the gods, the withdrawal of Being. For it is speech,
it is language, that is the 'house of Being'.

In the first verse of the poem there is hardly a noun that is
not enlivened by an adjective: the pears are yellow, the roses
'wild', the swans 'hold', and the water 'heilignüchtern'. We are in a
rich province of Nature; but the unadorned barrenness of the last
three lines is made by man, and Heidegger's belief that 'language
is the house of Being' might appear to be vindicated by the
'speechlessness' and coldness of those walls and the metal clatter
of the weathercocks. Their creaking shrillness is in the accumulated sounds of 'im Winde klirren . . .' (which of course is lost
in translation). The weathervanes point in any direction dictated
by the changeable wind – in any direction and therefore in none.
If language is the house of Being, it is that of Non-Being too:
it accommodates both that rich landscape and this waste land.

The oneness of thing and word, which is the essence of great
poetry, is the riddle of language. As the oneness of thing and
expression, as 'form', it is also the riddle of art; of all art apart
from music, the art that knows of no 'thing' or 'matter'. Heidegger
has little to say about it, so different in this from Schopenhauer
for whom music is the language of the Will itself; and the Will
reaches in Schopenhauer's philosophy as far as *his* intuition of
Being will take him. But this is beyond the scope of our discourse. As far as 'Thinking about Poetry' is concerned, nobody
has done it as devotedly and intensely as the Heidegger of the
time after *Being and Time*. 'If we go to a spring or stroll through
the woods, we are passing already through the word 'spring',

through the word 'woods', even if we do not utter these words or think of anything to do with language ...' Heidegger says this in his essay on Hölderlin's question 'Wozu Dichter?', 'Why poet?' It is one way of stating the riddle: How is it that words in poetry possess, or acquire, φυσιs, and thus partake of Being, and thus *are* thought?

5
Karl Kraus

KARL Kraus is among the most important and remarkable writers in modern German or any other literature, and yet he is hardly known beyond the reach of his own language. Born in 1874 in a provincial Bohemian town, the son of well-to-do Jewish parents, he spent almost all his life in Vienna, and died there in 1936. When he was young he thought of working for a newspaper or as an actor, but in 1899 he founded his own journal *Die Fackel* (The Torch). It was immediately obvious that a satirical talent of great force had arrived on the Viennese scene, a writer supremely thoughtful in his use of language and recklessly determined to attack those whom he regarded as the journalistic literary, and political corrupters of the human condition.

Among the early contributors to *Die Fackel* were such diverse writers as Wilhelm Liebknecht, Franz Werfel, Frank Wedekind, and Peter Altenberg, but before long the editor was writing everything himself, and did so until his death at sixty-two. From these writings for *Die Fackel* he selected the contents of his books. Nine volumes of his satirical essays and aphorisms alone were published, beginning in 1908 with *Sittlichkeit und Kriminalität* (Morality and Criminality) and concluding with the posthumous *Die Sprache* (Language) in 1937.*

It is not fanciful to suggest that 'Language' would be a fitting name for all these books – 'Language', or 'The Apocalypse'. For Kraus examined the language written, spoken, and degraded by his age and knew that Armageddon was at hand. Yet his tone was not at all reminiscent of Biblical prophecy. The place evoked was Vienna, not Babylon, and the time was every day, not the last one. And yet he wrote, 'I hear noises which others don't hear and which interfere with the music of the spheres that others don't hear either.' The noises were in the speech of both prominent public men and hack journalists, passers-by, tip-greedy

---

* In the intervening years he published *Sprüche und Widersprüche* (Dicta and Contradictions), 1909; *Die chinesische Mauer* (The Wall of China), 1910; *Pro Domo et Mundo*, 1912; *Weltgericht* (Day of Judgment), 1919; *Nachts* (Night), 1919; *Untergang der Welt durch schwarze Magie* (The Destruction of the World by Black Magic), 1922; and *Literatur und Lüge* (Literature and Untruth), 1929.

waiters, passengers in railway carriages, and patriotic or rebellious demonstrators in the city's squares. The satirist perceived evil omens in these voices: their pretence, foolishness, or illiteracy announced to him catastrophes to come. The voices drowned out 'the music of the spheres', upsetting, that is, what he believed was, or should be, the natural and spiritual order of the human domain.

The end of the world is frequently alluded to in the very titles of Kraus's books – for instance, *Day of Judgment* or *The Destruction of the World by Black Magic*. But he is at his most apocalyptic in his vast assemblage of scenes about and from World War I, *Die letzten Tage der Menschheit* (The Last Days of Mankind), written during the years of the war and finally published as a book of 800 pages of which thirteen are taken up with a list of characters. If performed on earth, Karl Kraus says in the preface, the drama would consume ten evenings, but this is not the reason why it was meant for 'a theatre on Mars'; no, the reason was that the audiences here and now would not be able to bear it. For it is 'blood of their blood', presenting as it does 'those unreal, unthinkable years, out of reach for the wakeful hours of the mind, inaccessible to memory and preserved only in nightmares . . .'

But he saw the horror of the war not simply in its obvious violence, its cruelty and slaughter; the horror lay in the casting done by a perverse stage director who allowed 'the tragedy of mankind to be enacted by characters from an operetta'. This was Karl Kraus's great and inexhaustible theme.

Our imaginations, he believed, had fed too long on the leftovers of the Renaissance and Romanticism; instructed by that past, we assumed that only heroic greatness could bring about great upheavals, and therefore relied upon the mediocre for our safety, and upon the trivial for the conduct of our affairs. Karl Kraus's satire relies on the recognition of the infernal dimension of the inferior, the gigantic shadow and freezing chill which the banal can cast over the world. In a way he anticipated Hitler long before anyone knew his name, just as he had, long before 1914, foreseen the bloodshed in the anaemia of civilized life, and discerned in the restless boredom of that life the menacing thud of marching armies.

When war did break out, he wrote and delivered his celebrated oration whose first words are: 'In dieser grossen Zeit ...', 'In these great times', the cliché he extracted from countless editorials that celebrated Europe's descent into the depths of ignominy as the long-awaited triumph of the age, and the rout of the human spirit as proof of its ultimate glory. His first sentence fills half a page. Like most of Kraus's work, it cannot be translated, only paraphrased:

In these great times which I knew long before they had become great and, if time permits, will be small once again; which, because in the realm of organic growth such transformations are impossible, we had better call fat times (for war profiteers) and surely hard times (for everyone else); in these times when things happen that could not be imagined, and in which the unimaginable must indeed happen because it would not occur, if one were able to imagine it; in these serious times which were dying with laughter at the thought that they might become serious; which, overtaken by their own tragedy, reach out for distractions and, catching themselves in the act of doing the unspeakable, grope for words; in these loud times which resound with the abominable cacophony of deeds that bring forth reports, and reports that are responsible for deeds; in these times here and now you should not expect from me any word of my own.*

The main clause is, of course, 'In these great times you should not ...', but the predicate is postponed again and again, just as in a world where wartime deeds and mendacious reports feed on each other, endlessly multiplying through their obscene couplings, the 'great times' could return to their proper scale only after an unconscionable delay. Indeed they would not return until the will to perform bloody deeds of war was as exhausted as the imagination must have been before the deeds could be done. The construction of the sentence is the product of Karl Kraus's superbly realized ambition not merely to express his thought but to do it so that precisely language itself would appear to be the thinker, would catch the rhythm of events in the rhythm of words,

---

* The first words in German show clearly enough why Kraus is untranslatable: 'In dieser grossen Zeit, die ich noch gekannt habe, wie sie so klein war ...' This manner of phrasing, with the highly colloquial relative clause set up against the solemnity of 'this great time', would not usually be used of 'times' but of people remembered from the past when they were still children ('klein'), just as children look forward to a time when they will be 'gross' (which here does not mean 'great' but grown-up, adult).

and make sentences the mirror of the world they describe – the mirror as well as the judgment passed on the world.

It should be clear that this use of language cannot be reproduced in any translation. For Karl Kraus's work is more deeply rooted in its own language than is the writing of any other writer of prose. Of the German language he said – echoing Goethe – that it is 'the profoundest of all languages' even if, as of course he had to add, German speech is the crudest and shallowest.

It was Goethe who believed that German, 'this strange and wondrous tongue', was so responsive to the subtlest stirrings of soul and mind that it could attune itself even to the spirit of any other language. He who knows German, he said, is well equipped for the literatures of the world, for German translations are more successful than any other. And it is certainly true to say that, compared to the awkwardness of Goethe's *Faust* in English, *Hamlet* in German is almost a German drama; and to render any philosopher's thought in German is child's play by comparison with the practically insurmountable difficulties of translating Heidegger. Neither the idea that language in its logical essence mirrors the world (Wittgenstein) nor the idea that it is 'the house of Being' (Heidegger) could have been thought in any other language. For German is – or seems: a difference that vanishes in faith as well as in love – 'the profoundest of all languages'.

A sober view of the matter may well be that modern German, having become a literary idiom later than French or English, is an adolescent language, malleable and ready to manifest the inarticulate, which lies buried beneath all languages, within its articulations. It is easily seduced by genius, idiot, or villain. Of course no language is immune from the mendacity of rhetoric and pretentiousness, but German has the lowest resistance. No translations of Hitler's oratory, alas, could convey the resonance of hell in it (had it been otherwise, perhaps the resistance of the world might have come earlier and at less cost). And if, to pass from the base to the sublime, all great lyrical poetry can only be approximated in any translation, Hölderlin's is nearly unapproachable; and this is so largely because he is a German poet. While every language is capable of purification by a writer of integrity, Karl Kraus's epigram about his love affair with language, his mistress who was a whore before he restored her virginity, would seem excessive, were it not said by him and in German:

> Sie war eine dreiste Dirne,
> die ich zur Jungfrau gemacht.

'In these times you should not expect from me any words of my own.' This is the statement of his satirical method: he often spoke merely in quotations. Merely? It was enough. For his genius for quoting was such as to perform the magic by which the real, faithfully rendered, was transformed into the stuff from which art is made. 'The most improbable deeds which are here reported', he says in the preface to *The Last Days of Mankind*,

... really happened; I have registered only what was done. The most improbable conversations which are here conducted took place; exaggerations and inventions are quotations ... Documents assume a living shape, reports come to life as persons, persons die as leading articles. The feuilleton is given a mouth to deliver itself as a monologue; clichés walk on two legs – men have kept only one. Inflections of voices rush and rustle through our days and grow into the chorus of the unholy plot. People who have lived amidst mankind and survived it, the executive organs and spokesmen of an age that has no flesh but blood, no blood but ink, are reduced to shadows and marionettes, the forms befitting their busy sham existences. Cyphers and lemures, masks of the tragic carnival, have living names because this must be so, and because nothing is accidental in this time conditioned by chance. But this gives nobody the right to regard it as a local affair. Even the noises of a Viennese rush hour are directed from a cosmic point.

'Cosmic points' are not easily come by in a time of scepticism, psychology, and relativity; and yet when Karl Kraus speaks of them it is not a *façon de parler*. He had no systematic theology or 'cultural anthropology', but his life was lived and his work was done from a firm centre of belief, so firm indeed that it refuses to be penetrated even by the sharpest definition. He was, however, able to see the history of his time from that perspective in which events, despite their satirical distortion, showed their true face; and by 'cosmic point' he meant the place where nature and spirit, world and language, meet. Although Karl Kraus may not have believed in a god known to theologians, he had the right to say that his satire did not deny God, but only everything that is denying Him; and if he wills it so, everything will once again be miraculous:

> Nicht Gott, nur alles leugn' ich,
> was ihn leugnet,
> und wenn er will, ist alles wunderbar.

Not only the bluebells, butterflies and kindly valleys of Karl Kraus's lyrical moments will be miraculous then, but above all language in its recovered integrity. He who judges what is said and written only after grammatical rules or aesthetic principles will find it hard to understand that for Karl Kraus language was the touchstone of morality; and this was so because like nothing else it is apt to serve as the tool of malevolent concealment, mendacity and falsehood. When – long before Karl Kraus – the corruption of language through irresponsible journalists began to spread and everybody appeared to be eager to contribute to it, Schopenhauer gave vent to his anger much in the blunt manner of Luther's saying: 'Das Wort sie sollen lassen stahn!', 'Let them not mischievously play about with the Word!'; in a style that fitted his temperament as well as the incipient deformation of language: 'Those wretched scribblers', the enraged Schopenhauer wrote, 'should be punished like obstreperous schoolboys.' The cause of his great indignation was the same with Karl Kraus, even if the advanced state of the disease in 'the last days of mankind' no longer allowed the simplicity of Schopenhauer's invective. 'Take your hands off language!' the philosopher demanded, 'for it is in language that great human beings have expressed themselves and great poets and thinkers have written their works.' This is undoubtedly one aspect of the ethics of language: language preserves the tradition of all speech poetry and thought. We have not acquired it as one acquires an article of daily use, but have inherited it with the inescapable commitment to hand it on to the next generations. Language is common property like the soil and the air; and how we treat it increases, reduces, or corrupts the inheritance. Reason enough to look after it with circumspection.

But the ethics of language has yet another aspect, so delicate and subtle that it almost eludes communication. For when someone versed in literature reads Goethe or Karl Kraus, he recognizes instantly not only that what he reads is written in German but also that it is by Goethe or Karl Kraus. Sometimes one sentence is enough: 'In keiner Sprache kann man sich so schwer verständigen wie in der Sprache' (There is no language in which it is so difficult to make oneself understood as in language). This is obviously by Karl Kraus. It has the unmistakable physiognomy of the paradoxical style distinguishing his writing.

What we call style results from the tension between the universality of language that belongs to all, and the unavoidable modification, be this a heightening or lowering of its level, it undergoes on the strength of the individual's character and sensibility. A writer like Karl Kraus who says of himself that language is his divining-rod which leads him to the sources of thought, has a relationship to language entirely different from one for whom words are nothing but signs that custom or fashion has placed at his disposal to utter what happens to enter his mind. Of course, he who has never quite realized that, apart from music, mathematics or formal logic, all thinking is inseparable from language, is prone hurriedly to take refuge in jargon that pretends to be scientific, yet is, particularly in matters pertaining to the psyche or to society, the deplorable outcome of the intellectual impatience that shuns the strenuous path of words, long and deeply pondered. What is new, particular, personal, in a person's idiom – in one word: his style – is like a human face. Although it is distinguishable from all other faces, it is yet what all other faces are: human. Only because this is so, are its particular features of interest. If they were so monstrously other as to be scarcely recognizable as human, we would avert our eyes with embarrassment and repugnance.

This applies in equal measure to individual styles of writing. 'What is incomprehensible in works of the literary arts,' Karl Kraus wrote, 'must not affect their surface meaning. This ought to be clearer than what Tom, Dick and Harry say to each other. It is only on the other side of such simplicity that the mystery begins. Art is something so lucid that nobody understands it.' Therefore, he rejected the unfortunate aftermath of symbolism and expressionism in literature that, with disrupted syntax and words that have shed the burden of meaning, threatened to cover with strange weeds the land on which poetry used to grow: the kind of poetry whose mystery begins behind the translucent clar-

ity of its literal sense. The originality of those who were 'original'
and nothing else – and very few remember that originality means
being close to the origins – violated, he believed, the ethics of
language. It was this morality that made him a mere 'epigone',
one of those who, as he said in an epigram, lived in the old house
built of words. For this house stood near 'the source' which he
faithfully believed was at the same time the goal. In his poem
'Zwei Läufer', two runners who race for victory, he undoubtedly
saw himself as the one who comes from the *Ursprung*, the source,
the origin, perhaps from that mythical garden where man was
as good as all the works of God were at the beginning of Creation,
and spoke a language which was as perfect as the works of that
beginning: the hives of bees, the nests of birds. The other, light-
heartedly starting from nowhere easily reaches what he seeks:
an empty goal in the nowhere of his breathless progress; while
the first runner, his heart heavy with anxiety lest he stray from
the destined course, dies by the wayside and, dying, wins out
against the other and arrives where he came from: his beginning.

> Und dieser, dem es ewig bangt,
> Ist stets am Ursprung angelangt.

T. S. Eliot, in some respects a later Anglo-Saxon relation of
Karl Kraus, had the same in mind when, in his poem 'East Coker',
he varied the prophetic words which the hapless Scottish queen had
chosen as her royal motto: 'In my beginning is my end'. Those
who have moved far from the unity of beginning and end try
to make themselves comfortable in the Waste Land of progress,
where houses go up in no time whatever and in no time whatever disappear again to make room for emptiness or a factory
or a parking lot or simply for glaring disorder. Yet the ethical
life is founded upon the intuition of a natural order. This is why
Immanuel Kant related the moral law to the starry sky above
us, the grand lawfulness of a world that the Greeks called cosmos.
And although the rules of language are certainly more changeable
than the cosmos, for Karl Kraus they had the force of a Categorical Imperative. 'What an order of life were to evolve if the Germans obeyed no other decrees but those of language', he wrote;
and also said that nothing could be more foolish than to assume
that it was merely an aesthetic need which is awakened or

satisfied by the desire for linguistic perfection. No, for Karl Kraus, this was an ethical demand, although at the same time he knew that the deep love for language was like the passionate love for Pandora or Helena: a sublime folly, even a chimaera, within the instability of world and history; and yet to him, the enslaved lover of language, it was the binding, unchanging image of eternity. He described in one sentence this paradox of illusion and love: 'Language is the only chimaera whose capacity for deception is without end, and the inexhaustible source of riches that will never impoverish our lives' (as other riches so easily do). And he added: 'Man must learn to be the servant of language.'

He detested the ruling aesthetic ideology of his time that regarded a work of art as a purely 'aesthetic phenomenon'. On the contrary: 'Ethics and aesthetics are one.' This sentence, which is to be found in paragraph 6.421 of Wittgenstein's *Tractatus Logico-Philosophicus*, would probably never have been written had the Viennese philosopher not been a devoted reader of Karl Kraus.

It is through the oneness of aesthetics and ethics that true satire – that is, satire as an art – transcends, like all arts, its subject matter. Just as *King Lear* transcends the foolishness and suffering of an old man, so does satire with the occasions it satirizes. The force of a satirical work solely concerned with its irritating material would vanish with the irritation; but the satire that succeeds in avenging its scandalous subject redeems it by the perfection of its language; the satire survives with the moral life of language itself. No less than the poet, the satirical artist knows how to make his angry tales of last winter survive throughout the years. No one remembers a garrulous Viennese reporter during World War I named Alice Schalek. She is alive now only on a few pages of *The Last Days of Mankind* along with the other forgotten journalists, politicians, industrialists, bankers, and generals in Kraus's drama. That no one remembers them did not prevent Karl Kraus's works later from being rediscovered, republished, and read widely in postwar Germany.

But doesn't the very negativeness of satire make it ephemeral? This would happen if the denials of the satirist were not the other side of affirmations: Alice Schalek, for Karl Kraus, was no more than one of the obstacles, small in themselves but endlessly effective because of their number, that stood in the way of the good.

For Karl Kraus's spiritual existence was not free of the terrible suspicion that man might have the power to erase the design of Creation. In such moments sin appeared to him omnipotent and salvation did not come through grace but only through lives led in obedience to the Law. He was a great Jew. Of course, this was contradicted by his saying that everything will be miraculous again if God wills it so; and yet the satirist's mind, again and again, was assailed by the tormenting idea that God may be prevented from working the miracle by the rule of the wicked. This is how his satire became a form of that 'modern ecstasy' that, in Shakespeare's *Macbeth*, rose from the 'violent sorrow' into which 'the poor country' was pitched by evil deeds. (This, by the way, occurs in the same passage from which, it seems, Bertolt Brecht derived the most impressive line that speaks of one who, in this frightening world, is still able to smile only because the terrible news had not yet reached him. In *Macbeth* this reads: '... Where nothing/But who knows nothing, is once seen to smile.')

'Modern ecstasy'. In his great essay 'Über naive und sentimentalische Dichtung' (On Spontaneous and Reflective Poetry) Schiller speaks of 'pathetische Satire', tragic satire. It flows, he writes, from a mind and soul, 'deeply imbued with the ideal. Only a powerful desire for harmony is allowed and able to bring forth the acute perception of moral contrariness and the passionate indignation at moral perversity that inspires the works of Juvenal, Swift, Rousseau ...' And Schiller insists that these very writers would have written poetry of affection and tenderness if the viciousness of their age had not diverted their sensibilities in the direction of satire; 'and even so, some of them *have* produced such works', namely purely lyrical poems.

Certainly Karl Kraus has done so: nine volumes of *Worte in Versen* (Words in Verse). Although he carried on his satirical attacks in some of his verse, most of his poems are the creations of moments of repose when a valley and a mountain stream rushing through it seem to be all that is left of friendliness in the world:

Karl Kraus

Staunend stand ich da
und ein Bergbach rinnt
und das ganze Tal
war mir wohlgesinnt . . .

In form, metre, and rhythm his poems are traditional, as befits the 'epigone', as he called himself in defiance of the stammering, blaring innovators who in his days as in ours thought they were probing the depths of a 'new soul'. Like Bertolt Brecht, the only writer among the contemporaries of his later years whose lyrical genius he acknowledged, Karl Kraus never left or rebuilt 'the old house of language' that stood near the 'Ursprung', 'the source'.

Nonetheless Karl Kraus was not a mystic if mysticism ultimately leads to the silence of the ineffable. For Karl Kraus everything that truly was, was sayable: war, killing, money, hunger, journalists, lies, machines, infamy; but also trees, fountains, dogs, love, and peace above the mountain tops on a summer evening. Compared to the real things conveyed by these simple words, anything that lay beyond the boundaries of language was, even if it lured the mind with vague intimations of the unknown, likely to be as trivial as the antics of ghosts from beyond the grave.

No doubt there is much that has never been said; but this is only because language has not yet reached it. The 'divining-rod' of words, this instrument of all true thought, is capable of finding it. For every truth that is meant for us is already there even though it may still be hidden in the folds of language, waiting to give itself to a great lover of words.

Karl Kraus's poetry is, like his satire, sustained at every point by his faith in the natural grace of language, indeed in the near-equation of language and human nature. Human corruption, he believed, could be revealed instantly in the corruption of language, and every correction of the tribe's faulty speech might induce a miniature catharsis of the soul. His poetry and his satire thus have a common source and this is why his satire, as if it were poetry, has outlived its occasions. Indeed, it is poetry of a kind, poetry in reverse. As Aristotle believed that the only worthy protagonists of tragic poetry were royal – for only in the fall from the heights of life was the fate of man revealed in all its

poignancy – Karl Kraus discovered the modern tragedy by showing how mediocrity, unexpectedly endowed with demonic powers,
had mounted those abandoned thrones:

> ... My business in this state
> Made me a looker-on here in Vienna
> Where I have seen corruption boil and bubble
> Till it o'er-run the stew ...

Measure for Measure, from which these lines are quoted, was
in the repertoire of the 'Theatre of Poetry', founded by Karl Kraus,
if 'founding' is the right word for his decision to counter-
balance, as it were, his own purely satirical dramas* by devoting
his great talent as a public reader to the tragedies and comedies
of Shakespeare. He wanted to restore the *language* of dramatic
poetry; for it had become almost inaudible in the ever noisier
machinery of the commercial stage, and enfeebled beyond recognition by the ever more 'naturalistic' – that is, slovenly –
enunciation of its actors.

Karl Kraus's stage was empty, except for the curtains that
covered its walls and the table at which he sat. His voice, face,
and gestures were all the cast he used and yet – although he
made no attempt at 'impersonating' – his theatre was richly
populated with the creatures of the poetic imagination. Like the
chorus of *Henry V*, he relied on his voice and the poetry of the
drama to bring forth on his 'unworthy scaffold' 'so great an object' as the proud triumphs and defeats of human worth in a
world endlessly embattled and yet, suddenly and incomprehensibly, at peace when lovers in the poetry of their love cannot
tell the skylark from the nightingale.

Kraus began by reciting on his little stage his own satirical
scenes, diatribes, aphorisms, and lyrical poems, as well as the
works of contemporaries he admired: Gerhart Hauptmann's early
dramas, full of compassion for the victims of social abuse, or
Frank Wedekind's plays, harsh, brittle, and eloquently indignant
at the sexual mendacity of the age; or the poems of Liliencron,
Georg Trakl, and Else Lasker-Schüler, the eccentric Jewish

---

* There was not only *The Last Days of Mankind*; there were also *Literatur*, 1921;
Traumtheater (Dream Theatre), 1922, *Traumstück* (Dream Play), 1922; *Wolkenkuckucksheim*
(Cloudcuckooland), 1923; and *Die Unüberwindlichen* (The Unconquerable), 1927.

poetess, always assailed by visions, words, and penury. Kraus once gave a benefit recital for Lasker-Schüler during which he remarked that she could not earn as much in a year with her own dreams as a psychoanalyst earns in a week with the dreams of others.

Before long, however, Shakespeare dominated his theatre, in the translation by Schlegel and Tieck (the greatest and most durable conquest Germany has ever made of foreign territory), which he only slightly adapted to the purpose of his one-man performances. He gave performances also of Goethe and of Nestroy, Kraus's nineteenth-century countryman who had examined Viennese corruption, and did so, as a writer and actor, with a *vis comica* that blended verbal wit, histrionic alacrity, melancholy pessimism, and moral exasperation. The excellent editor and biographer-critic of Nestroy, Otto Rommel, said of Karl Kraus's readings of his comedies that Nestroy lived in them while most other performances of his plays lived off him.

The closeness of Kraus's satire to his poetry explains what so often disturbed his readers: the fluctuation of his apparent political allegiances. The truth is that he had none. He said much that seemed political, and did so with inimitable satirical skill and force and great sympathy for the helpless and maltreated. Once or twice his 'politics' were even posted, angrily and succinctly, on the billboards of the city, demanding, for instance, that the head of the Vienna police resign.

He wrote and spoke about rulers and ruled, war-drunk or blackmailing editors, sadistic colonels, cliché-ridden writers and illiterate readers, about Christian power-seekers and unchristian socialists, about soubrettes singing of the slaughter of men and black marketeers swearing *Nibelungentreue*, about boiling corruption, 'carnal, bloody, and unnatural acts', 'accidental judgements', and 'deaths put on by cunning and forced cause'. But after all this, it became transparently clear that the secret of Kraus's 'politics' – so secret that he himself did not always have access to it – was that he was not political. He aimed at neither revolution nor reform, neither change nor conservation, but at aesthetic annihilation, wanting to dissolve into art all the vicious, inarticulate, obtuse stupidities that offended the moral and aesthetic intelligence. His verbal victories over the villainies of the world were not unlike the triumphs of Shakespeare's sonnets over the wicked fascination of the Dark Lady.

But there were moments in Kraus's recitals when the evils of life seemed to vanish into thin air, into the air that intoxicates, or into a music which, as in the finale of *Don Giovanni*, exuberantly rejoices at the city's being rid of a scoundrel. This was when Karl Kraus 'performed' the operettas of Offenbach. He had come to know them as a child and preserved his memories in the poem 'Jugend': of the enchanted summer days in the village of Weidlingau where the sky was blue and the butterflies red, and where, sitting before the stage of the summer theatre, he fell in love with Offenbach's Belle Hélène, with his Bluebeard's Boulotte, 'and not to forget: Gérolstein, Trapezunt, all the princesses'.

His performances of these works were imbued with such memories. Once again there was Weidlingau, and innocence was restored. Yet the delight he took in Offenbach was not merely nostalgic and certainly not sentimental. He found in those operettas – the libretti of which he partly rewrote and wholly cleansed of the dust that had settled on them – the ideal unity of satire and *joie de vivre*, the mirth that still vibrates with the echoes of great anger. Mauriac said that the laughter in Offenbach's music struck him as that of the Empress Charlotte gone mad. For Karl Kraus it was an entirely sane and witty celebration of the self-transcending power of the satirical spirit.

Such force was of no avail against Hitler. Of course Kraus knew this. In 1933 there appeared a very slim *Fackel*: four pages. Three of them contained the text of the funeral oration he delivered at the grave of his friend, the architect Adolf Loos. On the fourth page there was the – now famous – short poetic manifesto of his silence. 'Ich bleibe stumm', it began, 'I shall say nothing', and it ended with 'Das Wort entschlief, als diese Welt erwachte': the word expired as this world awakened. This was not tragic irony but tragic consistency. For the art of the satirist was bound to abdicate before rulers who left nothing to be transformed into satirical art; and this was so because the world they created was itself 'art' – the abominable art that perversely fulfilled itself in reality. It was not for nothing that Hitler was a bankrupt painter.

Karl Kraus had said of his *Last Days of Mankind* that its satirical humour 'was only the self-reproach of a man who had survived with his mind intact'. The satirical exaggerations of this drama, as he insisted, merely reported what really happened in those unspeakable years. What he uttered as his own words was simply an attempt to avoid a silence that would be misinterpreted. But it is still true to say that those times were not yet the worst; for satire could still say: 'This is the worst.' The worst was still to come; and it came when Germany insisted on outdoing even the exaggerations of satire, eliminating the breathing space the imagination needs to contemplate the event, and the event to grow into the sayable.

Nonetheless, Karl Kraus kept writing and went even so far as to have set up in type *The Third Walpurgisnight*, one of his last works. But he refrained from publishing it. Perhaps it should have been left at that. However, it was published posthumously, three times posthumously: after the death of its author, and of the Third Reich, and of satire itself in Germany. The title of the book declares the defeat of the satirist's art; for the first two Walpurgisnights are creations of Goethe's poetry, but the third takes place in a real country even if its scenes appear to overflow the embankments of reality. Now, for the first time, Karl Kraus's writing was out of date. For the Day of Satirical Judgment was – at least by the calendar of European culture – the day after the last days of mankind.

Karl Kraus was of that remarkable generation of men who, despite all their differences, unmistakably belonged to the last days of the Austrian monarchy. They were prophets of its end, or messengers of a radically new beginning, or subtle analysts of its decadence. Or they were searchers for an ultimate clarity which, however painful and unsettling it may be, was to do away with the fustian that had become the idiom of an age bent upon hiding from itself the vacuity at its core and the doom that awaited it. It happened once before that the disintegration of a great empire released extraordinary spiritual energies in men possessed by premonitions of the end. As happened at the time of the decline of Rome, the men of the Austrian 'apocalypse' were mostly Jews or at least not quite un-Jewish: Karl Kraus, Otto Weininger, Franz Kafka, Gustav Mahler, Arnold Schönberg,

Hugo von Hofmannsthal, Sigmund Freud, Arthur Schnitzler, Joseph Roth, Ludwig Wittgenstein,* Hermann Broch; and it almost comes as a surprise, or strikes one as an act of wilful 'racial' discrimination, that the names of Adolf Loos, Alban Berg, and Robert Musil cannot be added to this list.

Is there anything, apart from the sense of civilization's winter, that these men have in common? Yes, but it is not easily defined; and with Karl Kraus the difficulty is much enhanced by the fact that – with a few exceptions – he would not have liked being mentioned in their company, in *any* contemporary company: 'If I were told that I shall have to share immortality with certain people, I should prefer a separate oblivion', he once said.

Yet it may well be that the elusive awareness which to a greater or lesser degree they all share is the one that pervades the work of Karl Kraus: of the progressive diminution of human substance, or character, or 'nature', or 'virtue', or *Sein* ('being') in an age abandoning itself more and more to the lust for the technical enslavement of the natural, and to the displays of mere talent and virtuosity. Life exhausted itself in 'doing'. 'Who on earth was it who thought out the great compensation: that a man should be able to *do* what he *is not*?'

This is one of Karl Kraus's most revealing aphorisms, as revealing as his confession that he was puzzled by the fact that 'half a man should have the faculty to write a whole sentence'. These utterances show his profoundest concern. What followed from it with regard to his writing was his refusal to be called a 'master of language'. 'I only master the language of others',

---

* Karl Kraus was one of the very few contemporary writers that Wittgenstein read attentively. How attentively is shown by the comparison of two aphorisms:

'Philosophy results in the discovery of one or another piece of simple nonsense, and in bruises which the understanding has suffered by bumping its head against the limits of language. The bruises make us see the value of that discovery' (from Wittgenstein's *Philosophical Investigations*, published in 1953).

'If I cannot get further, this is because I have bumped my head against the wall of language. Then, with my head bleeding, I withdraw. And want to go on' (from Karl Kraus's *Nacht*, published in 1918).

But this is only one conspicuous example of affinity with Kraus revealed by Wittgenstein's style throughout his writings. When he had sent his *Tractatus* to the first publisher of Karl Kraus's works (Karl Kraus became his own publisher later on), he even tried, as a letter to a friend shows, to find out with incongruous curiosity what Karl Kraus thought of it; incongruous because Karl Kraus would not have read it. He maintained he was unable to understand technical philosophy.

he replied. 'My own does with me as it pleases.' About a poet
whose early poems he printed in *Die Fackel* and whose later works
he intensely disliked, he said that for a long time he had not
been quite sure of the quality of his poetry until he found out
that its maker was no good. This decided the matter.

To such a mind mere opinions meant little, and least of all
political ideologies, those cheaply priced substitutes for faith or
wisdom. Once confessing in verse his 'contradiction', he called
himself a revolutionary whenever lies threatened to get the better
of life, or laws set themselves up against nature; but, whenever
freedom was used to further commerce of the press or the
degradation of the arts, he was a reactionary, going back, in his
'reaction' as far as 'the origin'.

When in 1914, shortly before the outbreak of World War I,
socialist critics reproached him for his friendship with some
members of the Austrian aristocracy, he wrote an answer which,
after evoking once more a lamentable 'radical' scene where the
ancient dreams of paradise were psychoanalysed or organized or
subsidized or advertised, concludes with the following sentences:

> I know what is at stake: the salvation of our souls. I know and
> confess – at the risk of being considered, from now onwards, a pol-
> itician or, worse still, an aesthete, or both – that in the name of the
> spirit it is more important to save the wall that surrounds a castle park
> where between a poplar tree ... and a bluebell ... the miraculous works
> of Creation are protected from the destructiveness of the world – more
> important than all the agitations ... that merely impede the breath of
> God.

The castle and the park belonged to the woman he loved, then
and until his death: Sidonie Baroness of Nadherny. To sense in
Karl Kraus's satire the design of the wall that is to defend 'the
miraculous works of Creation' against the encroachments of a
decaying civilization is to understand and affirm his 'negativity'.

6
Literature and political responsibility
apropos the letters of Thomas Mann

I

L ITERATURE and Political Responsibility – a couple that have acquired some notoriety in the history of thought both by their mutual attraction and by their ceaseless quarrels. Indeed, the two have been married and divorced so often that the invitation to dwell with them is unlikely to be received with a sense of relaxed serenity; and the irritable antiquity of the entanglement only increases the sense of discomfort. The more one reflects upon this problem, the surer one becomes that it would have qualified for admission with the French Surrealist poet Robert Desnos who once proclaimed (and Surrealism relished such imperial gestures): 'The questions that I am willing to discuss are all unanswerable.' And like many another insoluble problem, this too has long since moved into a draughty halfway house situated between the banal and the unmanageably complex. Yet imagine a student who has been kept in ideal ignorance of the problem's bothersome history. Would it not be easy enough to keep him occupied for a very long time with respectable works of literature without his discovering anything problematical in the relations between writing and politics? Would he, reading or seeing Shakespeare's history plays, feel that the poet's blatant political partisanship is to the detriment of his poetic or dramatic effects? Indeed, that it produces any difficulties whatever? Or would he, if he studied the literature of the German Middle Ages, sense any betrayal of the pure Muse in the poems with which Walther von der Vogelweide, animated by the utmost partiality, joins the political controversies of his age?

Surely, history abounds in the kind of literature that wears its politics, as it were, upon its sleeve, the right or the left sleeve, leaving him who is bent upon examining the relationship between literature and politics with nothing to interpret or unmask; he would be defeated by the obvious. For there are, again and again, artistically effective alliances between literary talent, sometimes even genius, and social or political engagement. We need only think, apart from those just mentioned, of the young

Schiller, of Heine, Büchner, Dickens, Dostoevsky, Zola, Ibsen,
the young Gerhart Hauptmann, Heinrich Mann, Sartre, Camus,
to give a few of the more conspicuous examples, and not to
compose a list of men of letters whose names, by virtue of the
distinction of their style and the vivacity of their political ideas,
ought to be included in the manuals of both literature and
political thought: some of the French Encyclopedists, for instance,
or Burke, or de Maistre, or many among the nineteenth-
century Russian intelligentsia, or George Orwell – the kind of
writers, in fact, who prompted Thomas Mann, in that deeply
troubled period of his life when, overwhelmed by this unquiet
problem, he wrote *Meditations of an Unpolitical Man*, to say in anger
and in untranslatable German that literature was *identical* with'
politics; in untranslatable German, for he meant 'literature' as
distinct from 'poetry'; and only in German is – or perhaps rather
was – the word *Literatur*, as opposed to *Dichtung*, capable of con-
veying that contemptuous pride of the spirit with which Thomas
Mann invested it. Gone for good, it would seem, are those
German days when the radical distinction between literature and
the poetic spirit made some sense, yet it was only fifty years ago
that one of the most intelligent and certainly one of the most
gifted German writers could insist upon this opposition. As
his *Letters** fascinatingly and often disconcertingly show, he was
to take it back, and then take back a little of the taking
back, and then once more modify or altogether deny the original

* *Letters of Thomas Mann, 1889–1955*, selected and translated by Richard and Clara
Winston, introduction by Richard Winston. This volume is a well-chosen, well-
introduced, and, apart from some mistakes, well-translated selection. Well-
translated: this is to say that it is not only faithful to the meaning of the original (and
this is saying a great deal in view of the sheer faultiness of the available translations of Thomas Mann's works), but also fluent and 'readable', although this is a
term of praise that one would like to avoid; for to say of a book that it is readable
seems not much better than to say of a meal that it is edible. But here it is meant
to be applause. I have no doubt that Richard and Clara Winston are, like F. D.
Luke who translated *Tonio Kröger* and other stories of Thomas Mann, translators whom
Thomas Mann's publishers, assisted perhaps by a Foundation, should give the time
necessary for at last doing him justice in English. This will be impossible as long as
translators' time is paid not in terms of hours but of words or pages. Mann's
urbanity; his ironical and gentlemanly shyness in approaching the truth; the
precision of which his controlled diffidence is capable; his long-windedness which
breathes elegance into apparent awkwardness – this has, after all, a superb correlative
in English: Henry James. Translators of Thomas Mann ought to be given the
leisure to immerse themselves in James's prose.

position, and so on – a 'so on' that bears witness not so much to the changeability of Thomas Mann's mind as to the refractory character of the problem of 'literary politics'.

In the years of the First World War he put aside the – as yet slim – manuscript of *The Magic Mountain*, to do as Hans Castorp, the hero of that novel, later did when at last he broke the spell of the sick mountain to become a soldier on the battlefields of Flanders. Thomas Mann, pen in hand, fought the battle for the fatherland on the pages, ever growing over the years, of *Meditations of an Unpolitical Man*, a book as tortured, inspired, sinister, enthusiastic and German, as much later, and yet not *so* much later, was to be *Doctor Faustus*. Germany is the protagonist of both books. In the first it is a Germany that defends her soul and her aristocratic genius of music, poetry, and irony against the blatantly political rhetoric of 'democracy', 'civilization', and 'progress'; in the second a Germany that, in the same conflict, has perverted her soul and loses it. Soul defended or soul lost: he would be a poor reader who did not perceive that the author's love of the lost soul had become even greater, nourished as it was by an abundance of pain and dismay.

Meditations of an Unpolitical Man is the last great document of the conservative mind – a mind, in this case, both patriotically German and European, and at the same time endowed with a sensibility that clearly recognizes the historical decadence of the virtues and values it struggles to uphold. It is based upon the belief that 'literature', the literature produced by, for instance, Thomas Mann's brother Heinrich, the Settembrini, the *Zivilisationsliterat*, is the upshot of the French Revolution, the literary aspect of democratic politics, and the destructive invader of the domain of the unpolitical inner spirit expressing itself in music, poetry, and metaphysics. This was in 1916. Was there, then, after the Second World War, any reason to assume that from the soil of that 'unpolitical' domain grew not only the genius of the German nation but also its wickedness? Was it not simply 'the *Junkers* and industrialists' who had 'put Hitler into power'? An emigré German teacher from Australia asked such questions and wanted to be assured by Thomas Mann that, for instance, neither Hegel nor Nietzsche could be held responsible for the National Socialists' catastrophic misbehaviour. Well, yes *and* no, answered the writer who was just about to complete *Doctor Faustus*. His reply of 29 December 1946 concedes to the teacher that 'as a teacher' he is right in allowing his young Australians to immerse themselves in the minds of such German philosophers. And yet he, Thomas Mann, had scribbled a doubting *hmm* in the margin of the letter. For does this dismissal of responsibility not reduce the stature of the intellect, does it not make the works of the mind look more innocuous than they are or want to be? For that Hegel, Schopenhauer, and Nietzsche contributed to shaping the German mind and its dealing with life and the world is as undeniable as the fact that Martin Luther had something to do with the Thirty Years' War, whose horrors he explicitly took 'upon his neck' in advance.

Even giddier in renunciation, more eager in taking back the 'unpolitical' doctrine of *Meditations*, is a letter of 18 April 1945 to his 'brother in spirit – or cousin at any rate', Hermann Hesse. It combines his thanks for *The Glass Bead Game* with his announcement that for some time now he himself has been working on *Doctor Faustus*, a novel that has, he believes, a very close kinship to Hesse's book. And yet, he seems to imply, it differs from it in one important point: *The Glass Bead Game* is the product of an imagination 'hovering' ironically above the conventional opposites. Therefore, he says, it is not surprising that it is a plea for the mind's freedom from political ideologies. Very well, but what is meant by 'mind'? 'If "mind" is the principle, the power, which desires the good; if it is a sensitive alertness towards the changing aspects of truth, in a word, a "divine solicitude" which seeks to approach what is right and requisite at a given time, then it is political, whether or not this epithet sounds pretty. It seems to me that nowadays nothing alive escapes politics. Refusal is politics too; it is a political act on the side of the evil cause.'

Who, one is tempted to wonder, is the speaker? Of course, the radically converted author of *Meditations of an Unpolitical Man*. How radically converted? And what, in the case of an artist, does 'conversion' mean? In 1930 – long after he had abandoned his conservative nationalism and made himself an advocate of the Weimar Republic, even of democratic socialism – he proclaimed, in an essay on 'Culture and Socialism', that indeed he no longer held the *opinions* of *Meditations*, but its 'true insight' (*Erkenntnis*) remained undeniably right. How is this? Is there a way of distinguishing between 'opinion' (*Meinung*) and 'true insight'? There is; although it is impossible to do it in one sentence, even if it is helpful to recall another one, written by him in 1923 in his oration on the 'German Republic'. 'I recant nothing', he said then, 'I renounce nothing essential. I spoke the truth, my truth, then, and am speaking it now.' Nevertheless, he himself needed the four volumes of *Joseph and His Brothers* to *show* what he meant: namely that 'divine solicitude' – Jacob was its master and Joseph overdid it sometimes with charm and wit   consists in fathoming which variation on the constant theme of the Spirit was demanded by any particular moment of Time, this medium, ever-changing in its claims, of the Spirit's journeying toward its full realization in the mind and heart of Man. It is, in the last resolve, a Hegelian configuration of history, and, of course, there may occur errors in man's assessment, at any given historical instant, of the exact station of the Spirit.

Thomas Mann, in that letter to Hesse, was in error if, with his critique of the unpolitical intent of Hesse's *The Glass Bead Game*, he wished to imply that his own *Doctor Faustus* was a political book. True, he inserted (and 'inserted' is unfortunately the right word) an exhortatory passage into *Faustus* – Leverkühn's last speech, the oration the composer delivers in the idiom of the Lutheran German Faustbook of 1587, in which he confesses his pact with the Devil, and introduces the event that is not to take place: his playing of the score that reveals his 'break-through', by means of the most rigid musical calculation, into the sphere of ecstatic genius – the bargaining price paid by the Devil. It is a madman's speech, and ends in the madman's paralytic collapse, and contains those political sentences, the only ones which in that masterfully written scene may give rise to some doubt about the speaker's musical accomplishment: they strike an utterly wrong note. Leverkühn, there, takes the guilt of the age, in Luther's phrase, 'upon his neck'. For in abandoning himself to his genius's 'infernal drunkenness', he disregarded the commandment that a man should be 'sober and vigilant' and prudently see to it that here on earth an order is established that would provide the proper soil for beautiful works to grow from,

works that would not, at their source, be in need of devilish
prodding.

This is completely out of character: not even in the remotest
nook of Leverkühn's unconscious could there ever have stirred
the impulse to become a supporter of 'causes'. (Not to ask the
unanswerable question, what the ingredients are of such 'soil'.
They are certainly not social justice or political morality. The
mere thought of the slaves of Greece, or the serfs of the Middle
Ages, or the riches of the aristocrats for whom Mozart made
his music, does away with such noble surmise.) But it is not only
out of character, it is altogether foreign to the *historical*
philosophy that pervades the whole novel. The 'danger of sterility', so intensely felt by the artists of the epoch, 'is not to be
blamed on social conditions', says the Devil in his conversation
with Leverkühn, and, as so often in this interior dialogue, he
is right. Certainly, these 'conditions' may be truly felt to be incompatible with the self-sufficient harmony of a work of art. But
this is 'accidental'; for 'the prohibitive difficulties of the work
lie deep in its own nature. It is the historical development of
the musical material itself which has turned against the idea of
harmony.' No, if a category has to be found, then *Doctor
Faustus* is not a political but a historical novel. *Mario and the
Magician* is, by comparison, a simple political allegory, and yet
its author said of it in one of his letters that he did not like 'to
have this story considered a political satire'. In the case of
Doctor Faustus he certainly did not dismiss a political interpretation as energetically, but wherever he invited it in the work
itself, the work itself refused to endorse the invitation: nowhere,
for instance, is it less successful than in the task of illuminating
the intended parallel between 'my friend' and 'my fatherland'
(the narrator's last words in the novel), between the story of
Leverkühn and the story of Germany. It was Thomas Mann's
will that it should, but the book knew better.

'The book wanted it so.' The words occur in a letter to Agnes
E. Meyer, the American recipient of many a letter from him,
and concern Fitelberg, the formidable Jewish impresario who
makes an important episodic appearance in *Doctor Faustus* (the
Riccaut scene, Thomas Mann called it once, referring to the
celebrated anti-French scene in Lessing's *Minna von Barnhelm*). The

correspondent seems to have expressed the fear that there might be some anti-Semitic rejoicing at the figure of Fitelberg. 'Curious', Thomas Mann replies, the same worry was expressed by his son Klaus 'when I first read the chapter to the family'. And to make matters worse for the Jews, their other 'representative' in the book, 'the Fascist Breisach', is also far from being an endearing character. Surely, political considerations would have made it advisable to avoid even the slightest suspicion of anti-Semitism. But 'the book wanted it so'. For clearly it was *Dichtung*, not *Literatur*.

2

Literatur versus *Dichtung*, literature which for Thomas Mann *was* politics, versus poetry which within that juxtaposition enjoyed the reputation of being unpolitical, and this despite Shakespeare and Walther von der Vogelweide and Bertolt Brecht (quickly to drop the name that in recent literature is likely to be thought of first in any discussion of literature and politics, and who may indeed be this problem's most problematical problem child) – well, despite Shakespeare and Walther and Brecht and many another perpetrator of political poetry, there *is*, of course, a formidable amount of *Dichtung*, and certainly of *lyrical* poetry which might be put before our imaginary student; and if we are sure that he was not disturbed by the obvious political affections and disaffections of certain literary works, he will now remain equally unworried by the blissful absence of any 'politically responsible' thought from the mind of, for instance, Keats as he lyrically addresses the Grecian Urn or the Nightingale; or of Blake as he laments the sickness of the Rose; or of Goethe as he strolls through rhymes and woods with the sole purpose of enjoying his purposelessness:

> Und nichts zu suchen,
> Das war mein Sinn.

> And naught to seek,
> That was my goal.

And even if it becomes the fashion here and there, a fashion created by moles of the mind burrowing deep into the 'structure' of lyrical poems so that its analysis might bring to light the 'social motivations', and therefore political bias, indeed a kind of insidious class-subconscious, from the layers below the humus in which 'pure poetry' has its shallow roots, we may still slip into the hands of our unsuspecting reader a few poems of Bertolt Brecht himself: the one, for instance, which sings in the most private of lyrical moods of lovers' embraces, and how quickly love is forgotten, much more quickly than the white cloud that hovered in the blue September sky above the scene of love; or that lyrically perfect *Mahagonny* song of the Crane flying with the Cloud, allegories of lovers who are utterly given up to their love and lost to the world of sober, dependable conduct, and who are yet utterly affirmed by the poet in the manner only good poetry or great love are capable of affirming. It is the poem ending with the line that may well be the consummate message of social irresponsibility:

Wohin, ihr? – Nirgend hin. – Von wem davon? – Von allen.

You, up there, where are you off to? – Nowhere. – Away from whom? – From all.

'Away from all' – it is undeniable that this cry of Brecht's lovers is also the voice of poetry itself in some of its most exquisite phases: namely when, in Yeats's words, the Imagination is brought

... to that pitch where it casts out
All that is not itself ...

or when the poet is entirely immersed in the business of making a poem, the phase that Goethe, rather angrily, once defended against any kind of moral or social interference: 'Certainly, it is possible that a work of art is of moral consequence, but to demand of the artist moral intentions and goals is to spoil his craft.' Small wonder that Plato, despite the excellent relations his great mentor Socrates entertained with Apollo and the Muses, emphatically crossed out the 'and' between 'Poetry' and 'Social Responsibility'. To look back then for a moment to the *locus classicus* where, together with many other problems, this too received its first and stubbornly enduring articulation: poets, Plato thought, were by their very nature debarred from being responsible citizens of the ideal Republic. Divinely or demoniacally inspired as they are, they may claim citizenship in some kind of musical *Civitas Dei*, or rather *Civitas Musae*; yet the summit of Parnassus is no breeding ground for civic virtues. Where civic virtues count, poets disturb the peace. Poetry *and* social responsibility? You might just as well try to turn Zeus himself into a husband faithfully abiding by the virtuous conventions of monogamy.

If time is the test – no, not necessarily of the truth but of the power of an idea – then that celebrated ruling about the poets in Plato's *Republic* has passed it: again and again this doctrine, in one form or another (and mostly without its expositors being conscious of its source), has found acceptance: not only with the rulers of some republics, but also with the poets themselves, sometimes even in poetical households boasting famous political commitments. Platonic, following from the *Republic* directly or inversely, is both the absolute aestheticism of nineteenth-century French coinage and, vice versa, Hitler's ostracizing what he regarded as degenerate art. And surely, it is an echo from Plato's *Republic* that is discernible in the French Symbolists' emphatic and emphatically anti-Saint-Simonist abrogation of any social contract that may have been concluded in the past between Art and Life (an abrogation through which artists exhibit a kind of Platonic and 'unpolitical' beggars' pride); and Platonic indeed was, before them, Schopenhauer's definition of Art as the exercise of minds rendering with the materials of this world, with words and colours and sounds, the visions obtained in another sphere, the sphere, ironically enough, of Platonic Forms, sights attainable only to those who have freed themselves temporarily of all ambitions, purposes, social responsibilities of this Will-driven life.

Plato was present, *malgré lui*, in the young Nietzsche's belief that only the purest aesthetic contemplation of the world can justify the world's existence: 'only as an aesthetic phenomenon is the world forever justified', the most audacious artistic theodicy ever attempted; and Plato has, not without Schopenhauer's and Nietzsche's mediation, a say in Thomas Mann's *Tonio Kröger*, the story of the young artist who – not quite unlike Rimbaud, Mallarmé, Valéry, Rilke – was painfully convinced that he had to lose his citizenship in the commonwealth of honourable and virtuous men in order to reach the heights of art. Again, Plato altogether dominates the scenery of ideas that Mann has arranged for the action of *Death in Venice:* beginning with the moment when the 'classical' writer Aschenbach, struck by the 'irresponsible' passion for the beautiful boy Tadzio-Phaedrus, socratically warns himself, by dreamily warning the youth, that although beauty is 'the lover's way towards the spirit', it is 'only the way, little Phaedrus', and issuing in the catastrophic recognition that, along that way, 'we poets are bound to go astray', and will, worshippers of beauty that they are, be destroyed by their idol; and the more they aspire to the classical role of educators, the more blatantly ludicrous will 'our magisterial style' look one day: it will be seen as 'folly and false pretence', and farcical 'all the honours bestowed upon us'; and 'to teach the young by means of art is a dangerous thing and ought to be forbidden' because Form, the preoccupation of artists, is 'in its innermost core indifferent to good and evil'. All this, and more, is prefigured in Plato's banishment of the poets from the company of morally dependable citizens.

Equally clear is the link that connects Plato's pronouncement about the poets with the repeated declarations of the Russian Communist party against an art 'alienated' from the social realities and responsibilities of Soviet society. For while the totalitarian states have tried to prove – to Plato, as it were – that there could, after all, be an art 'shouldering' its prescribed political obligations (and the art that did such shouldering was the well-known and excruciatingly well-behaved 'Social Realism' in both the German and the Russian tyrannies), poets, from the Parnassians' *l'art pour l'art* to the Symbolists' absolutely 'pure poetry', have been passionately intent upon making the highest artistic virtue out of precisely that which Plato regarded as the ineradicable vice of poetry: its detachment from the body politic, its unreliable ambiguities and ironies vis-à-vis the seriousness demanded by the moral life, and its helpless exposure to the seduction of fantasy, play, and pure form: in brief, its tendency to climb up to 'that pitch where it casts out all that is not itself'. *Les extrêmes se touchent*, and the point at which the extreme anti-aesthetic philosophy of the totalitarian state *and* the extreme aestheticism of Absolute Poetry meet, is that passage from Plato's *Republic*.

Caught between these extremes of literary theory and practice, many critics, interpreters, and teachers of literature were unfortunately inclined to follow suit, and either ran with the hares of aesthetic 'escapism' or hunted with the hounds of the totalitarian ideologies. Few, alas, remained immune from the infection. For critically to receive a work of literature as if it were truly nothing but an aesthetically organized assemblage of words on a page, or a sequence of lines containing varying or recurrent 'images', or a concert of rhythmically ordered sound and artistically transmuted fury, means uncritically to accept a strange, if not pathological, belief in sheer formal perfection which, on the part of the artist, may lead to the frantic illusion that all *contents* are but tiresome obstacles impeding the poet's progress towards absolute poetry. The form is the content: it was this creed that Nietzsche, the very inventor of the 'theodicy' of aestheticism, called perverse. For he knew that the artist may become obsessed with form *as* content – just as if the thing to be given form did not exist, or had to be annihilated rather than moulded; and Baudelaire, so often himself under the spell of such aesthetic despotism, wrote of 'le goût immodéré de la forme', 'the immoderate taste for form', which bred 'disorders, monstrous and unheard of'.

To look upon such formal excess as the norm, indeed to derive from the 'monstrous disorder' a method of literary criticism, means to accept the extreme situation that, at the other end, has called forth the politico-ideological judge of literature who absurdly measures literary creations by degrees of their 'realism', or, worse still, by the relative conformity or dissent regarding the political 'opinions' they seem to utter or imply. The philosophy of the type of criticism which many years ago was New represents merely a novel aspect of that betrayal of which, in a classical treatise, Julien Benda accused the intellectuals: their readiness to give a hand in the operation which removes from the fabric of man's social and political arrangements the spiritual conscience – that conscience which must be one of the chief inspirations also of literary criticism if it is to justify the important place we have allotted to it in our higher education; and the subtlest variant of the surgery that severs the link between aesthetics and ethics, between the disciplined life of the imagination and the social-moral reality may well be to encapsulate literature in a sphere all its own. For literature is certainly many things, but few of the things that literature is would be worthy of our attention if the spiritual conscience were altogether absent from it. Then indeed Plato would not have been so wrong in advocating its prohibition in the commonwealth of men; and yet again not so right either: for literature would then simply be trivial, and would not matter, and the hypnotic glimmer of deranged profundities and the blinding glitter of broken mirages would try in vain to make up for its lost meaning and beauty. W. H. Auden, not so long ago, charmingly repudiated this radical aesthetic operation, and in doing so, he spoke with the voice of poetry itself, a voice unmistakable in its power to please and to shock. You hope, the poet in that poem says to himself, you hope that your works, aesthetically successful as they are, may one day serve as the grand justification of your existence, no matter how otherwise you have conducted it. But will this apology be accepted? Perhaps not. For

> God may reduce you
> on Judgment Day
> to tears of shame,
> reciting by heart
> the poems you would
> have written, had
> your life been good.

Nonetheless the problem persists, and seems to have invaded the consciousness of poets themselves with ever greater force. Nietzsche, in saying that there must have been a time when the moral and the aesthetic domains were one (Wittgenstein, in philosophic daring, maintained that they are identical), was surely more regretful about their present dissociation than confident about the indefinite past of their oneness. This anticipatory spokesman of many modern poets knew neither Kierkegaard nor Keats, but he would have supported much of what these men wrote about the moral dubiousness of the aesthetic state; indeed, he did, as it were, write it himself. There are numerous Nietzschean utterances on art and artists that are almost indistinguishable from certain passages in Kierkegaard's writings; and even a thorough student of Nietzsche would, if he did not happen to know that it was by Keats, readily believe that it was Nietzsche who spoke of 'the poetical Character' as having 'no character', as taking 'as much delight in conceiving an Iago as an Imogen'; and:

'What shocks the virtuous philosopher, delights the chameleon Poet.'

3

To move from a poet and a poetic thinker to a writer of novels and letters: in his *Meditations of an Unpolitical Man* Thomas Mann summons witnesses from every corner of the world's literature to make his case for the 'chameleon Poet' and against the prodigal brother Heinrich, the *Zivilisationsliterat*, the political moralist. Has he, Thomas Mann asks, really not enough self-knowledge to see the lie in his politico-moral 'commitments'? Not to recognize that, as a writer of literature, he will forever remain an 'aesthetic opportunist' to whom the aesthetic success of his sentences is bound to matter more than the success of the moral or political opinions those sentences may advocate? '*Bellezza* radicalism' – this is what Thomas Mann calls the irresponsible politics of his aesthetic brother seized with political enthusiasm. In the denunciation of this *bellezza* radicalism Thomas Mann is most formidably inspired. Some people, he says, allow themselves to be etymologically misled into taking radicalism in literature for depth. But no, it is 'a pretty superficiality, a cult of the generous gesture which at times assumes an almost choreographic quality'. And indeed, the *Zivilisationsliterat* once exclaimed: 'Liberty – that is the Dionysian dance of Reason'. And Thomas Mann, calling this 'ballerina politics', quotes Goethe who, in his *Italian Journey*, said: 'Liberty and equality can only be enjoyed in a state of giddy lunacy.'

The radical *littérateur*, even by declaring his political hostilities in stylistically ennobled frenzy, surreptitiously wants his enemies to be impressed by the style of his attack, and even in indicting the world for its state of misrule and mismanagement, he wants the accused to be fascinated by the phrasing of his indictment. And even the *littérateur* has in him enough of the disposition of art to know that the artist still woos with his aggression, seduces with the chastity of his language, and seeks the admiration of those he damns with his last judgments. Therefore, there is always a subtle kind of insincerity in his proclaimed opposition to the 'world' as represented by the society of his time. He wishes to please. What ultimately matters to him is success – not necessarily, of course, in the crudest but certainly in the most fastidious sense of the word: success as that delicious contentment achieved in the perfection of a sentence, the happy appropriateness of a cadence, the conclusiveness of a metaphor. Beliefs and opinions – what are they to him if not building material for the great aesthetic artifice, 'matter to be consumed by form', as Schiller once defined the artistic process. What pleases the artist more than one conviction, is the splendid clash of two. Indeed, he does take 'as much delight in conceiving an Iago as an Imogen', and even if sometimes he chooses politically to commit himself and to forswear the 'culinary' ambition to give pleasure, he may, perhaps even to 'the general regret' of his followers, a little later be compelled to follow the natural call of art and settle down once more 'in the domain of the agreeable and the pleasurable'. Bertolt Brecht announced this in 1948 as his intention after all the alienating and political moralizing of the preceding years. There is little political authenticity to be found in the aesthetic sphere. Therefore, it would seem that, vis-à-vis all forms of moralizing politics, it befits the artist to remain sceptical and ironical rather than 'committed', quite apart from the question of whether, if he truly be an artist, his would not be more a tragic or comic reading of the human lot than a political and ideological one.

Turgenev once confessed that he felt always a little lost when asked to speak his own mind on this or that question, and deprived of the chance of hiding behind the exchanges of imaginary characters: 'Then it always seemed to me that one might just as well and with equal right assert the opposite of what I am saying. But if I talk about a red nose or fair hair, well, then the hair is fair and the nose is red, and no amount of reflection will reflect it away.' It is even possible to say that a man, capable of authentically speaking his own mind in a direct, straightforward way, would not and could not create epics or dramas or novels where the truth of the work's totality – 'the whole is the truth', said Hegel – always limits, or modifies, or even refutes the truth presented or uttered by any particular character in it. This makes it almost symbolically right that we know nothing or little about the individualities of some of the greatest poets, of Homer or Aeschylus or Sophocles or Shakespeare; and helps to explain why Dostoevsky so often had to outshout – to the point of hysteria – the many voices speaking in him and therefore in his novels when he wished to speak with his own religious, moral, or political voice (can he who has conceived the story of the Grand Inquisitor still believe in the Church, in any Church?); and why Tolstoy felt he had to cease writing novels in order to become a religiously and ethically integrated person.

Great works of art are made after the creative principle of Nature herself; and Nature, wrote Schopenhauer, 'does not do as had writers do who, when they show a knave or a fool, are so full of clumsy moral purpose that behind every such figure we glimpse, as it were, the writer himself, disavowing their minds and words, and warning us with a raised finger: "This is a knave, this a fool: do not listen to what he says!" No, Nature does as Shakespeare and Goethe do, in whose works every person, and be it the Devil himself, is, while he speaks, in the right; because he is conceived so objectively that we are compelled to sympathize with him: for, like a product of Nature, he has grown from an inner principle by virtue of which everything he says and does appears natural and therefore necessary.'

Beheld with the eyes of art, the world appears *sub specie necessitatis*, under the aspect of Necessity. Art's idea of man remains more 'natural' and 'chthonic' than 'social', even where the discourse is about man in society. Therefore it may happen that the artist's imagination makes a mockery of his declared political intentions; and this not by means of ideological inconsistencies creeping into his work but, far worse, through the imagination's insistence upon its own autonomous truth and knowledge; and what the imagination knows is the denial of all great political or moral expectations. There is about the characters, for instance, of Balzac or, at his artistically best, even of the 'literary scientist' and political reformer Zola, or indeed of the revolutionary Bertolt Brecht – there is about their successfully created characters a quality of natural destiny and monumental inevitability which reduces to all but irrelevance any hope of radically affecting their good or evil by changing their social functions through a changed social environment. Certainly, it may well be the writer's wish to show his characters as pawns in a social game the rules of which he abominates and desires radically to change. Yet the better he is as an artist, the more likely it is that his imagination will defeat his purpose by setting these figures in their course more like celestial bodies whose revolutions appear indifferent to anything except their centre and fields of gravity. Look how much trouble Brecht took to make his Mother Courage or his Galileo 'politically relevant', and how little his trouble was rewarded!

We can be sure he did not know that, to all intents and purposes, he quoted Thomas Mann's *Meditations of an Unpolitical Man* (he would probably have been rather alarmed if he had known) when in July 1934, in Svendborg, he talked to his friend Walter Benjamin about the nature of his political engagement: 'Often I imagine a tribunal', he said, 'a tribunal, questioning me: "What about it? Are you really in earnest?" Then I should have to admit: "No, not altogether. I think far too much of artistic matters, of what profits the theatre, to be entirely serious about the political." ' This is admirable, and it is true. Equally true is what he said afterwards: that the really great poets are those for whom there is no rift between the 'art' and the 'commitment'. As an example of such *Substanz-Dichter*, as he called them, that is, poets creating from the undivided integrity of their inner substance (Schiller called them 'naive' poets), he mentioned Gerhart Hauptmann. Well, yes, Hauptmann. He should have, to be equal to the grandness of the question, named Aeschylus or Sophocles or Shakespeare. And then Brecht said: 'Assuming you are reading an excellent political novel, and after you have finished it, you learn it was by Lenin. You would change your mind, would you not, about Lenin as well as about the novel, and not in favour of either.' Thus speaks a politically committed poet, but a poet happily not committed enough to make his intelligence immune from the ironies with which the relationship between literature and social responsibility is so amply afflicted.

Walter Benjamin, at that time, had just written his essay on Kafka, and asked Brecht to read it. For weeks there was no response. In the same conversation in which Brecht spoke of the imperfections of his political commitment as a poet, Kafka was at last talked about. It emerged that Brecht thought he was a great writer – 'like Kleist, Grabbe, or Büchner'; and, like these, ultimately a failure, one who suffered shipwreck. Why? At this point Brecht proved to be an extraordinarily perspicacious critic. He answered: Because Kafka was meant to be what Confucius was: he had the disposition and the gift of a great teacher, a prophet; yet as there was for Kafka – and here I enlarge a little on Benjamin's sketchy diary jottings – no society to teach or prophetically to inspire, his Confucian parables became 'literature', 'mere' literature. ('If I were a Chinaman', wrote Kafka once to Felice, and 'but at bottom I am a Chinaman'.) The parables grew into 'art', even into novels, and thus lost their ultimate seriousness. Yet from the beginning, probably on account of the historical absurdity of a teacher without a school to teach, of a prophet without a people to guide, they showed signs of wanting to become what they did become: literature. 'They were never quite transparent', said Brecht. This is also the reason why the apparent precision of Kafka's style is so deceptive: it is the precision of an exact dream confusingly dreamt in a place between prophecy and art.

There are not many interpretations of Kafka of which it seems certain that Kafka himself would have found them revealing or even interesting. This is one. When Brecht said it, he did not and could not know that Kafka was indeed tortured all his life by the consciousness of the two half-realities of which his world appeared to be made up – without the two half-realities ever amounting to anything felt to be wholly real. There was the half that was his writing, that hateful unreal thing to which, as he once put it in a letter to his fiancée, he was bound with invisible chains; and there was the sphere of his 'real' responsibilities: his profession which he hated, his city which he much disliked, the woman he would not marry, the house he would not inhabit, and the garden he was not to plant. There was, in fact, an 'unreal' literature and an 'unreal' life. What, after all, must be called his life, seemed to him without meaning and therefore unreal; to find meaning, he gave himself to literature – like someone, as he once said, who, equipped with only a lamp and pen and paper, withdraws forever into the deep, dark vault of a cellar. But as in the cellar, in his tomb, there was no life, literature too became meaningless. It is an extreme case of that laceration which, on the one hand, has ever more acutely raised the question of the writer's responsibility and, on the other hand, has made it ever harder to answer it. For where 'meaning' and 'reality', 'literature' and 'life', are felt to be irreconcilable, the one can hardly be responsible to the other; responsibility presupposes correspondence. In order for literature to be truly responsible, there would have to be such correspondence; and it would have to be the correspondence between language and reality – a correspondence whose questioning appears to have become the foremost concern of both our philosophers and our writers.

What to us has become so deeply questionable was a certainty for Confucius. When once his disciples asked him what he would do first if he had to administer a country, he answered: 'The first would be to correct language.' 'Surely', they said, 'this has nothing to do with the matter. Why should language be corrected?' The Master's answer was:

If language is not correct, then what is said is not what is meant; if what is said is not what is meant, then what ought to be done remains undone; if this remains undone, morals and arts will decay; if morals and arts decay, justice will go astray; if justice goes astray, the people will stand about in helpless confusion. Hence language must not be allowed to deteriorate. This matters above everything.

What a grand definition of the writer's social responsibility, and what confident faith in the very correspondence between language and reality, and therefore between literature and life! Shall we ever regain the confidence of both this definition and this faith? It is the very condition of literary responsibility, and on it depends the future of our liberal education.

The years 1889–1955: this is the span of time over which the *Letters of Thomas Mann* were written. They record, among a multitude of other and not quite so grave concerns, also his progress from the position of the 'unpolitical' artist to what he took to be a political platform. Progress? The trouble is that during those decades the terms 'political' and 'unpolitical' 'lost their names', and if not their names, their meaning. What was meant by politics in 1900, by 1940 had ceased to be applicable to the public conduct of nations, above all the German nation. In German, certainly, the word 'politics' was by that time an archaism. When Thomas Mann claimed to be an unpolitical writer, the claim made good sense and was, moreover, supported by the very cast of his sensibility. It was destined to be violated by the violence of the age; and gently chiding Hermann Hesse in 1945 for his refusal to be 'political', Thomas Mann sang out of tune, but only because the tune was no longer singable. For truly, what can 'politics' mean to a mind – a mind as fine as his – coming face to face with what to his humanity must have looked like the failure of the human enterprise? Thomas Mann, with the great courage and often with the rhetoric of great moral resolution, avoided saying so as a man speaking in letters to other men. Yet his writing said it in *Doctor Faustus*, the novel that cancels man's heavenly apotheosis at the end of Goethe's *Faust*, takes back the celebration of the 'subjective harmony', the harmony between soul and world, in the last movement of Beethoven's Ninth Symphony, and unweaves the configurations of faith in that carpet of Confucius.

7
The taking back of the Ninth Symphony
reflections on Thomas Mann's *Doctor Faustus*

for Michael Tanner

As Goethe unavoidably comes to mind whenever Doctor Faustus is mentioned, we may as well begin, choosing a short-cut to the centre of our theme, with a sentence from the sixth book of Goethe's autobiography *Dichtung und Wahrheit*, Poetry and Truth: 'No doubt, there is no more beautiful worship of God than the heart's communing with Nature'; and this, varied, deepened, expanded, he repeats a hundred times as, for instance, in July 1786 when he writes to Charlotte von Stein that he no longer needs strenuously to 'brood' over nature because her immense variety 'simplifies' itself ever more in his mind, allowing him to hope that one day even the hardest problem that arises from thinking about her will solve itself 'naturally'. Yet as early as the third chapter of Thomas Mann's *Doctor Faustus*, we meet Jonathan Leverkühn, the farmer father of the novel's Faustus, Adrian; as is his wont, father Leverkühn 'speculates the elements' (a quotation from the first German Faustbook of 1587) in a manner that much contrasts with that 'simplification' Goethe hoped for. For Jonathan does so with an ominous captivation that would seem to be proper to the charms of black magic. He is drawn particularly to those manifestations of nature that show her at her most ambiguous, indeed deceitful, as in the case of the butterfly *Hetaera esmeralda* (a name that is to develop into a *leitmotiv* of the novel). She displays on her transparently glassy wings a dot of pink and purple, giving her the appearance of a wind-blown petal. Thus the creature, as it were, fraudulently, escapes her voracious enemies, just as do her equals in cunning, those butterflies that positively attract attention as they slowly wing along in their glaring colours and are nonetheless knavishly safe because every bird in the wood knows that they taste abominable.

Of course, Jonathan Leverkühn's interest in such machinations of nature is radically different from Goethe's nature-enthusiasm as it expresses itself most fervently in Faust's monologue in the scene 'Forest and Cave'. There Faust rapturously thanks the 'erhabnen Geist', the very spirit of earth and nature, for having granted him everything that ever he desired, namely 'nature, the magnificent, as his kingdom'; and not only as his

kingdom but as his most intimate friend who is ready to reveal
to him the secrets of her heart. *Dramatically*, this superb poem
proved rather troublesome. When Goethe, despairing of ever
completing *Faust*, published in 1790 the *Fragment*, this monologue
followed with almost intolerable irony upon the scene 'By the
Well' in which Gretchen for the first time fully realizes the 'sin'
she had committed through the surrender to her love for Faust,
a scene that prepares her heartbroken prayer to the *mater dolorosa*:
'Help me! Save me from shame and death . . .'

> Ach neige
> Du Schmerzensreiche,
> Dein Antlitz gnädig meiner Not!

And immediately afterwards her lover, cause of her disaster, is
shown, announcing his happiness in words so glorious that the
reader cannot help wondering why neither Faust himself nor
Mephistopheles recognizes that this *is* the moment of fulfilment which, according to the pact in the completed *Faust I*, was
to deliver him into the hands of the Prince of Hell:

> Werd' ich zum Augenblicke sagen . . .
>
> If ever I feel like imploring the fugitive moment
> to stay because it is so beautiful . . .

And 'Forest and Cave' was to remain even after the scene of
the pact with Mephistopheles was at last written. True, now
Faust's monologue of bliss comes, more suitably and at the same
time even more inappropriately, after that declaration of love,
in which Faust, almost with the words of the wager, *does* say
that this moment must become what in its innermost nature it
is: eternity: 'No end! No end!'

  With these two scenes of *Faust I* Goethe exposes his dramatic
plot to the danger of collapsing; and this is not a matter of mere
oversights or superficial inconsistencies on the part of the dramatist. No, these breaks in the dramatic coherence of *Faust* are caused
by the collision between the sensibility of the later Goethe and
the nature of the story that the tempestuous young poet set out
to dramatize. For the fundamental – and fundamentally tragic
– *disunity* between nature and man's soul and mind, the very

spring of Faust's restless striving, is at odds with Goethe's pro-founder faith in the essential *harmony* prevailing between him and nature. Ultimately he aspired, as he put it, to 'the synthesis of world and mind' (*Geist*) and to that truth which, 'rising from within and revealing itself in the external world' blessed him with the assurance of 'the eternal harmony of existence'.

Yet the crux of the drama *Faust*, the *conditio sine qua non*, is the irreconcilable tension between Faust's inner being and the character of the eternal world. It is this that makes for Faust's certainty that he *must* win the wager with Mephistopheles. For there is – so different in this from everything that the En-lightenment stands for – a *pre-established disharmony* between the highest aspirations of man and the world in which he is destined to live. It is only because of this discord, utterly resistant to all human or devilish arts, that Faust knows that he is condemned to never-ending dissatisfaction, and challenges Mephistopheles by passionately asserting that life will never fulfil as much as *one* wish of his, for the unfulfilled and unrealizable desires of his have their source in an *inner* nature that has no correspondence in *outer* existence. This is why Faust can never reach the goal of happiness and, therefore, cannot be the loser in his wager with Mephistopheles:

> Der Gott, der mir im Busen wohnt,
> Kann tief mein Innerstes erregen,
> Der über allen meinen Kräften thront,
> Er kann nach aussen nichts bewegen . . .

Which means that the creator of the outside world lacks the power to order things in it so that man – Faust – may find contentment. How could Faust's striving not be unending? How could he, ac-cording to the condition of the wager – an extremely strange, indeed perverse twist within our theological tradition – *forfeit* his soul by *finding* the peace that passes understanding? Faust must strive endlessly; Faust must win.

It is obvious that the monologue 'Forest and Cave', this song of songs intoned in praise of the blissful peace between within and without, mind and world, appears to undo the postulated con-flict of the drama. But even if the *drama* cannot be saved, Faust perhaps can. The truth of the matter is that Goethe, during the sixty years it took him to complete both parts of *Faust*, was unable consistently to maintain the Storm-and-Stress conception of the young man. To show this, a thorough reading of the whole 'Forest and Cave' scene might suffice. For the untranslatably beautiful 'strenge Lust' with which the first part of the monologue ends, the exuberant delight that is yet held in bounds by disciplined restraint, leads a little too abruptly to the regret that such perfection is not meant for him. The 'erhabne Geist', the sublime spirit who had granted Faust such pure happiness, also saw to it that its purity was defiled by the spirit's other present (that Faust had surely asked for): the degrading and yet by now indispensable companion Mephistopheles whose contrivances, rather than satisfying Faust and thus securing the Mephistophelian victory, drive him into ever deeper depths of discontent as he staggers from desire to pleasure and, desire once gratified, yearns again for desire:

> So tauml' ich von Begierde zu Genuss,
> Und im Genuss verschmacht ich nach Begierde.

This is the young Faust as it is the young Goethe himself; and if Goethe decided to preserve the monologue in the drama, then certainly not only because it was such a beautiful poem. The answer may well be that he sensed that it might bring out the truth behind Faust's restless striving and with it the justification of Faust's final salvation and transfiguration. Justification? After all has been said to show the striking inconsistencies of the dramatic plot, the poetry of the dramatic (and not all *that* dramatic) poem may again and again persuade us that the extraordinary wager between Faust and Mephistopheles which Goethe found so difficult to invent, is poetically unnecessary. For the *poetry* incessantly insinuates that Mephistopheles cannot possibly win the bet because Faust's soul is in no need of a saviour. Despite his unquiet mind it seems that the god who dwells within Faust's innermost being is destined to become one with the divine guarantor of the universal order. For it is unthinkable that Faust, Goethe's problem child on whose education he gave sixty years, should *not* partake of the faith that his creator had achieved and maintained despite uncounted bewilderments and temptations: his confidence that the human world was permeated with the stuff of which grace is made. Time and again it is the *poetry* of *Faust* that, disregarding the *plot*, not only promises such fulfilment but *is* it. This faith has always been called pantheism. Yet with regard to Goethe, it may be more helpful to think of the pre-established harmony, a world order which in the long run would render it impossible that 'the god who is enthroned above all my powers', as Faust refers to him in his moment of desperation, should forever ignore or even refute 'the god who dwells within me'. No, all manner of thing shall be well in the end when it will be seen that there is no discord between the spiritual and ethical striving of man and the true nature of Being. Therefore, the only imaginable damnation of *Goethe's* Faust would come about through his ceasing to strive for that *self*-realization which is in profound agreement with Creation itself. Certainly, more than once Faust appears to jeopardize his salvation: for instance, when he curses love itself, love, hope, faith, and patience, causing the chorus of spirits woefully to accuse him of having destroyed 'the beautiful world' so that now he will have to rebuild within himself what outside lies in ruins; or when, ruler of land re-claimed from the sea with the help of the devil, he rages against the order of a world that he has to share with others, even if only with the old couple Philemon and Baucis. Yet despite all this, *it ought to be* that Faust, in the conclusion of Goethe's drama, is raised to the sphere of that imperishable goodness of which everything that is mortal is a symbol: 'Alles Vergängliche/Ist nur ein Gleichnis.'

'It ought not to be', says Doctor Faustus-Leverkühn in chapter 45 of Thomas Mann's novel, in that shattering scene when the child Nepomuk, innocent victim of Adrian Leverkühn's love – for love is according to *his* pact with the devil forever for-bidden him – lies dying and Serenus Zeitblom, Adrian's friend, tries to say consoling words to the disconsolate man. And as Serenus is about to leave, Adrian speaks the words: 'It ought not to be ... It will be taken back. I shall take it back.' Un-comprehendingly, Serenus turns around, asking what it is that his composer friend will 'take back'. Leverkühn answers: ' "The Ninth Symphony." And then he fell silent.' It is as if at this point

133

Thomas Mann quoted the seventh chapter of book 8 of his *Buddenbrooks* where little Hanno Buddenbrook, upon being scolded by his father for the childish misdeed of having drawn a double line under his own name in the family tree, stammeringly explains: 'I thought – I thought – there wouldn't be any more.' And if there is indeed nothing more in Thomas Mann's first novel after Hanno's death, in *Doctor Faustus*, his all but last work, there follows upon this leave-taking Leverkühn's greatest work, the cantata 'Dr. Fausti Weheklag' – 'The Lamentation of Dr. Faustus' – which does 'take back' the finale of the Ninth Symphony, the symphonic equivalent of the homage Goethe's Faust pays to the 'sublime spirit' that had granted him everything he desired.

What the 'Ode to Joy', as Beethoven set it to music, has in common with Faust's monologue 'Forest and Cave', is the 'Dionysian': the ecstatic certainty that the individual is safely at home in the totality of the world and has there, despite his metaphysical fate of being a *dividuum*, a being divided from the whole, his true *'in'* (to use Nietzsche's brilliantly wrong etymology). At the same time it is true to say that it is precisely the ecstatic nature of these utterances that reveals how imperilled this certainty already is. Epochs and souls that are surer of their place in the world conduct themselves less boisterously when they bear witness in their art to such integrity. Bach's music is sobriety itself compared to Beethoven's intoxicated jubilation that Adrian Leverkühn 'takes back'.

'Es kann dir ja nix g'schehn' (meaning: don't ever doubt that you are safe) – this is how the most popular character in one of Anzengruber's plays (*Die Kreuzelschreiber*) – Anzengruber wrote very successful dialect dramas in nineteenth-century Austria – unassumingly speaks of such metaphysical confidence; and this is probably the reason why the philosopher Ludwig Wittgenstein was once so deeply moved by that play that, even years later, he spoke of it as a religious experience. It is the same Wittgenstein whose *Tractatus Logico-Philosophicus* is the last powerful attempt to demonstrate by logical analysis this correspondence between world and man, and to prove it by an examination of what is most human: language. Later he took this work back himself (and 'himself' means, of course, Wittgenstein with all his philosophical idiosyncrasies). In his *Philosophical Investigations* he encircled language with every imaginable doubt in order to discover that, after all, it may be related not all that fittingly to the world which it pretends to describe. If here I might make a personal observation, I would say that it is always the person Wittgenstein who appears before my eyes whenever I try to imagine what Adrian Leverkühn may have looked like. (Thomas Mann, the most pedantic 'portraitist', took pains *not* to 'portray' him.) Also, Wittgenstein, just like Leverkühn, demanded so much of himself that often he seemed paralysed by his philosophical task, so hard for him because he, like Thomas Mann's composer, suspected that work and authenticity had become almost incompatible. Authenticity was only in the coldest mathematical –logical precision. Where there was the 'animal warmth' of sentiments, as Leverkühn called it, the work was threatened by the mendacity of imprecision, and by the temptation to play false as soon as the soul began to speak.

Adrian Leverkühn, then, wants to take back the Ninth Symphony, just as his author, Thomas Mann, takes back the salvation that Goethe had granted his Faust. For this salvation was only possible because Faust, with all his restless striving, aspired to what fundamentally he already possessed: those gifts that the 'sublime spirit', the 'erhabne Geist', could only bestow upon him because he was meant to receive them – as the bees are made for the sweet offerings of blossoms. 'Gift' here is not to be understood literally; for what is 'given' is the predestined correspondence between the need of the creatures and the nourishment provided by nature to feed their hunger. No doubt, from time to time there occur catastrophic mishaps and uncontrollable shortages, devastating landslides, volcanic eruptions, earthquakes, droughts when nothing grows, famines, changes of the climate, those in particular that prove fatal to a whole species of animals. These, as it were, wake up one morning and find not what they need for their survival. One may well ask whether similar catastrophes do happen in the history of the human soul. If Nietzsche is to be believed, they do; and the death of God was one of the worst. This event that he diagnosed, though not as the first and not as the only one, moved him warningly to predict the emergence of nihilism, even to prophesy the end of the human species, at least of that subspecies whose minds and souls have, throughout millennia, found their spiritual sustenance in faithfully believing in gods, in God, in Ideas and Categorical Imperatives; who, consciously or not, trusted in a kind of spiritually balanced economy existing between the requirements of their inner being and the provisions of the external world. Only the *Übermensch* could survive after human kind was forced back on its own resources, and would even splendidly flourish after the withdrawal of the accustomed food.

The hero of Thomas Mann's *Doctor Faustus* is modelled on Nietzsche. It is a grandly desperate gesture with which Adrian Leverkühn 'takes back' the Ninth Symphony; above all its last movement which resounds with the joy, the 'schöner Götterfunke', the divine spark, the ultimate inspiration of the human heart. The 'spark' is no longer to be 'divine'. *Doctor Faustus* is a Nietzsche novel cast in the mould of a humanism that has come to the end of its tether. At least fictionally, the book is written by a humanist narrator, Serenus Zeitblom, Adrian's oldest and perhaps only friend who, terrified, outraged, uncomprehendingly intimidated, copies out for posterity the most frightful document in the story of Leverkühn's life. Zeitblom has found it among the composer's papers. Written in his own hand, it reports the uncanny dialogue between him and the devil, a scene clearly suggested by a chapter of Dostoevsky's *Brothers Karamazov*. The uncanny exchange 'ratifies' the satanic pact which Leverkühn, without as yet realizing it, had concluded with the 'adversary' when, warned by herself, he was given the gift of syphilis by the prostitute 'Hetaera Esmeralda', the fatal disease that, for some time, was to 'free' his mind of its sceptical sobriety and thus inspire his greatest work. This is the Faustian pact that puts in the place of the 'divine spark' the inflammation of hell as the fiery agent of art.

It is in keeping with the Nietzschean character of the novel that the story of the pact 'parodies' the *Zarathustra* section of Nietzsche's autobiography, blasphemously called *Ecce Homo* by him. What Thomas Mann parodies is Nietzsche's account of an inspiration, in the grip of which the 'creator' feels that he is not himself any more but the mouthpiece of superior powers. 'I am blessed', such an artist rapturously exclaims,

The taking back of the Ninth Symphony

I am beside myself. That I call new and great! Seething bliss of inspiration! My cheeks glow like molten iron! I am raging, you will all be raging when this comes to you! Then God succour your poor souls!

Such creative ecstasy the devil promises his victim Leverkühn; and in an utmost of blasphemous mockery he adds that this is the very gift for which Goethe, 'the classical poet, the lofty and stately genius, so beautifully thanked his gods':

> Alles geben die Götter, die unendlichen
> Ihren Lieblingen ganz . . .;

meaning that the gods grant everything to those they love.

It is, then, no longer the gods who are the givers of such gifts, above all the gift of great art, but hell; and this means that human beings have lost the ability intuitively to understand the *spiritual* design of creation, to contemplate it in devotion, dedication, or enthusiasm, and to be inspired by it. On the contrary, for their inspiration they must turn to the powers that negate the creation of the world or, as in Leverkühn's case, to the spirochaetes or, in other instances, to pharmacology. There they seek those transports that change the colours, the sounds, the coherences of the world. For the soberly *rational* order of the world, as it is accessible to the sciences, cannot induce such elation. Even the man of reason, the humanist Serenus Zeitblom observes: 'I shall never understand the "Hosanna" mood which befalls some people when they contemplate the "works of God" as these are presented by astrophysics. Can an arrangement be properly called the "work of God" when one may just as reasonably say about it: "Well, what of it?" instead of "Glory be to God"?'

Wendell Kretzschmar, the stuttering organist who taught young Leverkühn musicology, demanded of the small circle of his provincial listeners to whom he lectured on the theme 'Why did Beethoven not write a third movement to the Piano Sonata Opus 111' (his extraordinary performance is superbly rendered in chapter 8 of *Doctor Faustus*) that they should impress upon themselves the difference between *harmonic subjectivity* and *polyphonic objectivity*. Although Kretzschmar maintained that this distinction was no longer valid for the Beethoven of the five late piano sonatas – the composer had transcended it by that time – it certainly applied to the Ninth Symphony. Kretzschmar's pedagogical admonition had clearly made a deep impression upon the narrator Serenus Zeitblom. For he remembered it years later when he took part – more as a listener than a contributor – in the 'agonizingly clever' discussions of Munich intellectuals, described in chapter 34 of the novel. Their theme was the precarious state of our civilization – was, in fact, the end of 'harmonic subjectivity' even if they did not use the musical term that, according to Wendell Kretzschmar, characterized the music and art of a whole epoch. The artists of that epoch confidently believed that their subjectivity, even in its most radical expressions, mirrored the lawful order of the world; and this could not be otherwise because the relationship between the individual's mind and the mind of Creation itself was spontaneously felt to be sanctioned by the 'pre-established harmony'. It is this that the end of the Ninth Symphony celebrates: an embrace that is truly all-embracing – just as is the Goethean Faust's panegyric to the 'lofty spirit'.

'Rühmen, das ist's!' To sing the praise of life is the beginning and end of poetry. This exclamation, from the *Sonnets to Orpheus*, is Rilke's; and Rilke was the exact contemporary of Thomas Mann. If intoned in a less exalted manner, it states the essence of the 'harmonic subjectivity' and all its works. One of these are the *Sonnets to Orpheus*, or so it seems. If they truly are, that late triumph has been achieved at an enormous price. The price may be assessed by our remembering Rilke's biography preceding the *Sonnets*, the history that, almost literally, for one ecstatic moment, led to that rapture of praise. What precedes that moment are above all the anxieties and dejections of the time of Rilke's novel *Malte Laurids Brigge*: 'This world, suspended over a bottomless pit, is impossible', says Malte, the uncanny double of his author. And why did Rilke, in the poetology of his *New Poems*, a collection that contains his best lyrical poetry, insist upon the total suspension of the 'harmonic subjectivity', the absolute elimination of the individually subjective element from the evocation of 'things'? Why is his discovery of Cézanne, in his letters about the painter, entirely determined by the revelation of the 'impersonal' Cézanne, that 'impersonal' element which for

Rilke had emerged as the very principle of the only art that was still possible? Because he now regarded the 'subjective individual' as a kind of cosmic mischief-maker among the 'objectivities' of the world. And when there came the turning point in this chimeric pursuit of unconditional objectivity – 'Wendung', 'Turning Point', is the title of his poetic proclamation of 1914 – it led straight into his exploration of the other *extreme* possibility that the distressed and upset 'subjective harmony' seemed to allow in its *extremis*: poetically to dispense altogether with the 'objective', the external world. This is the way at the end of which the *Duino Elegies* are reached, above all the Seventh with its apotheosis of absolute, purified subjectivity: 'Nirgends, Geliebte, wird Welt sein, als innen ...' – Nowhere will world exist but within ... Certainly, Rilke survived ('To survive is everything', he once wrote) where Leverkühn succumbed; yet if it is at all permissible to compare the work of an imaginary composer with that of a real poet, it could be said that according to the will of Thomas Mann's imagination Leverkühn's cantata which voices the 'Lamentation of Dr. Faustus' is undoubtedly meant to be a mightier work than Rilke's sonnets of praise that came into existence despite the *Elegies'* renunciation of the 'subjective harmony'.

At the end of the sixth section of his book about *Doctor Faustus*, *The Genesis of a Novel*, Thomas Mann said that the most important theme of his work is the menacing approach of artistic sterility *in these times*, and thus the 'innate despair that inclines the artist to conclude a pact with the devil'. As the gods are no longer in the mood to 'give', art knocks at the devil's door. This is how the *fleurs du mal* spring up in the fields of art.

What about 'these times'? What is it that makes for the epochal discomfort of the arts, an unease so troublesome that in the opinion of *Doctor Faustus*, and not only of this one work, it renders *great* art all but impossible? Is it, as is so often and so readily held, the fault of the prevailing social conditions? The devil who is aware of many things is even convinced that Leverkühn has been in the habit of saying that society lacks everything that is spiritually binding and compelling enough to sanction the self-sufficient harmony of works of art. But here the devil would seem to be in error. The reader has not overheard all that much in Adrian's utterances that would justify the devil to speak of such a 'habit'. Only once or twice, for instance in his dispute with the devil, does he strike that note; and certainly at the end, in the mad sermon of chapter 47, he confesses that in his 'hellish intoxication' he has been guilty of never having cared to ask what could be done on earth to improve the lot of mankind, and of not having contributed anything to the founding of an order of society that would be fertile ground for creative works.

This affects the reader like a foreign body in Adrian's distressingly deranged speech for it is at odds with his character. Of course, social injustice and violent misdeeds rightly arouse moral indignation, yet it is extremely doubtful whether one may speak of the relationship between art and society with such simple-mindedness; and it is even more unlikely that, after all we have come to know about Leverkühn, he would ever judge his 'profound sinfulness' in so naive a manner – surely not when his self-indictment rises from the depths of madness. (R. H. Tawney, in the succession of Max Weber one of the important and not quite un-Marxist sociologists of the past decades, knew better when in his 1949 lecture about 'Social History and Literature' he said that, apart from a few commonplaces, we know next to nothing about the connections, if any, between the achievements of art in a certain period and the conduct of its economic life, and that in all honesty we should admit our ignorance. And it is certainly true to say that there was plenty of lamentable social injustice at the time of Bach or Mozart without their music betraying any infernal assistance although they concerned themselves not much with the social mismanagements of princes or archbishops.) 'Correct but unimportant', the devil, in chapter 25, replies to Leverkühn's attempt at social criticism. No, the social conditions are not responsible for the fact that art has become 'too difficult' to attain greatness without 'hellish fire' burning under its cauldron. On the contrary, 'the prohibitive difficulties', originate in the work itself. And the intelligence with which the devil treats these 'prohibitive difficulties' is Nietzsche's or even Hegel's, while the theory of society to which Leverkühn appears to adhere for odd moments comes from other minds (domiciled, like the publisher of the first Faustbook, in Frankfurt).

The taking back of the Ninth Symphony

Adrian's teacher Wendell Kretzschmar believed he knew the cause of those 'prohibitive difficulties' and no devil was needed to teach his disciple the lesson. The music of past centuries was founded upon the concord between the *individual* sensibility seeking expression, and the *general* order of forms and conventions readily accepted by the subject as the mould of art. It was this concord that Kretzschmar called 'harmonic subjectivity' in his memorable lecture. But this is no more. The individual in whom critical knowledge, in the course of history, gained the upper hand over the seeming spontaneity of emotions and sentiments, now rejects the convention, and the old rules are felt to rule against the truths of a changed subjectivity. Now it is as if the law had established itself in a vacuum, and the individual had turned its back upon the universal. The law no longer knows how to come to terms with the subject's inwardness; and even if it tried to win the assent of the heart, the heart would never yield to such wooing, for in every single case it has come to regard itself as the exception that does *not* confirm the rule. And if a human being did say sincerely what he felt in his soul, his 'authentic' speech would be non-sense not art. For art cannot be without measure, lawfulness and the dictates of form. Therefore, the artist whose inner existence has become inexpressible, submits to an *impersonal* order that is the more rigid for having shed any claim to 'subjectivity', and creates in obedience to a new version of what Wendell Kretzschmar called 'polyphonic objectivity'.

At the gatherings of those Munich intellectuals much used to be said about all this without Adrian's contributing anything to it. He was conspicuously silent when the talk became socio-critical and all agreed that bourgeois culture had reached the point of no return. For its individualistic-aesthetic ideal had, individualistically and aesthetically, luxuriated so ferociously that it had deprived the human being of its place in the community and thereby severed the links between art and its true sources: the universal, the community. This has been for a long time painfully noticeable in the bourgeois theatre. It had come to serve almost exclusively the needs of a doomed class that asked for ever stronger nervous titillations, and expected of art that it should abet the occasional tired flights of the bourgeois self from its boringly empty duties and occupations. This is what was said in those circles, and one of the group added that dramatic art had long since betrayed its origins in the collective. Was it Bertolt Brecht? If these speculations give the impression that he was a member of that group, they are at the same time characteristic of the ideological flirtations of highly individualistic intellectuals with 'the people', the 'collective', the 'tribe' and tribal virtues. Some of these ideologues were prone to join movements that moved in very different political directions from the dramatist who so much disliked the 'culinary' theatre of bourgeois amusement.

Serenus Zeitblom, then, thought of Adrian's compositions when he listened to those Munich debates, and also thought of Wendell Kretzschmar who, convinced that the music of 'harmonic subjectivity' had come to the end, acquainted his pupil with the 'polyphonic objectivity', a musical principle that pointed towards a formal logic and cogency after the model of the 'pious fetters of pre-classical rigid forms'. And as, according to Kretzschmar, the history of the sonata had reached its pinnacle with Beethoven's Opus 111 and at the same time its true conclusion, music itself was soon to discover that it was at its wit's end and did not know in which direction to turn. For when Kretzschmar, in the novel's chapter that is entirely devoted to him and his lecture, answers the question why the Sonata Opus 111 that he has played to his scanty audience, has no third movement, exclaims in his stuttering-rhetorical style whether a new beginning is imaginable, a return after this leave-taking, he means not only this particular sonata. No, when this particular sonata has reached its end with this enormous movement, an end without return, it is, as we read, 'not only this one, in C minor, but the sonata in general, as species, as traditional art-form'. Is it too audacious to suspect that he who has thought out Kretzschmar's lecture, Thomas Mann, had music itself in mind, indeed the whole sphere of art? It would not be too surprising. A considerable time before him, Hegel had prophesied the end of art; no, not prophesied it but diagnosed it as a fact – not to mention him who was closer to Thomas Mann: Nietzsche.

Adrian was the more receptive of Kretzschmar's thinking as, from his earliest years, his sense of order was most conspicuous. 'Order is everything', he once said when he was still very young and blushingly misquoted the Bible by declaring that everything that comes from God is ordered. ('It transpired that he was religious', adds the humanistic author of his biography.) When Adrian and Germany were a few years older, that religious belief became: 'Even a silly order is better than no order at all.' It referred to the music of the primitively eccentric composer Johann Conrad Beissel who, in the middle of the eighteenth century, invented a grotesquely naive compositional system of great austerity that he practised in a Christian community of emigrants in Pennsylvania. But within the network of allusions in the novel we have, of course, to think of a much more catastrophic total order than the one excogitated by that 'musical peasant' in Philadelphia: the totalitarian system of the German tyranny whose victories, 'break-throughs', defeats and monstrosities form the background to the lives of the humanistic narrator as well as the composer-genius. (*Tonsetzer* is the untranslatably archaic word that Thomas Mann uses instead of *Komponist* because he sees as the other side of Germany's military 'break-through' her falling back on archaic modes of thought and conduct, just as modern art often explores the possibilities offered by a new primitivism and calculated barbarism.) *Doctor Faustus* does intend to establish the unequal equation between the agonies that the totalitarian dictatorship inflicts upon those who cannot or will not 'conform', and the creative agonies which, according to the devil's announcement, hell visits on the artists among its exquisitely chosen victims, the stubborn resisters to History's suspension of art. It certainly is not implausible that the total order of the coarse political domain emerges from the same confused helplessness of souls and minds that Adrian Leverkühn, with the help of the devil, seeks to transcend through sublime works of art. When Zeitblom, on the last page of his 'biography', takes leave of its subject – 'God have mercy upon your poor soul, my friend, my fatherland' – this intended symbolic identity becomes as perfect as it never is in the book itself. But this does not diminish the importance of the work.

If despite such times a man is meant to be an artist by nature and the grace of God (if it is permissible to speak of grace and God in the case of Adrian Leverkühn's genius), what is he to do in order to produce works? Leverkühn had once before answered the question – in the sense of Hegel and Nietzsche. At that time he had said that the 'play of art' had played itself out; and this was because the imagination had been catastrophically devalued in the economy of human faculties. Our sense of truth forbids us still to take seriously the imaginative play. The poets lie too much, said Nietzsche's Zarathustra, and what he had in mind was not merely the fictiveness of literature. No, what he meant was that traditionally art used to buoy up the soul with false beliefs in any meaning, order, lawfulness and harmony gracing a world which suggests that, if looked upon with truthfulness, to believe in anything of this kind is sheer superstition. The fair illusion of art is nothing but lies and deceit, and lies and deceives the more the fairer it is; and lies and deceives no less where it tries to deny its illusiveness and pretends to be the mirror of what really is. And Adrian says of music what Nietzsche says of poetry and literature.

As Serenus Zeitblom, the humanist who desires to believe in the imperishable nature of art, listens to his friend whom he so anxiously loves, and of whom he knows that he is deeply immersed in the business of composing, he wonders what strenuous efforts, intellectual stratagems, devices, and ironies are necessary to enable an artist nonetheless to create. He had heard Leverkühn say: 'Illusion and play run counter today to the conscience of art; it has arrived at the point where it abhors illusion and play and wants to become knowledge'; and yet Adrian is capable of producing works which, as 'travesties of innocence', betray the devastating insight against which, or from which, they are won. ('Travesty of innocence': is this what the Romantics hoped for when, again and again, they spoke, like Schiller, of a spontaneity that will be reborn if the reflective poet – he called him 'sentimentalisch' – becomes reflective enough; or like Kleist who, in his great essay-story about the Marionette Theatre, predicts a regained paradise if knowledge has achieved its ultimate goal of completeness; or even like Nietzsche-Zarathustra who prophesies a new childhood of the spirit in the third and highest form of its metamorphoses?)

Adrian Leverkühn, then, composed according to the rules of that new 'objectivity'. For if the 'play of art' is over, there is nothing left but earnest work. Technique sets itself up as art's alpha and omega, because the 'method' too has become so devilishly difficult that the artist exhausts himself in its elaboration. There is nothing left to him but the unuttered, stealthy expectation that technical perfection may yield something like meaning, even if this meaning is not much more than the critique of art itself, the kind of critique that strains to become an art in its own right. This was yet another Romantic hope: Friedrich Schlegel toyed with the idea of such a future art. Leverkühn's devil is less optimistic; he sees in this, as he says in his dialogue with Adrian, 'the danger of sterility'. And as Leverkühn is busy composing his great work 'Apocalypsis cum figuris', Serenus Zeitblom receives a letter from him, signed 'Perotinus Magnus', whereupon the apprehensive humanist ponders the question of the possible seriousness and legitimacy of a work that, with all its earnest devotion to problems of technique, allows for such jokes full of self-mockery. For this Perotinus directed, in the twelfth century, the church choir of Notre Dame and became famous for musical instructions that led to a significant improvement of the young art of polyphony. But did Adrian have a historical and, considered more gravely, a legitimate *spiritual* claim to the religious sphere in which this music was at home? And which Adrian yet pursued 'with the most extreme, most refined application'?

Adrian once said in the hearing of Serenus that the opposite of bourgeois civilization was not barbarism but the communal life which one day would replace the living arrangements of the bourgeoisie. Yet for Serenus the question remains whether barbarism and the ideological cult of the community are necessarily opposites. Might not the purely aesthetic-profane exploitation of principles that were developed by the ritualistic music of a long-past religious epoch, call forth the barbarism? Saying this, one need not think of the Christian ritual, but of times when the transcendental was the business of medicine men and magi. And it is this form of the magical that comes to life again in Leverkühn's 'Apocalypsis'. This, at least, is how it affects the humanist who describes in chapter 34 some passages of the work:

You have there ensembles which begin as 'speaking' and only by stages, by the way of the most extraordinary transitions, turn into the richest vocal music; then choruses which pass through all the stages from graded whisperings, antiphonal speech, and humming up to the most polyphonic song – accompanied by sounds which begin as mere noise, like tom-toms and thundering gongs, savage, fanatical, ritual, and end by arriving at the purest music. How often has this intimidating work, in its urge to reveal through the language of music the most hidden things, the beast in man as well as his sublimest stirrings, incurred the reproach both of blood-boltered barbarism and of bloodless intellectuality!

What affects Zeitblom as most barbarous, are the glissandos which play so big a part in the 'Apocalypsis'. They sink back to the level of a primitivity, mastered, indeed, by Adrian in a most sophisticated manner, when no tonal system had as yet been won from chaos and no sound had as yet been 'denatured', that is, 'cultivated', but 'song' must have been a howling throughout several pitches. Serenus regarded these glissandos with the suspicion that they were expressive of a demoniacal obsession and utterly inimical to culture and humaneness. 'Howling as a theme', he writes, 'what horror', a horror the more horrible as it was the product of thought and superb technical virtuosity: a 'bloodless intellectualism' that, from its opposition to bourgeois civilization, has allied itself to barbarism *as well as* collectivism.

Quite apart from the music of Adrian Leverkühn, Thomas Mann's tragic parody of the Frankfurt Faustbook of 1587, is such a going back to the primitive, or at least to the more primitive. It is so radical a parody that it reverses, turns around, the meaning of that old 'morality'. For the Faustus of the chapbook desires of the devil the power to rise above the spiritual order of his age. But Adrian Leverkühn, Thomas Mann's Faustus, is eager to come into the possession of the objective, binding, cogent, of a firm order that, paradoxically, would liberate him from the monotonous sequence of the never-ending variations, banalities, boredoms of that tired liberty – the 'mildew liberty', as he calls it – of this civilization; and expects to be given this liberty from something akin to the 'magic words, figures, characters and conjurations' of the ancient Faustian adventures. If, to top it all off, he achieved the 'break-through' from the rigid order of the new 'polyphonic objectivity', conceived only intellectually and aesthetically, into a 'subjectivity' which, though tied to formal stringency, issued from such intellectual frigidity into a world of audaciously new feelings, he would be 'the saviour of art'. Would be. For the sake of such salvation he hands himself over to the devil.

When Adrian, in his great disputation with 'him', put before the devil the idea that, even with the *play* of art having ended, it might be possible to raise the play to a higher level by *playing* with traditional forms that, taken seriously, are now lifeless, the devil replies: 'I know, parody. It could be fun if only it were not so sad in its aristocratic nihilism. Do you think such tricks would bring you happiness and greatness?' And as Adrian angrily answers 'No', there occurs the most astonishing self-negation of a writer whose parodistic 'playing', even if 'raised to a higher level', began as early as Hanno Buddenbrook, his little Richard Wagner, reached a first climax with *Death in Venice*, a classically measured one if compared with this satanic jocularity. Surely, the devil has better things to offer and grants the prayer which Serenus Zeitblom believes he can discern in one passage of Leverkühn's 'Apocalypsis cum figuris', the only deeply 'personal' utterance of the work in which the taking back of the Ninth Symphony is not only announced but done: the perversion of sublimity. 'The whole work', says the observer in chapter 34, 'is dominated by the paradox that dissonance is the characteristic of everything that is elated, serious, pious, spiritual, whereas harmony and tonality is the preserve of hell.' For hell is now the place of the concord between the individual and the world, the point at which 'harmonic subjectivity' emerges again. In hell it is now where the Goethean-Faustian 'Indescribable' comes to pass. What, in Adrian's apocalyptic composition, to Serenus sounded like a prayer, was the heartbreaking request to be given a soul. The devil does give it.

Adrian Leverkühn's and the devil's triumph is 'The Lamentation of Dr. Faustus', parts of the old Faustbook set to music. The form of this cantata is even more severely disciplined than Adrian's preceding compositions, and yet it is the 'break-through'. For just because the order of this work is total – not a single 'free note' is to be found in it – the artist can, without any fear of violating the unassailably solid construction, entirely surrender to his 'subjectivity'. This is why Zeitblom, in chapter 46, can say of this work, that, although it is the composer's most austerely calculated, it is at the same time 'purely expressive'. This, then, is the profound scandal of the profoundest of Thomas Mann's books that, although so much in it is parody, is yet his most personal, the outcome of suffering *and* construction. And it is its most scandalous invention that the lost soul of Leverkühn's final and

147

greatest work was regained in hell. For the new, the 're-established harmony' is attained in the subject's yea-saying to his being un-redeemable. An utmost of virtuosity comes together with an utmost of authenticity; and the utmost of authenticity is – lamentation. At the same time it is the jubilation of hell. Who, the devil had asked Adrian in 'his' chapter, still leads nowadays a genuinely religious existence if not I? Dostoevsky's devil had said the same; but he was successful with only one of the brothers Karamazov, with Ivan who is not quite unlike Adrian Leverkühn.

What is most perishable in Thomas Mann's *Doctor Faustus* is the equation Adrian Leverkühn = Germany. It has never been quite convincing. As once before, in the *Meditations of an Unpolitical Man*, written during the First World War – a book that considerably helps to understand *Doctor Faustus* – he gave to Germany too high a value in the mathematics of the spirit. But what will remain, in spite of much that is questionable in some of the book's musicological reflections, is the suffering and even the greatness of Adrian Leverkühn, and with it the art of Thomas Mann; and, of course, the terrifying possibility that hell has arrogated to itself the gifts which, with Goethe, the gods had prepared for those they loved. Listen to the conclusion of the 'Lamentation of Dr. Faustus' as Zeitblom describes it at the end of the last-but-one chapter: 'The finale is purely orchestral, a symphonic adagio movement into which gradually issues the chorus of the lamentation that had powerfully emerged from the gallop of hell. It is, as it were, the reverse way of the Ode to Joy, the inspired negative of the transition of the Symphony from the orchestral to the vocal jubilation, it is the taking-back ...' A German orchestra was meant to play this; yet the world outside Germany does not seem disinclined to join in the playing. May it be said that the hovering cello sound that, at the end of 'Dr. Fausti Weheklag', shines in the night as a mild glow, promises a future daybreak? Can anyone be sure of it after this crossing-out of the Ninth Symphony?

8
Thomas Mann's diaries and the search for identity

THERE is nothing unusual in keeping a diary. It is certainly the least reprehensible among all the signs of a person's attaching importance to himself. A diary is a kind of private bulwark against the endless inroads made upon the memory by time. On the grander scale of nations or even mankind historiography serves the same purpose. The work of Thucydides, the Old Testament, and indeed the histories written in nineteenth-century Germany during her Romantic period – all are concerned with the sense of national identity, creating, fostering, extolling or debating it. Indeed, it is the question of identity that lurks behind all events, experiences, thoughts, trivial or weighty, recorded by the diarist. Why is 'identity' so highly prized that the loss of it is looked upon as the severest pathological affliction of the mind?

'Who am I?' is the central question of every autobiography, and a diary is nothing if not the raw material for the potential self-representation of a person. 'Who am I?', Thomas Mann asks in his *Meditations of an Unpolitical Man*, and it was consuming doubts about 'who he was' that, among many other doubts and dubieties, compelled him, during the First World War, to spend three years and 600 pages on this question and all its ramifications, interrupting thereby his work as a novelist, in particular the writing of *The Magic Mountain*. Yes, certainly, he was a novelist, close even then to being acknowledged as Germany's greatest writer. He had produced *Buddenbrooks*, the book that was on its way to becoming the country's best-known and most widely read novel – the rarest of successes for a book on so vast a scale and on so high a literary level. Immediately afterwards he had written *Tonio Kröger*, the intellectual idyll that soon won the enduring affection of its readers, especially those of the younger generation; and a few years later he published *Death in Venice*, the story that, like no other serious book of the time, instantly became a resounding success and was felt to be a deeply stirring challenge. Although it was conceived in 1911 as an utterly unpolitical story, inspired as it was by a very private experience, it vibrates with the tremors of the approaching political catastrophe, the 1914 war. In any case, the yearning that the adolescent Thomas Mann once dared to pronounce publicly in an immature poem: the dream of one day being crowned with a little laurel wreath, had long since come true; and the 'little wreath' proved rather sumptuous. That by 1914 he was a much-admired writer, a celebrated artist, was an indisputably correct answer to the weighty question: 'Who am I?' Thousands of aspiring young people would be supremely satisfied with it. Not so Thomas Mann. He now had to write a book, he said, that, though the work of an artist, was in his own judgment by no means a work of art: the *Meditations*; and the artist who wrote it was a man 'whose existence was shaken to its foundations, whose self-respect was brought into question, and whose troubled condition was such that he was completely unable to produce anything else.' The sincerity of this is unmistakable, as well as the intense pressure that had given rise to it: 'Who am I?'

It signalled a crisis and asked a question that any thinking and feeling person may have to face during some periods of his life: in times, above all, of an agonizing loss or public upheaval. For Thomas Mann, the upheaval was the war in which, as he firmly believed, *his* Germany, had to win, not only to ward off the devastating effects of defeat but to save her *Kultur*, the culture that was his as much as it was the culture of Aschenbach's, the writer of Thomas Mann's creation and his *alter ego* in cholera-infested Venice, who one day wakes up from a chaotic-Dionysian dream 'with his moral existence annihilated'. And Thomas Mann's loss was that of the close, if always precarious, friendship with his older brother Heinrich, his respected fellow-novelist at the beginning, but later, with the onset of the war, the hated *Zivilisationsliterat* of *Meditations*, the 'un-German' champion of the West, of 'civilization' as against '*Kultur*', of political rhetoric as against musical inwardness, of democratic enlightenment as against the metaphysics of art: 'There is no longer any other word for him but idiot', Thomas Mann noted in his diary as late as 20 January 1919. The occasion seems to have been Heinrich's proclaiming somewhere that now at last, in defeated Germany or revolutionary Russia, 'thought and art are going hand in hand with government'. Although later the brothers became reconciled, the scars left by the fraternal war never disappeared completely.

The *Meditations* are themselves a compendious intellectual diary of the writer's existence as he saw and defended it in the years of the First World War. It is an agitated and fascinating book, beautifully written and, as a logbook of a rich mind's journeyings, restless in its organization. Yet there was still room for a diary not meant for publication. Secrecy is what distinguishes the 'real' diaries from those that, 'literature' themselves, are from the beginning intended to be published. It is most unlikely that Thomas Mann would have divulged to anyone those many 'secret – *very* secret' things that made him burn the diaries of his early years in the winter of 1896, when he was twenty-one. He reported this to a childhood friend, advising him to do the same: 'One is, as it were, rid of one's past and cheerfully lives in the present', without having to fear that the 'very secret' secrets would become known to others. Strange, this liberation from the past the chronicling of which is the diarist's sole purpose. Not so strange is that he soon embarked upon keeping a new diary. It multiplied in the course of the years; for it was a sizable compendium that had accumulated between 1896 and 11 February 1933 when, leaving it safely, as he believed, in his Munich villa, he went, accompanied by his wife Katia, on a lecture tour abroad – never to return to his house. Hitler who had only just come to power was consolidating it more and more. Soon Thomas Mann realized that his exile would not be over in a few days or even weeks, and with that realization, *beginning a new diary*, he also began to worry about the fate of the old ones. His worries were justified: they fell into the hands of the Gestapo.

How this happened is a story of 1933-Germanic intrigues and officially sponsored crimes. In early April he had asked his son Golo, sending him the key to the safe, to place the diaries, without reading them, in a trunk (what a voluminous collection it must have been!) and have them shipped to him in France. They were late, very late, in arriving. The trusted family chauffeur in Munich, so Golo decided, was to look after the dispatch of the trunk at the railway station. The young man saw to it that they made their way to the Secret Police. Small wonder they were not received in time. Upon learning in the end what had happened, Thomas Mann was frantic with apprehension. On the last day of that April the compulsive diarist noted in his new diary: 'My fears now revolve first and foremost, almost exclusively, around this threat to my life's secrets. They are deeply serious. The consequences could be terrible, even fatal.' The apparently highly explosive piece of luggage finally arrived at the end of May, thanks to the adroit manoeuvring of the family's Munich lawyer. (Conditions in Germany deteriorated rapidly after these first weeks of the deplorable new masters' regime. Soon no advocate's skills would have persuaded them to release their easy prey.) With the exception of the notes he had written between September 1918 and December 1921, these 'deeply serious', indeed 'fatal' documents came to share the fate of their earlier companions in secrecy. After twelve years and two far-reaching family moves – from Switzerland to Princeton and then to California – the author threw them into the incinerator behind his house in Pacific Palisades. The notes he reprieved concerned the end of Imperial Germany and the initial years of the Weimar Republic. He knew he would need them one day. He did – for *Doctor Faustus*. Some of them were even published before: in the limited edition of the slender volume *Leiden an Deutschland*, a title that might have been invented by a previous exile, Heinrich Heine. It appeared in 1946 in Los Angeles.

Leiden an Deutschland (Sorrowing over Germany), purged no doubt of all too private entries, also provides a highly significant example of the insecurity and ambivalence of Thomas Mann's political judgments. The diary of 1933 speaks, apropos the Leipzig trial of the presumed incendiaries of the *Reichstag*, of the 'kinship, yes, even the identity, of National Socialism and Communism' (November 24). This is not only left out in *Leiden an Deutschland* but actually replaced by ' "Fascism or Communism – it makes no difference?" – Nonsense. Although Communism would not provide the right atmosphere for me to live in, it would allow me to exist, would not bestially kill me, indeed we would mutually respect our humanitarian concerns.' Stalin, at that time, administered the humanitarian concerns of Soviet Russia.

The protection of private secrecy is taken for granted in a humanely ordered society, even safeguarded by the Constitution that solemnly acknowledges the division between the public domain and the individual's privacy. And yet, what a problem-ridden separation it is, particularly at a time that has raised the virtues of honest disclosure and sincerity to such an extent as to make them impinge on the sense of shame. Before long nobody will be sure what the difference is between the much-vaunted 'openness' and that unashamed exhibitionism that threatens to become the hallmark of much in our literary and artistic commerce. Yet, despite this cult of frankness, human beings appear, more than ever, burdened, oppressed, disturbed in their souls, by having 'secret selves'. They take this to be a pathological state of affairs, condemning them – no, not to be sinners, but patients. While there are no lines of people waiting to be forgiven at the confessionals, psychoanalysts have – or had until recently – long waiting lists. The urge to unburden oneself of one's secrets seems to be a universal human disposition. It becomes exceptionally troublesome in a society that produces ever more 'complex' individuals while lacking the spiritual institutions that enjoy the authority of public trust.

The diaries of Thomas Mann: twice destroyed, once because they contained secrets, 'very secret' secrets; another time anxiously – and expensively – wrested from the clutches of a ruthless secret police because the secrets in them were so 'weighty' that they might have had, in those new political conditions, 'fatal' consequences; and yet begun anew after each conflagration. What is the source of such compulsion? On one level it is the paradox of a man who knows that he is, like every human being, an ultimately incommunicable self and, as a modern writer, at the same time this self's embarrassingly omnipresent observer; a man who is, therefore, driven to articulate, at least to himself, what by its nature is inarticulate and, therefore, unavoidably secret. This leads to his confusing the diary articulation of socially concealed desires for a help in illuminating to himself the dark ground of selfhood. Of course, he is bound to be puzzled himself by this compulsive enterprise.

During the days of the turmoil that invaded his life immediately upon leaving Germany, the diaries, he says, are 'a comfort and support' to him. He may not necessarily read them again, but just now they enable him to take stock and achieve perspective. On another occasion, much later, he asks himself whether he wishes that the world should come to know him as thoroughly as possible upon his demise; and certainly, in the end he saw to this by decreeing that the diaries could or should be opened twenty years after his death – and this meant, of course, published. Elsewhere he sees them even as a prayer-like communion. Nothing in the diaries can possibly bear out this ambitious characterization. Besides, communion with what, with whom? And if it was to be, as he also hinted, a matter of bestowing eternity upon the fleeting moment, the artist who wrote on one parcel of these diaries (1933–51) 'without any literary value' knew only too well that there was only one way of arresting the relentless flux of time and giving it permanence – or at least the highly comforting and noble illusion of permanence: making works of art. However disagreeable a dental treatment may be, or time-consuming a visit to the barber, or tiresome an upset stomach, or irritating the inadequate plumbing installations in a southern *albergo*, they are deserving, perhaps, of the attentions of a comic genius like Wilhelm Busch, but hardly, in the raw, of the 'permanence' of print. There exist only grotesque relations between constipation and eternity.

Homosexuality is, undoubtedly, a more serious theme in the life of a happily married man and father of six children. But which perceptive reader of Thomas Mann's work would not have known of his erotic ambivalence? Tonio Kröger's love for fair, blue-eyed Hans Hansen may still be regarded as perfectly 'normal' for an adolescent. But we soon come upon middle-aged Aschenbach's Venetian – indeed 'fatal' – passion for the beautiful boy Tadzio, or upon young Hans Castorp's enchantment with Przibislav Hippe, of which his later love for Clavdia Chauchat is merely an adult re-enactment. Thus initiated, the reader will soon come to sense that Jacob's devotion to the Rachel-child Joseph is not entirely what a crudely distinguishing world would call purely paternal. And very little instruction is needed (one or another of the author's photographs suffices) to recognize the author himself in the Scottish Lord who, in *Felix Krull*, shyly but insistently woos the handsome 'waiter' Felix. And who would not suspect that in the exuberantly outrageous love scene between Felix Krull and Diane Philibert 'alias Madame Houpflé', a writer of novels 'qui sont énormément intelligents', the 'alias' may be replaced by quite another one, and even by a different gender? Does such a reader need the revelations of the diaries? Does anyone?

Some are 'piquant' enough to deserve a place among the 'very secret' matters that made Thomas Mann destroy his diaries. There was, for instance, a time when he was much in love with his son Klaus, deeply disturbed by observing the boy in the nude 'up to some nonsense' at his younger brother's bed; and was emotionally so preoccupied with this involvement – 'Find it quite natural that I should fall in love with my son' – that his conduct as a husband demanded apologies to his wife Katia ('the serenity, love, and equanimity with which she takes this are remarkable'). Or he asked himself, upon coming to sit on a train journey next to an attractive young man in white trousers', whether he was perhaps 'once and for all done with women'. Other confessions and reflections of this kind are touchingly naïve, such as when he was smitten by the sight of a handsome young worker in a plant nursery, 'bare to the waist' and was (Thomas Mann was close to sixty at the time) enraptured by the beauty of the youthful body, describing it in some anatomical detail. The 'extraordinarily articulate' Madame Houpflé comes to mind as she rhapsodizes about Felix Krull's bodily charms even while she is in bed with him. Yet Thomas Mann is moved to the following meditation about his erotic attraction: 'It requires no fulfilment at all, neither intellectually nor physically. This is likely thanks to the influence of the reality principle on the imagination; it allows for the rapture, but limits it to just looking.' One cannot help remembering Aschenbach and Tadzio in *Death in Venice* where no Freudian vocabulary intruded and the 'rapturous looking' led to the most celebrated *Liebestod* in modern German literature. *Death in Venice, Felix Krull* – these are not the only works of Thomas Mann's that may be linked to quite 'unliterary' entries in the diaries. If a literary historian were to search for links between 'life' and 'art' in the works of this writer who was inclined to deny such connections, he would certainly be indebted to some of the diarist's most blatant indiscretions. But is this sufficient reason to make them known? And then the reader is suddenly asked to puzzle over the relationship Thomas Mann asserts, on 17 September 1919, between his erotic tendencies and his most troublesome work: '... there is no doubt in my mind that "even" the *Betrachtungen* (Meditations of an Unpolitical Man) are an expression of my sexual inversion'. This is said at the very time when the ambivalent

German nationalist who had done, as he once said, his war service by writing that book, is about to transform himself into a soldier of the Weimar Republic and thus ultimately into the exile who, in *this* role, is better known to the world than he is as a writer. It is as if he had forgotten what, after the success of his early novella *Little Herr Friedemann*, he wrote in April 1897 to the same childhood friend whom he had told that his youthful diaries were no more: 'Now I am suddenly able to find the *discreet forms and masks* in which I can show my experiences to people, while formerly I needed . . . a secret diary.' Clearly, the forms and masks, the discretions and metamorphoses, did not render the secret diaries superfluous. Truly, who was he?

How is this autobiographical fury related to Thomas Mann–Tonio Kröger's apprehension that the art of the artist is fated to be at the expense of his 'life', even to the cursed point where life becomes unlivable to him, in fact nonexistent? When he read to his wife from *Gesang vom Kindchen*, his rare exercise in hexameters that were to celebrate the recent addition to his family, his youngest daughter, the mother 'was very moved, and only objected to my describing our most intimate experiences. But it is these intimate things that are really the most universal and human. I don't know any such scruples' (German edition of the complete diaries, 10 January 1919).

This is the extreme consequence of naturalism and psychologism and – in his customary ambivalence – he deplored on many an occasion the 'unscrupulous' non-art perpetrated by writers in the name of naturalistic 'truth'. Still, when at the end of 1918, the year of that *Gesang*, he 'dipped' into Tolstoy's diary and was sometimes repelled by it, he yet 'thoroughly agreed' with the following: 'The main purpose of art . . . is this, that it tell the truth about the soul . . . Art is the microscope that the artist focuses on the secrets of his own soul, and that then *reveals to men the secrets common to them all*.' 'Very good', Thomas Mann applaudingly adds without remembering that it was this characteristic of the realist novel which, after *Anna Karenina*, persuaded Tolstoy that, for moral and religious reasons, he should abandon the corrupting business of art. Tolstoy's 'hysteria' (that abated before long) had healthy roots. For where indeed is the line to be drawn between having 'no such scruples' and the threatened collapse of civilized living through the insistence of 'souls' to express themselves uninhibitedly and enact all their secret drives? When civilization is *felt* to maintain itself only through taboos put up against the 'universally human', it is ripe for death. For the 'secret' of any culture lies in the delicate refinement of its 'secretiveness' with regard to much that is only natural and 'commonly human'. Thomas Mann himself was to use the strongest possible words, his most inspired invective, when he tried to rouse an indifferent, opportunistic, or paralysed world to realizing the horrors of a Germany awakening (*Deutschland erwache!*) to the chance of murderously living out her secret desires.

When in *Meditations of an Unpolitical Man* Thomas Mann asked the question 'Who am I, whence do I come that I am as I am, and am neither able nor willing to be anything else?', the first answer that came to his mind was that he was a child of the German burgherdom. He even believed he recognized his distant forebears when looking at the portraits of German citizens painted by Dürer or Holbein. Did he really? Their features, in their seriousness and dignity, betray nothing of the nervousness to which Thomas Mann's *diaries* constantly testify. Only their 'true being', their *character indelebilis*, shows in those pictures. Within their frames they look as if they knew very well 'who they were' without even having to question their identity. The same would apply to the artists who painted them. Neither they nor those who were sitting for them would have understood what, for instance, Tonio Kröger worried about: the persistent dilemma between his being an artist *and* a burgher, a defective *Bürger* because of his art, and a shy artist for being a *Bürger*. Imagine their utter incomprehension as their prodigal son tells them that he is, as an artist, 'often sick to death of having to represent what is human without myself having a share in it'. They would, without saying a word, shake their heads, and by not saying a word teach us a lesson in the tyrannical nature of history, in the inescapable dictates of the *Zeitgeist*, the ever-changing qualities imposed by the spirits of the ages. Thus, perhaps, they would explain the irrepressible urge of the diarist Thomas Mann to include any triviality in his attempts to give permanence to the fleeting moment. How is this?

Tonio Kröger's distress has a long history or histories. It must have begun at times, impossible to determine with any accuracy, when art, probably more than once in the lives of peoples, their cultures, religions and rituals, emancipated itself from the crafts that, even when they supplied aesthetically most pleasing objects and works, served 'practical' needs. For also the 'spiritual' made highly practical demands; for instance, it demanded places of worship worthy of the divine, sacred spectacles that would not offend the gods, God-pleasing churches and cathedrals He would not frown upon, and music that would be music to His ears. When art became Art, ultimately purposeless and even proud of having no 'practical uses' apart from satisfying the creative urges of the artist and the aesthetic appetites of his clients; when the Parthenon became something merely to wonder at, the 'alienated' artist had arrived. Finally there came the house of little Tonio Kröger, Thomas Mann's early 'alienated' artist, little when compared to grander ancestors, for instance Shakespeare. For it was Shakespeare who wrote also the great drama of the art that was only art: the art of acting. What is Hecuba to the actor? Surely not what the gods were to Antigone or even to the masked speaker who enacted her destiny. At one high moment of his imagination and art Hamlet's actor sheds tears, real tears, over Hecuba's fate; at the next, returning to 'life', he counts the money he has earned with his performance. To disown the 'unreality' of the artist's existence, Shakespeare in the end made his Prospero bury the magic wand of his 'so potent art' and gave him back to life with a prayer.

It is like the beginning of much modern aesthetic thought. The actor is, of course, Shakespeare himself and the name of Hecuba stands for all but countless other names, names like Othello, Desdemona and Iago; of Hamlet, Gertrude, Ophelia, and Polonius; of Shylock and Jessica; of Macbeth and his Lady. Enough! Enough, surely, to wonder who Shakespeare himself could possibly be. It is most fitting that so little should be known about the man himself even if he is not quite as anonymous as that bard who has no existence except through the deeds and adventures, the friends and enemies, of Achilles and Odysseus. In the glorious company of many a man of the Renaissance, Shakespeare is the first great artist of a new age. Having dwelt in so many minds and souls, he may in the end – and in the end was Prospero – not have known who he himself was. There are years and years and yet only a few steps that separate him from Schopen-hauer's belief that the 'true artist' must 'disown for some time his whole personality and survive alone as . . . a medium of lucid visions'; from Keats's 'wretched' confession that he is a poet and, *therefore*, has no identical nature; from Kierkegaard's melancholy diagnosis of the aesthetic person being condemned to never achiev-ing ethical self-realization; from T. S. Eliot's 'continual extinction of personality' as the condition 'for the progress of an artist'; from Tonio Kröger–Thomas Mann's discovery that nobody may 'pluck a single leaf from the laurel tree of art' without 'paying for it with his life', his life as a definable personality. 'Who am I?'

It is, I suggest, the desire nevertheless and against all odds to define and ultimately even reveal himself as a 'real person' that accounts for Thomas Mann's pedantic zeal of keeping diaries (and *vice versa* for the unprecedented eagerness of people to read publica-tions of this kind: biographies, autobiographies, letters, diaries). It is as if this writer decided to refute his mind's persistent companion, Nietzsche, who wrote that 'the perfect artist is for ever and ever shut off from all "reality"'. These diaries abound with every imaginable and scarcely imaginable wavering and in-decision, ambivalence and contradiction; yet toothaches and indigestion, insomnia and sleeping tablets, haircuts, having tea with so-and-so – all these trivia are at least irrefutably, un-ironically, unambiguously 'real'.

9
Knut Hamsun

IT is strange for a critic to introduce, almost as if he were a new arrival on the literary scene, an author whose many novels, in German translations, accompanied and enchanted him during his student years and afterwards. Knut Hamsun was a renowned, much read, and much admired author then, above all in German-speaking countries but also in pre-revolutionary Eastern Europe. A recent fellow Nobel Prize laureate, Isaac Bashevis Singer, said in 1976 that for years he was under the spell of Hamsun's prose. When Hamsun himself, in 1920, received that royal Swedish bonanza, he had merited it, it seemed, with *The Growth of the Soil* (1917), a work that to this day is often judged his masterpiece. It was not necessarily apropos its title that he remarked on that occasion that he would use the money for planting more flowers in his garden – in accordance, perhaps, with the founder's will to make up for the dynamite that is behind the Swedish reward. When Hamsun's seventieth birthday approached, he left his farm and house, Nörholm, that was in danger of becoming a kind of Norwegian Yasnaya Polyana, and withdrew to a little hotel at some distance from there in order to escape all celebrations. He really treasured only one present: a large consignment of fertilizer sent to the farmer Knut Hamsun by a portland cement factory. But he could not stem the flood of congratulatory messages from the representatives of European literature such as Gorky, Gide, Galsworthy, H. G. Wells, Heinrich and Thomas Mann, etc. The president of Czechoslovakia, T. G. Masaryk, sent a telegram. All this is to be set up against the neglect he has suffered in recent decades. The young generation of readers may well look upon him as a newcomer.

Even where he used to be most famous, in Germany, his works are not read. It is a fascinatingly ugly story that has led to his eclipse, a story inseparably linked to the bigger and uglier one: Hitler's European conquests and mass murders. Ezra Pound might have had the same fate when his poetic reputation became entangled in political notoriety. He did not. This, however, was not due to the greater durability of his immensely overrated achievement as a poet, but rather to the determination of the Anglo-Saxon lettered liberal to keep aesthetic judgments strictly apart from political ideology – if indeed the devastating performance in which Pound played his small, noisy part comes under the heading of either ideology or politics. In saying this, I hasten to add that Hamsun, who outraged the vast majority of his fellow Norwegians by publicly applauding the power that occupied his country in April 1940 – he was, we should remember, eighty-one years old at the time – not once in his novels expressed sentiments as vicious as the anti-Semitism voiced by Pound's *Cantos*, attitudes no less vicious for being conveyed in metres and rhythms that reputedly have significantly enriched the poetic possibilities of the English language. On the contrary, in *Wayfarers*, published in 1927, to give only one instance, Hamsun has lavished great imaginative affection on the Jew Papst, the good-natured, kind-hearted, and humorously fraudulent itinerant, peddling watches that certainly could not compete with the astronomical predictability of his appearing, boisterous and melancholy, at every village fair throughout the region.

Melancholy and boisterous, good-natured and fraudulent – such play on the contradictoriness of a character who nonetheless emerges as a perfectly convincing person suggests the particular quality of Hamsun's art and, therefore, his cast of mind and, therefore, some of the causes of his downfall. I shall come back to this.

The best of his many novels evoke in a highly sophisticated manner – this is the irresistible charm of the paradox that Hamsun embodies – the complex primitivity of life lived in the villages and small towns (such as the Segelfoss of his novels) on the islands and along the fjords of Norway; and if, as in the first work that spectacularly initiated his career, *Hunger* (1890), the scene is a city as large as Oslo (called Christiania at the time), the action – or what in more conventional novels would be the action – takes place entirely within the one character who is the story's protagonist and narrator. Yet this 'inwardness' needs explaining. When Hamsun, one year before *Hunger* – before, that is, he had established his reputation – published his determinedly biased book on America, *The Cultural Life of Modern America* (1889), he prefaced it with a sentence, intended no doubt simply as an apology, but remarkable for the reverberations it set off in its aphoristic succinctness: 'Truth is neither two-sided nor objective; truth is precisely disinterested subjectivity.'

The word 'subjectivity' is hardly ever used in this way – except perhaps by that other self-willed Scandinavian Kierkegaard. *Hunger*, by being the book it is, was to define Hamsun's meaning. For it is precisely through this subjectivity that Christiania, in its 'objective' facticity (even the names of its streets and squares are factually correct) comes to life as intensely as cities hardly ever do in the naturalist literature of the epoch. Certainly the Christiania of *Hunger* is a fact verifiable by anyone who knows the city. Yet it is a fact of the poet's soul, just as is Baudelaire's Paris and Rilke's too (in *The Notebooks of Malte Laurids Brigge*), or Kafka's Prague (and the America he imagined in his first novel), or T. S. Eliot's London, the 'Unreal City' of *The Waste Land*. If Kierkegaard had written novels, they would possess this concrete inwardness.

Indeed, Hamsun's *Hunger* vigorously attacks our senses with Christiania's sights, sounds, and smells. For days on end, after closing the book, we feel that we have actually met its shopkeepers, pawnbrokers, policemen, and prostitutes; climbed staircases to deserted addresses on streets given by name, trying to find a long-neglected friend who may help us, desperately hungry as we are, to some food; or we sit on a bench at the harbour, watching the ships on the mother-of-pearl-coloured sea. At the same time all this is piercingly unreal, not in the manner of an evanescent dream, but by virtue of an absurd enhancement of the real as occurs in nightmares or hallucinatory states induced by exhaustion. After Hamsun, only Kafka, who was an avid and admiring reader of his, had the power of effecting such metamorphoses; and certainly Kafka could have said of Prague (did he not actually say it?) what Hamsun says of Christiania right at the beginning of *Hunger*: 'All this happened while I was walking around starving in Christiania – that strange city no one escapes from until it has left its mark on him.' Kafka, too, went around Prague, indelibly marked by it and starving, not literally but allegorically, because like his 'hunger artist' he could not find the spiritual nourishment he needed.

Never before had hunger, physical hunger, been explored with such elaborate intensity and pursued to the ultimate fantasies and derangements it causes in the mind; and never before had it been so true to say of a man starving in a big city that he had only himself, and not society, to blame for his starvation. A novel called *Hunger*, published at that time, by its very title certainly would have raised expectations that Hamsun disappointed. His hero's misfortune is not due to cruel social circumstances but is a matter of free choice, if there can be free choices in Hamsun's universe of preordained and irrevocable destinies. Choice lies only in the acceptance of fate. There is no rebellion in *Hunger*, most certainly no protest against society – that hazy entity that performs for sociologically minded modern people the same function that ether did for pre-Einsteinian physicists. It is all more like a hunger strike against God. In extreme moments of near-fainting, this hungry man does curse, but he curses – the curse. 'When nothing helped, no matter how hard I tried, ... I shouted and roared threats up to the sky, shrieked God's name hoarsely and savagely, and curled my fingers like claws.' What is the curse? It is his knowing that he is meant to be a writer and nothing else, and nobody's sharing this knowledge with him. Nobody? With regard to Hamsun himself, thousands of readers, after they have been enslaved for hours by his ability to transform hunger into a work of art, see him become what he was sure he was all the time, an artist. Although Hamsun's hungry man, like Kafka's hunger artist, is, in his own way, an allegorical figure, Hamsun's is more successful in practising his art: he survives. Survivors, resilient and competent men and women, always commanded Kafka's respect. Perhaps Hamsun gave him more cause for admiration than the author of *Hunger* could possibly have known.

The editors of the almanac that his Norwegian publisher prepared for Christmas 1927 sent Hamsun the kind of useless questionnaire on which the famous are requested to satisfy the public's unholy curiosity. The man who had written *Hunger* was asked what his favourite food was. Hamsun answered morosely that he was no gourmet and ate what was put before him. Honesty, he said, was the quality of character he valued most highly (and he meant nothing to do with any virtue in the code of conventional morality, but what Nietzsche called *Redlichkeit*, truthfulness to and with one's self); and almost all politicians found themselves in the questionnaire's category of 'historical personalities' he most despised. And finally: 'What is the worst you can imagine?' 'To die', he answered: 'I certainly wouldn't put up with it if I didn't have to.' He almost succeeded in avoiding it. When in February 1952 he died at Nörholm, where he had built his house with the study, the 'Dichterhaus', separate from it (a neat symbol of the separation of art from his life), he was ninety-three, a deaf and almost blind man, a survivor of himself, deeply at odds with his own people, prosecuted for high treason in its law courts, and almost forgotten as a writer. Would he still have maintained that dying was the worst?

How did it come to this? Here was one of the greatest writers of his time, the author of *Wayfarers* and of the earlier and certainly not less powerful enchantments: *Mysteries* (1892), *Pan* (1894), or *Victoria* (1898). Here was the poet of changelessness whose every character was conceived by his imagination as if to reveal the ingrained mendacity of all manifestos that aimed at changing human beings by engineering a change of social circumstances. (Ibsen once sat in the front row of the hall when the young lecturer Hamsun assailed the dramatist-reformer's belief — and perhaps made him write *The Master Builder* afterwards.) Here was the creator of the truest, tenderest, and, in their verbal restraint, most sensuous love scenes in modern literature, and the artist who knew how to play most captivatingly on the muted strings of language. How did he avoid being repelled by that loud-mouthed, cheap painter who killed millions of people because they did not fit his cheap notion of what the picture of mankind ought to look like? All answers to these questions are bound to be unsatisfactory, but the question marks at their close may at least illumine some of their impenetrable blackness.

He was called Knut Pederson when he was baptized in the little village of Garmo which, far back in almost legendary days, was believed to have been built by one of his mother's ancestors who, they said, was bidden to do so by St Olaf himself. The distinguished family gradually lost its distinction and wealth; and when the beautiful Tora Olsdatter Garmastaeet, daughter of the village vet, married the tailor and small farmer Per Pederson Skultbakken in Lom, a parish in the interior of southern Norway, in the poor and austere Gulbrandsdaal, it was considered a perfectly suitable match. They had seven children – Knut was the fourth – and little to support them with. Tora's brother, a moderately prosperous tailor and merchant in Hamaröy, high up in the north, persuaded the family to try their luck on less unyielding ground. When Knut was three, they settled on the little farm Hamsund in Hamaröy. The journey from Lom was long and strenuous. They went in rough vehicles over the mountains to Trondheim, continued north by ship along the rugged coast, and finally arrived in a rowing boat at their destination, at the three-year-old boy's destination. The sea, which he saw for the first time, the ships, the fjords, the woods of Hamaröy, the mountains, the parish tailors and cobblers, peasants and fishermen, and the names of people that sound as if they had their real place in Nordic sagas, stayed with him all his life; and of course the name of that Hamaröy farmstead, Hamsund. He chose it as his pseudonym when, after his first sojourn in America, he published an article on Mark Twain in a Norwegian journal. Through a misprint the author's name appeared as 'Hamsun'. He liked it and kept it; but henceforth, one of the many voices within him, not the least troublesome, persisted in questioning if it was not due to a cosmic printer's error that he was destined to be a writer. Was it not too 'civilized' an occupation? Too removed from the woods and soil? Could writing ever be an honest man's work? Was it not appropriate that the attempt to make a living at it should be punished by starvation?

It is surely not without malice against the writer's vocation that August – the unforgettable wayfarer of *Wayfarers*, sailor of the seven seas; bragging of immense treasures stored in boxes god knows where on the Indian continent; hatching scheme after scheme of how to become rich, with all the mountains he suspects to be full of gold turning out to be 'big rubbish heaps', yet sometimes hitting upon a capital idea as, for instance, when he insists that the bog outside the town, devourer of cattle and even men, could be drained and turned into benevolent farm land – that this superb braggart whose every résumé of life is 'So it comes and goes ... It cannot be otherwise' or 'Good luck and goodbye' and who, like Blake's fool, travels the road of excess, but rarely enough becomes wise, discovers his kind of Knut Hamsun:

... there's a marvellous man here who wants to write down everything I've been through in my life. Wants me to talk and he'll put it all down in writing. I met him on one of the quaysides, and I sat and talked to him for a long time ... I've never seen a man who could write like that, though I've been all around the world. I can talk as fast as I like, but he still gets it all down. He says it will be a whole book with my picture and everything ... We'll make a mint of money, this writer says ... Just like Gjest Baardsen, who went and wrote a big book about all the things he'd stolen in his life. What do you think?

The writer as the collaborator of liars, the usurper of stolen goods, stolen experiences, stolen feelings, as an exhibitionist of sentiments as if they are honestly his own: traces of this distrust of literature remained with Hamsun throughout his life. His mother, whom he deeply loved, was a taciturn woman; when she did speak, she spoke with a strange oracular emphasis, faintly reminiscent of the magical invocations of witches. Hamsun's style at times appears to be indebted to her. She never read a book of her son's. And when the young man Edevart, the main character of *Wayfarers*, to whom August's question is addressed, 'did not know what to think ... For him books were an unfamiliar world. Faced with them, he shook his head ...', it could be the response of Hamsun's mother, just as she might have spoken the words of the old man in *Victoria* who has read very little in his life: 'I read what is within myself if ever I feel like reading.' In *The Growth of the Soil* Hamsun said of an old peasant that his age was 900 years, that he had been resurrected from the remote past and yet pointed towards the future, a man from the time when the first plough furrowed the soil, and yet a man of today. When Hamsun was in his eighties, Hitler unbelievably succeeded in making him believe that he, the leader, had come to lead the insurrection against the lettered, clever, and hollow men.

Many of Hamsun's fellow Norwegians sought in America an easier and more lucrative life than their homeland offered them. Their numbers swelled in the 1880s. 'Dragging their torn roots behind them', as Hamsun says in *Wayfarers*, they are shown again and again in his novels. Before he and the world knew he really was a writer, he himself might have settled in America. He tried twice. He had suffered, as a boy, five years of being exploited by his Hamaröy uncle to whom his penurious parents gladly abandoned him. In 1873 he became an assistant to the wealthy shopkeeper Walsöe, the virtual ruler of his village and archetype of all the ambitious merchants in Hamsun's books; in 1876 he was apprenticed to a shoe-maker, taught at an elementary school, and wrote, even published, stories that now are forgotten. Having found a wealthy supporter who believed in his literary talent, he managed in 1879 to be received by the famous Björnstjerne Björnson who looked first at the manuscript of Hamsun's novel *Friola* and then at the tall and handsome man of twenty: 'Why don't you become an actor?' he asked and gave him a letter of introduction to the theatre in Christiania. Hamsun showed no histrionic talent, but he lived now, often hungry, in the capital city. Thus was the stage set for *Hunger*. In the meantime he worked with a road construction gang, read Strindberg and the French novelists. At last, in January 1882, he crossed the Atlantic. Norddeutscher Lloyd, the Hamburg shipping company, was persuaded to give him a free ticket. He marvelled at the splendours of New York where the railway, as he wrote in a letter home, made its way above the roofs, and the bridge to Brooklyn stretched for almost a mile. Then he moved to Elroy, Wisconsin, where his brother had settled before him. He was a shop assistant there and later worked as a farmhand in North Dakota. In the autumn of 1884 he was received into a more intellectual milieu: he met the Unitarian minister and writer Kristofer Janson in Minneapolis, who befriended him and employed him as his secretary because he was good at lecturing to his flock. Hamsun, of course, did not become a Unitarian himself, but read Nietzsche. He fell ill in that year; galloping consumption was the doctor's diagnosis. Hamsun returned home.

The tuberculosis proved to be not terminal and probably not even tubercular. He recovered in the agreeable climate of a mountain-sheltered place in the south of Norway and again went to Christiania, once more trying to become a writer. He *was* already − if Thomas Mann defined a writer correctly as a man who finds writing incomparably harder than anyone else. 'For two weeks', Hamsun wrote to a friend, 'I have pored over one page. It isn't done yet. Imagine, two weeks . . .' He showed what he had written to an author well known in Christiania. 'Your writing is too strange for Norway', he said. 'You have learned too much from

Dostoevsky.' At that time Hamsun had not read a line by Dostoevsky. Still, despite his 'strangeness', he succeeded in obtaining promises from two Christiania newspapers that they would publish his articles about America. He went there again in 1886. 'He could not do without *food* and for the second time he fled across the Atlantic', as Kristofer Janson in Minneapolis explained. Hunger again. He became a tram conductor in Chicago and, unable to learn the names of streets, used to call out the wrong stops and lost his job. After once again working as a farm labourer, he made a slim living as the journalist he had promised to be and by lecturing to the many Norwegian communities in Minnesota. In the summer of 1888 he left America, sailed to Copenhagen, ready magisterially to pronounce on the culture of the new continent. *The Cultural Life of Modern America* is a witty, eloquent, amusing, and, more often than not, wrong-headed book. He might have been warned by what he himself said in print about Mark Twain's *The Innocents Abroad*: that it was marred by the author's rather superficial acquaintance with European traditions, the inadequacy of his aesthetic perception, his provincial nationalism, and the all too blatant intrusion of his political persuasion. The persuasion was, of course radical-democratic.

Although Hamsun's own political or quasi-political convictions made themselves heard at least as loudly in his book on America, it certainly could not be said of them that they were democratic. Rather they were Nietzschean in their intellectual-aristocratic bearing, and radical only in their aversion to the tyranny wielded by the masses over the works of the mind, to the naive religiousness and the numbing of the tragic sense through the optimism of the therapeutic popular pedagogues. It is, certainly, Walt Whitman's 'marvellous naiveté' that has won 'a couple of followers' for his mediocre 'tabular poetry, those impossible inventories of people, states, housewares, tools, and articles of clothing'; and it is Emerson's preachiness that made this 'Aesop of the American mob of moralists' the supplier of 'mottoes for their most ingenuous goody-goody books'. Later in his life Hamsun recanted his harsh pronouncements on America, called the book 'my youthful sin' and its views 'lopsided', and opposed its republication. Yet many passages of it are magnified projections of his abiding belief that 'we become more and more civilized and lose in spirit'. After 1889 and 1890, the years in which *America* and *Hunger* were published, Hamsun's biography is that of a more and more successful novelist and – at least outwardly – secure family man until in old age catastrophe overtook him. He married twice (the second time at the age of fifty to an actress twenty-two years younger), had four children, and, although in 1925 he fell into prolonged depression, emerged from it victoriously with *Wayfarers*.

The mob of moralists ... One of the *Wayfarers* episodes that is bound to haunt the reader's mind for a long time is the dying of Skipper Skaaro, one of the more powerful men of the fjords, owner of the vessel *Seagull*, and notorious womanizer. He hires the girls of the village for good money to stack the catches of herring in the hold of the ship. The prettier women he would then invite to his cabin. One day he invited Ane Maria, a married woman, but as it turned out in the end, his end, invited her not insistently enough. When she played coy and fussy, he angrily left her. This was his undoing, for the passionate and emotionally unstable Ane Maria felt rejected by this and was determined to have her revenge. A little later, on a Sunday, after having put on her best finery, she lured Skaaro to that bog near her village where, at the time, many berries ripened. He expected the gifts she had withheld from him before:

'So I can pick myself a few berries?'
'Yes', she replied. 'As many as you like!' She pointed across the bog and said: 'The ripest ones are over there!'
He followed her direction, and sank deeper and deeper into the quagmire with every step. Ah, such diabolical evil – to point where she did, and not warn him that the bog there was bottomless. She knew that if he went out far enough, if he did not turn around and come back, he'd never be able to lift his legs clear, but simply sink – sink.

He does, and on the pages that follow, Hamsun unflinchingly describes his slow sinking, his futile pleas for help, her resolution to let him perish, her turning away from the bog, pretending to call rescuers, but only in order to watch secretly the final moments of his being sucked in by this fiendish piece of nature; and Hamsun's description is so detached as to avoid any possible identification of his own moral feelings with the victim's desperate outcry against the 'diabolical evil'. When a year and a half later, as once again the 'dark days of autumn set in', she was plagued by her conscience and gave herself up, 'there was a kind of pride, of hauteur about Ane Maria' — very different from the somnambulating Lady Macbeth's immersion in her guilty nightmare, or Raskolnikov's longing for atonement. It is neither incommensurate with Hamsun's genius to evoke such comparisons nor irrelevant to the large question of how imaginations differ with regard to their moral textures. That Hamsun, whatever his advanced age may have contributed to his failure, was, despite his aristocratic stance, so stubbornly indifferent to the abysmal words and deeds; so blind to the glaring deceptions of that German seducer of the masses; and — no doubt because of his own love of the earth — so willing to believe in the false prophet's prophecies of the blood and the soil while he at the same time cunningly manipulated all the available technologies, is surely related to an imagination capable of maintaining its moral composure in describing Ane Maria's 'pride and hauteur': 'When the authorities asked her whether she had anything against Skaaro, she replied: "No. Quite the reverse." And asked why she had done away with him, she replied frankly: "It was because he wanted me but didn't ask me enough . . ."' Indeed, August's 'It cannot be otherwise' is very close to his maker's sense of life.

In trying to explain the inexplicable, there is one more point to be made. In 1943 Hamsun, aged eighty-four, went to Berlin to be received by Hitler. He asked Hitler to remove from office the *Reichskommissar* of Norway, Josef Terboven, under whose rule patriotic Norwegians were imprisoned or sentenced to death. (Terboven committed suicide in 1945.) Of course Hitler refused, but he was much upset by his interview with the old man, as Hitler's public relations chief, Otto Dietrich, reports in his book *Twelve Years with Hitler*.

Hamsun's quite extraordinary last work, *On Overgrown Paths* — it appeared one year before his death — is a strange collection of moving memories, expiring poetic perceptions, and disquieting descriptions of the poet's agonized life as a patient in an asylum for the insane (Ezra Pound comes instantly to mind), as an inmate in a home for old people, and as an accused before a tribunal that, after long hesitations and delays, found him guilty and made him poor by ordering him to pay a vast sum of money (collaborators had to make amends for Germany's extortions). From this last book Hamsun emerges as an obstinate and stubbornly misguided Norwegian patriot. He had believed in Hitler's assurances that his country would play an important role in the Germanic empire to come. Sometimes he sounds as if he looked forward to a Norway that would be as triumphant in the world as Kirsten Flagstad was in its opera houses; or, had he felt less defeated, he might have added: as his novels were in the literary world. In the meantime he showed little sympathy with things that conquer: for instance, with the mighty poplar tree in a neighbouring garden about to kill a young fir that tried hard to grow in the giant's shadow. He asked the owner to cut off the lower branches of the poplar: 'I am so sorry for the little fir tree.' The neighbour did not even answer. 'He has probably read in his paper that they examined my mental condition', Hamsun notes. 'Midsummer 1948' is the date of the last line of *On Overgrown Paths*: 'Today the Supreme Court upheld the sentence and I stop writing.' Halfway through the book he had said: 'God bless everything that is not merely idle talk. Silence, too, is blessed by God.' It should be engraved on the tombstone standing above the silence of a great writer.

10
Observations on
psychoanalysis and modern literature

In the history of thought it occurs again and again that a privileged mind turns a long-nurtured suspicion into a system and puts it to the good or not so good uses of teachers and learners. When this happens, we say that it has been in the air for a long time. This is so in the case of psychoanalysis, and, whatever its future fate, its historical importance is beyond doubt. For it is impossible not to come into contact with it or to avoid the collision, even if one merely wanted to say to it that it has no business being there. A theory owes this kind of inescapability to its long maturation in the womb of Time. It is born and casts its spell upon a world that seems to have been prepared for quite a while to receive it. Pallas Athene, it is said, emerged from her father's head in full armour. But surely, before this birth took place, Zeus must have spent many a day pondering Athenian thoughts and must have done so in the Athenian dialect; and our world had awaited Freud long before it heard his name.

This is why psychoanalysis appears to be more than merely one among many possible theories about the psyche; rather, it comes close to being the systematic consciousness that a certain epoch has of the nature and character of its soul. Therefore it would be an endless enterprise to speak of Freud's influence on modern literature; and literature, whatever else it may be, is also the aesthetic form assumed by the self-awareness of an age. If a writer today speaks of fathers or sons, of mothers or dreams, of lovers or rivals, of accidents that determine destinies or destinies rooted in character, of the will to live or the longing for death – and what else is it that poets and writers talk about? – how can he remain unaffected by Freudian thoughts even if he has never read a line by Freud? And the more he were to try to extinguish or 'repress' this 'influence', the more he would become its victim. Could a post-Freudian poet say what Goethe's Egmont says: 'As if whipped on by invisible demons, the sun-born horses of Time rush along with the fragile chariot of our destiny, and nothing is left to us but intrepidly to hold fast to the reins and keep the wheels from pushing against a wall of rock or driving into an abyss' (*Egmont*, II, 2) – could a contemporary writer put such words into the mouth of his hero without suspecting that he has learned it from Freud? That the invisible demons with their whip are really the Unconscious, the *Id*, and the rather helpless charioteer the *Ego* with its good intentions?

From Goethe, Novalis, the German arch-Romantic, and Kleist, the one and only naturally tragic poet of German literature (even if Goethe once cursed him as 'Unnatur' – 'Diese verdammte Unnatur', he said), and certainly from the literature we have uppermost in mind when speaking of the later nineteenth century, from Stendhal, Flaubert and Maupassant, from Tolstoy and Dostoevsky, there is a much shorter way to Freud than the maps of literary history usually show; and the subsequent literature is altogether domiciled in a country the cartographer of which is Freud. It may not be the most pertinent of questions to ask whether Hofmannsthal, Schnitzler, Broch, Musil, Kafka, Rilke, Hermann Hesse or Thomas Mann have been 'influenced' by Freud, or whether Joyce or Virginia Woolf, Hemingway or Faulkner have 'learned' from him. For the question – to which the answer may be in some cases Yes and more frequently No – is almost as irrelevant as it would be to ask whether the first builders of aircraft were inspired by Newton. Planes fly in Newtonian space, trusting, as it were, in the validity of the law of gravity. What then are the qualities of the sphere of the psyche traversed by modern literature?

Out of its multitudinous characteristics I wish to select two from the writings of Thomas Mann. The first bears upon the problem of man's responsibility for his decisions and actions – that is, the problem of morality itself. A masterpiece among novellas, *Death in Venice*, supplies our first example. We remember the episode (in the third section of the story) that is decisive in the development of the plot, when Gustav von Aschenbach for the last time tries to take the moral initiative in the encounter with his destiny. He wants to escape from the sickly oppression: from the Venetian air, heavy and sultry with the sirocco, where the deadly epidemic would soon luxuriate, but also from his growing passion for the beautiful boy Tadzio. He determines to leave and orders his luggage to be taken to the railway station on the hotel's early morning motor boat, whereas he himself, believing that there is enough time for an unrushed breakfast and, without acknowledging this to himself, perhaps for a last silent encounter with Tadzio, chooses to take a later public steamship. But when he arrives at the station, his luggage has gone off on a wrong train. This accident makes his moral determination collapse. He decides to wait for his trunk in Venice, returns to his Lido hotel and to his erotic enchantment. He is ready now for the approaching disease and for death.

Fate and accident are ancient allies; yet only in the Freudian era could *this* accident have been woven in this manner into the texture of destiny. For as Thomas Mann tells the story, the accident is not, as any similar event in Greek tragedy would be, a weapon in the hands of a divine antagonist with whom the hero's will is interlocked in combat, and not a cunning manoeuvre of that friend or foe called Fate. It is rather the revelation of Aschenbach's true will that gives the lie to his declared intention to depart. If Aschenbach is clearly innocent of the mistake made in the dispatch of his luggage, he is innocent only after the canon of traditional moral judgments. According to the new dispensation he is responsible; and in his soul he knows this or comes to know it as he ecstatically welcomes that travel mishap as if it were the gift of Freedom itself. 'Aschenbach', we read, 'found it hard to let his face assume the expression that the news of the mishap required, for he was almost convulsed with reckless delight, an unbelievable joy.'

The basic idea of Thomas Mann's novel *The Magic Mountain* can be stated almost in one sentence: Hans Castorp, a seemingly 'well-adjusted' young shipbuilding engineer from Hamburg, has planned a visit of three weeks in a Swiss sanatorium for tubercular diseases where his cousin is a patient, but remains there for seven years. Certainly, he becomes ill himself, but his physical symptoms are by no means serious. What then is the *real* reason for his tarrying? It is his hidden wish, a secret perhaps to himself, to await the return of Clavdia Chauchat. He has fallen in love with the Russian woman and she, as she leaves, promises that she will return: and Hans Castorp waits seven years. His illness is the mere pretext for his waiting. Against all 'humanistic' reasonableness and moral principles, his *true* will has asserted itself. And Thomas Mann began to read Freud only after he had written *The Magic Mountain. Violà*, the *Zeitgeist!*

Both *Death in Venice* and *The Magic Mountain* would be unthinkable were it not for the Romantic fascination with the alliance between love and sickness and death; and this is almost as much as to say: unthinkable without depth psychology. These works are situated in a territory of the psyche the ethics of which are radically different from those of the Enlightenment (to name only one of the preceding epochs). It is strange that the strongest hostile response evoked by Freud's teaching was, at least to begin with, moral indignation. Freud, it was held, undermined morality and catastrophically narrowed the domain in which ethical laws could be applied unquestioningly. A profounder criticism would have been to show that, on the contrary, he extended a person's responsibility so immeasurably that it became in practice all but unworkable. The rationalistic doctrine of morality, which until the Romantic period had dominated the moral philosophy of Western civilization, saw the moral person triumph or succumb in a *conscious* struggle with forces which, no matter whether they were called 'nature' or 'instinct' or 'inclination', were the simple antagonists of the ethically wakeful human being. In Freud's doctrine, deeply indebted to the Romantic sensibility, the moral conflict becomes total warfare. It is waged even in places where once upon a time the warrior sought and found relaxation from the strains of morality: in sleep, in dreams, in fantasies, in innocently involuntary action. Let anyone say now: 'I have only dreamt this', or 'I did not intend to say this; it was a mere slip of the tongue', or 'I was determined to do what I promised, but then I forgot': instantly he will be persuaded that he dreamt what he dreamt, said what he said, forgot what he forgot, because he was prompted by his deepest and truest will. While the moralist of the rational Enlightenment proved himself or failed in what he consciously *willed* or *did*, the Romantic and Freudian morality is once again concerned with the innermost character of a person, with his *being*. Once again: for there was a time, long ago, when a prophet struck fear and terror, albeit by speaking in a different idiom, into the minds of the Pharisees by putting the goodness of the hidden soul or the rebirth of the whole man ethically above the righteous observance of the law by the publicly displayed goodwill. This was the essence of the moral revolution of Christianity.

As psychoanalysis, with all its variations and eclectic modifications, is a dominant part of the epoch's consciousness, it has a share in its calamity. This manifests itself – speaking, as would seem appropriate, in medical terms – in the vast superiority of presumed diagnostic insights over therapeutic possibilities. Has there ever been a doctor who has diagnosed as many pathological irritations as Freud? The psyche is to him an inexhaustible reservoir of abnormalities, precariously dammed in by the most delicate concept of health. All pleasures and all oppressions of the soul, all sins and all virtues, the restlessness of the heart as well as the great constancy of love, the fear of evil as well as the faith in God – all these may in the twinkling of the diagnostic eye degenerate into signs of psychic imbalance. But what is the health of the soul? Compared to the resourcefulness and ingenuity of the diagnosis, the only answer that can be given within the limits of psychology is primitive, pedestrian and simple-minded: the ability to control the controllable conditions of existence and the adjustment to the unalterable. But who has drawn the frontier between the controllable and the unalterable? Where exactly does it run? Is it fixed by God, this fabrication of the father-bound neurotic psyche? Or by Nature who has created the boy after the image of Oedipus and then handed him over to the healing practices of psychological *ratio*? Or by society or the State? By *which* society and *which* State? By that Victorian society whose numerous pathological symptoms have called forth psychoanalysis? Or by the enlightened, generously liberal, thoroughly 'demythologized' society that on both sides of the Atlantic sends swarms of patients into the consulting rooms of psychologists? Or by the tyrannical State that prohibits their activities?

The questions are endless and unanswerable. For it is true to say that if there were an answer, there would be no psychoanalysis. It would not have been invented, had it not been for the disappearance from our beliefs of any certainty concerning the nature of human being. Thus we have become the incurable patients of our all but nihilistic scepticism, indulging a conception of the soul that stipulates more, many more, psychic possibilities than can be contained in one existence. Whichever possibilities we choose, we miss out on the others – and distractedly feel our loss without being able ethically to justify it. Inevitably foregoing uncounted possibilities, we experience this as the betrayal of a vaguely conceived 'fullness of life'. For our beliefs do not acknowledge any reason to sacrifice possibilities in order to gain our reality – a reality that for us has assumed the character of the arbitrary and the indefinable. Thus we are haunted by as many dead possibilities as there is room for in the wide region of frustrations. It is the accomplished hypochondria of unbelief.

Paradoxically enough, Freud himself, over long stretches of his enterprise, was securely at home in that rationalistic Enlightenment faith whose increasing instability was the historical occasion of this doctrine, just as the doctrine in its turn added to the disturbance. But because he himself was hardly affected by it, he had no ear for the question his own theory raised, and certainly did not have the *philosophical* genius to meet it. With astonishing naiveté he examined the 'How' of psychic conditions, as if such labours could yield clear answers to the 'What' of psychic phenomena, of their meaning and their possible relatedness to the possibly true nature of being. Thus he believed, for instance, that primeval murderers of their fathers created from the agony of their guilt a god–father to be conciliated by worship – a theory which presupposes that those savage creatures in all their savagery possessed a conscience and the psychic disposition to believe in God. Yet Freud did not ask to what end human beings should have the ability to feel guilty or the capacity for religious beliefs, but took for granted that the conscience and the faith of his savages corresponded to nothing real in the world and fed on sheer illusions; and his readers, just as he himself did, looked upon certain *contents* of guilt and faith understandably as antiquated, without paying attention to the *form* and quality of these psychic dispositions. But are those dispositions not exceedingly curious if they have no correlative whatever in the order of reality? Of course, Freud would rightly have said that this was not a psychological question, but a metaphysical or ontological one. True; but to doubt the very validity of such questions, quite apart from the inability to answer them, is the main psychological characteristic of the epoch that has produced psychoanalysis as its representative psychology.

One of its most important tenets is the theory of repression. From the beginning of his history, man has suffered from the compulsion to 'repress', and only because he 'represses' has he a history; for historical epochs or cultures differ one from the other by the changing moulds in which they cast some human possibilities at the expense of others. This is why the ancient Greeks were, despite Pythagoras and the Pythagoreans, not rich in great natural scientists, but in artistic accomplishments unsurpassed by any other age; or why we have the most self-assured and effective technology, but arts that are exceedingly tentative, uncertain, restless and experimental; or why creations of nature have been, ever since the discovery of Nature, the great comfort and pleasure of the Romantic sensibility: because this tree or that range of mountains appears to be the sum total, without loss or sacrifice, of *all* its potentialities, and therefore never hurts our aesthetic sense by insinuating to us that it might have done much better had it only chosen another career. For one of the things that set man apart from all other beings is that the sum of his potentialities by far exceeds the measure of their realizability in one human life or even in one historical epoch. Man has been given language (in the sense of all his means of expression) so that he can say what he has not chosen to be silent about. He is such an eloquent creature because he is unspeakably secretive. This is the natural-historical aspect of human transcendence, the psychological side of his 'existential problem'. Human existence is choice, resignation, sacrifice – and indeed neurotic repression if a man has to make his inescapable choices and sacrifices under the dim enforcement of social norms he no longer believes in, instead of basing his decisions upon the belief in the greater virtue of what he has chosen, no matter whether he does so consciously or unconsciously, from lucid insight or from faithful unreflective obedience. If he no longer feels that there is any compelling reason why he should forego this in order to achieve that; if his existence is not illuminated by any shimmer of its transcendence, then his rejected potentialities (or, for that matter, injuries sustained by the child in his religiously or ethically 'agnostic' society) grow into neuroses in the darkness of the unconscious. And psychoanalysis shares with existential philosophy the tragic fate that, although it is, of course, founded upon the awareness of the universal human need to choose, to select and to sacrifice, it is at the same time, deprived of a world in which the nature of such choices would have any compelling moral significance.

From this follows the 'scientific' intention of psychoanalysis to disregard any hierarchy that religion or metaphysics or ethics or tradition has set up concerning the activities of consciousness. It may well be true to say that this has been the first such attempt in the history of man's efforts to know himself. There is for psychoanalysis no pre-established order of the psyche: it is impossible to discern, at least initially, what is important to it and what is unimportant. It is a theory that lets itself in with chaos. If there is to be any order, it has to be created – somewhat in keeping with the *aperçu* of that arch-Romantic Novalis (in his celebrated fragment of 1799 'Christendom or Europe') that only anarchy will once again beget a true spiritual order: 'Religion will rise from the chaos of destruction as the glorious founder of a new world.' Psychoanalysis – like the sensibility of Romanticism (as opposed to that of Classicism) – is imbued with the suspicion that everything, every tatter of a dream, every scrap of memory, every seemingly arbitrary association our thinking makes between this and that, may be of hitherto unsuspected significance within the economy of the soul, just as Marcel (in the first volume of Proust's vast novel *À la recherche du temps perdu*) receives those sudden messages of a great and hidden truth, those unpredictable intimations of eternity, from a stone the surface of which reflected the sunlight, or from the clanging of a bell, or from the smell of fallen leaves – 'a confused mass of different images, under which must have perished long ago the reality' – the absolute reality he was seeking. Nietzsche's great and truly dreadful experiment consisted in his assuming that the history of the Western mind was nothing but a conspiracy to conceal the truth; and where such concealment is looked upon as the rule, the suspicion is bound to arise that, vice versa, anything, literally anything, may unexpectedly 'conduct' the mind towards a tremendous illumination. It is precisely this that distinguishes modern literature from, above all, the myth-bound poetry of ancient Greece. And what Hofmannsthal said in his poem 'Lebenslied' of the 'heir' of this long process of disinheritance, is as true of psychoanalysis as it is of the artist of the psychoanalytical age:

Ihm bietet jede Stelle
Geheimnisvoll die Schwelle,

meaning that he who is without a home in an ordered world will entrust himself to any current of chance to take him anywhere, for anywhere may be the threshold of the mystery.

Proust's great novelistic *oeuvre*, the attempt to catch hold of a withdrawing world by means of an exquisitely woven net of memories; James Joyce's *Ulysses*, this monster work of genius that turns the experience of one day into a kind of lyric-epic encyclopedia; Hermann Broch's time-consuming record of Virgil's dying; not to mention the many minor 'stream of consciousness' novels – all this is the literary product of an epoch whose soul has been analysed by Sigmund Freud. And whatever will remain of this literature will bear the imprint of a consciousness that Freud has helped to become conscious of itself and thus, given the nature of consciousness, has helped, in fact, to create it. But can a consciousness that is so thoroughly conscious of itself ever achieve that 'geprägte Form', as Goethe called it in 'Urworte-Orphisch', the oneness of deliberate form and 'naive' spontaneity that has always been the hallmark of great art?

Speaking of Freud and modern literature, we cannot help concerning ourselves with the unusual and in all probability critical situation of literature in an age that constantly is in search of an acceptable theory of its soul. For the relationship of art to that self-understanding of the soul which culminates in Freud is by no means free of conflicts, and these tensions have been in the making ever since the truth about man has been sought not in myth or religion but in psychology. Psychology – the psychology, for instance, that dominates the novel of the nineteenth century – is the science of disillusionment. Its climate is, as some of the Romantics believed, unfavourable to poetry; and in a serious sense it is true to say that the history of the psychological novel is the progressive dissolution of what traditionally has been regarded as poetic. Novalis, who believed that psychology is one of the 'ghosts' that have 'usurped the place in the sanctuary where the monuments of gods should be', knew what he did when he opposed the Romantic enthusiasm for Goethe's *Wilhelm Meister*, indeed his own fascination with that novel, by calling it a 'Candide aimed at poetry', a satire of the poetic mode.

Goethe, in his turn, accused Kleist, this *Ur*-patient and *Ur*-practitioner of depth analysis, of aiming at the confusion of feelings. What he meant by this was very likely the war that Kleist's imagination, in love with the heroic and the mythic, fought with his analytical intelligence; and this intelligence was at the same time in unrelenting pursuit of the psychological truth. It is a feud that reverberates throughout Kleist's dramatic verse and prose. Indeed, the source of the particular fascination wielded by his dramas and stories is the clash, and at times the unquiet marriage, between poetry and neurosis. Goethe was bound to abhor this poet as intensely as Kafka admired him. For Goethe believed – at least at times – that poetry prospered only when it was left to grow and mature in the unconscious. He said so to Schiller and added that poetry presupposes in those who create it 'a certain good-natured and even simple-minded love for the real which is the hiding-place of truth'.

Unconscious, good-natured, simple-minded, trusting that the hidden truth may, after all, reveal itself to the naive mind in the phenomenal world – if one were to define Kleist's genius, indeed the spirit of modern literature by means of its perfect opposite, this would be its negative definition. Should it ever happen that a history of modern literature is written in honour of Sigmund Freud – by a literary historian who also possesses a thorough knowledge of psychoanalysis without having become intellectually enslaved to it – it might begin with Goethe's highly conscious praise of the unconscious, contemplate afterwards the Kleistean tension between mythology and psychology which is at the same time so characteristic of a whole literary epoch, and then arrive at the writings of Nietzsche, that astonishing prompter of psychoanalysis, 'the first psychologist of Europe', as, not very modestly, he called himself (and Freud himself all but acknowledged his claim) – Nietzsche, who at the same time never tired of pointing to the perils of the mind's psychological pursuit of itself, and believed he knew that there was a kind of knowledge that might become 'a handsome instrument for perdition'. Such an essay in literary history might conclude with Kafka's dictum from 'Reflections on Sin, Suffering, Hope, and the True Way': 'Never again psychology!'

In honour of Sigmund Freud? Would it not rather be a polemical performance? No. For is the stance of the polemicist appropriate to the inevitable? Our imaginary historian of literature would show that there is a compelling logical development from German Romanticism, the fountain-head of so many currents in modern literature, to the works of Sigmund Freud. How is this? The medical sobriety of the founder of psychoanalysis brought into the vicinity of a literary-philosophical movement that is reputed to have fostered every conceivable extravagance of the fancy? Still, the connection exists; and it is a mistaken belief, hardly more than a facile superstition, that the early German Romantics were bent simply on discrediting realistic wakefulness in order to rescue the dreamily poetic, or on fortifying the domain of the imagination against the encroachments of the real. True, the poet in Novalis was sometimes outraged by the prosaic realism of Goethe's *Wilhelm Meister*. On these occasions he would say of it that it elevated 'the economic nature of man' to the rank of his 'only true nature' (and he might have said: the nature of man insofar as it is accessible to psychology); or that it was 'a piece of poetic machinery to deal with recalcitrant material'; or that with this novel he made his final bid for quasi-bourgeois respectability: 'The Pilgrim's Progress toward a knighthood'. But in a different mood he called it a supreme masterpiece, 'the novel *par excellence*', and its author 'the true vicar of the poetic spirit on earth'. It is clear that even Novalis, the true poet in the first group of German Romantics, played his part in the strategy of Romantic Irony, an attitude of mind which would surely be useless in any ferocious defence of the imagination against the attacks of rationality. No, Romantic Irony is a play played around a centre of great seriousness. Its ambition is to save the authentic life of the imagination from the wreckage of illusions. Just as lifeboat instruction is given on luxurious ocean liners, so Romantic Irony aims at teaching the spirit of poetry how to keep afloat in the approaching floods of what Goethe named the Prosaic Age: the Age of Analysis.

Friedrich Schlegel, the Grand Intellectual Master of the early Romantics, demanded that Poetry should be practised like a science, while every science should become a new kind of poetry. This was Schlegel's *outré* manner of expressing what Schiller, in his celebrated essay 'On Spontaneous and Reflective Poetry' ('Über naive und sentimentalische Dichtung'), hoped for: that at the highest point of consciousness man would acquire a new and higher 'naiveté'. Novalis said even more: 'Those who uncritically believe in their health make the same mistake as those who uncritically regard themselves as sick; both are diseased' – because, one assumes, of their wanting in critical alertness; and still more: that certain kinds of physical sickness are best remedied by treating the psyche because the soul has the same influence upon the body that the body has upon the soul. If these sayings were offered as utterances of Freud's, the attribution would not meet with much incredulity. And the following *is* all but by Freud although it too was said by Novalis: 'All that is involuntary must come under the control of the conscious will.' This means the same as 'Where *Id* was there shall *Ego* be'.

As one reads what Freud says of the relationship between 'I' and 'It', of the wounds which the struggles between the two inflict upon the soul, and how the soul may regain its lost integrity through the enhanced consciousness of itself, it is impossible not to relate this great psychological utopia to the vision of a future paradise with which Kleist ends his meditations 'On the Marionette Theatre' – or rather, on the neurotic derangement, the false self-consciousness, of the inhibited psyche; and even though the Eden of the original innocence and unselfconscious grace is shut for ever, we must, Kleist writes, 'embark on the journey around the world in order to find out whether we may not be received through a back door': In the future *perfection of consciousness* we may recover what we have lost in the Fall; we shall have to 'eat of the Tree of Knowledge again to fall back into the state of innocence'.

Schiller, in that essay on 'Spontaneous and Reflective Poetry', means something similar, if not the same, when he speaks of our gaining a new and purified spontaneity through the infinite increase of our reflective power. And what else is it that the philosopher of Romantic pessimism, Schopenhauer, has in mind when he, intimately knowing the terror of the *Id*, the dark impulses of the Will, glorifies in his *magnum opus, The World as Will and Representation*, the freedom that the *Ego* may conquer through the understanding of that *Id* and itself? And finally Freud and Nietzsche: Even if the mountain tops of the prophet Zarathustra seem worlds apart from the consulting room of the analyst, they are nonetheless neighbours, and not only in the sequence of time. For one of Nietzsche's two divinities is Dionysus, the god of the intoxicated will to live, but the other is Apollo, the god who possesses the power of clear articulation and disciplined insight. Nietzsche too longed for the ultimate rule of Apollo – not *over* Dionysus but *together with him* in a utopian oneness of Mind and Will, intellect and impulse. Yet Nietzsche and Freud are neighbours above all by virtue – virtue? Well, sometimes it seems a necessity imposed by history – by virtue of the determination with which they pursued the truths of psychology, a psychological radicalism intolerant of any gods that were not more than the illusory comforters of sick souls. But if ever there comes the unimaginable day when men, beyond sickness and illusion, live in the integrity of being, then the spirits of Freud and Nietzsche may give their assent to Kafka's resolve, unrealizable in his time: 'Never again psychology!'

II

The dismantling of a marionette theatre; or, psychology and the misinterpretation of literature

a lecture

WITHOUT wishing to preach, I shall be following the example of preachers in basing my discourse upon a text, not from Holy Scripture (although I shall not avoid the story of Adam and Eve and their Fall) but, on the contrary, from a recent issue of a psychoanalytical journal read and respected, I believe, by the practitioners of that discipline. The article in question is about Heinrich von Kleist (1777–1811), the only modern dramatist whose genius was cast in the tragic mould, 'tragic' to be understood in the sense of the tragedians of both Greek antiquity and Elizabethan England. Wieland, one of the literary celebrities in 'classical' Weimar, the Weimar of Goethe and Schiller, recognized this. After Kleist had read to him 'some of the essential scenes and several *morceaux*' from his unfinished *Robert Guiskard*, Wieland concluded that Kleist was destined 'to fill the gap in our literature which even Goethe and Schiller have left'. For neither Goethe nor Schiller was in Wieland's judgment a tragedian. Kleist was: 'If the minds of Aeschylus, Sophocles and Shakespeare united to write a tragedy, it would be what *Robert Guiskard* is' or promised to be if the whole work were as good as the fragments Wieland came to know (and in the end only fragments were left to posterity). Yet Goethe found Kleist 'unnatural'. But is this, coming from Goethe, perhaps synonymous with 'tragic'? 'Die verfluchte Unnatur!' he exclaimed after reading one of Kleist's plays, *Das Käthchen von Heilbronn*, and threw it into the fire. Yet we should remember that this was the same Goethe who said that the mere attempt to write tragedy would be his undoing. On the other hand, immediately after the Second World War, when the sense of the tragic was livelier than it was in Goethe's Weimar, Kleist's dramatic masterpiece, *The Prince of Homburg*, was one of the great successes of the Paris theatre, not only because the ideal actor, Gérard Philipe, acted the part of the protagonist, but despite – and so soon after the German occupation – the defiant apotheosis of the Prussian spirit that pervades the whole drama and rings the curtain down with the notorious curse wished on all the enemies of Prussia: 'In Staub mit allen Feinden Brandenburgs!' If we add that Franz Kafka admired nothing more in German prose literature than the stories of Kleist, we have suggested the place held by him in the canon of literature. Therefore, I would insist that there exists not only a level and manner of discourse, a tone of voice, that is appropriate to his rank, but moreover, as we shall see, a deplorable possibility of speaking of him 'out of tune', or with utter tactlessness – and this in deference to a 'method'.

I see that I shall be quite unlike an expert preacher because I shall be dallying on the way to the promised 'text'. For it has to be prefaced by two more pieces of information, one biographical, the other about the particular occasion of the 'text' to be used. First, then, the biographical. Kleist's life, more than that of any other celebrated figure in the literary history of his epoch, abounds in unsolved puzzles, both factual and emotional, and biographies of him, therefore, often engage in purely speculative constructions. But one thing is quite certain: he was a very unhappy man. 'There is no help for me on this earth', he said in his last letter before committing suicide. Apart from being a great writer, he was what today would be called a neurotic character – not quite unlike Franz Kafka, who, of course, sensed this kinship. There was undoubtedly a great deal of 'elective affinity' at work in Kafka's fascination with Kleist (as there also was in his being so powerfully attracted by the writings of Kierkegaard). And, as with Kafka, we would, if it were not for Kleist's genius, be left with nothing but his neurosis. But what an 'If' is this! It is a conditional that is at the same time a warning to 'the doctors' not to treat his case, posthumously, as if it were simply a pathological one. True, he himself once said that it might be up to the science of medicine rather than to political moralists to understand his attempt, in 1803, to join Napoleon's armies preparing to attack England – he, the Prussian patriot. He appears to have looked upon this design as a heroically disguised suicide: 'Mine will be the glory of dying on the battlefield', he wrote to his half-sister Ulrike.

Certainly, he was in love with death, above all with the idea of dying in the company of others, of comrades-in-arms, and especially with persons he believed he loved. He would ask his favourite cousin, Marie von Kleist, or, more than once, his closest friend Ernst von Pfuel, to die with him. On one sad occasion, when

Pfuel refused, Kleist destroyed instead what at the time he regarded the best of himself: his unfinished drama *Robert Guiskard*. In the end he found what he most desired: the death *à deux*. After elaborate preparations and in a serene, even ecstatically joyful, mood, he shot himself on the shore of the Berlin Wannsee a few moments after having killed, with her consent, of course, a mortally sick woman companion whom he was determined to see as a profoundly kindred soul. Before this conclusion to his life, there had been several persons who evoked his passionate devotion, most of all his half-sister Ulrike and Pfuel with whom he soldiered, studied, travelled, with whom he often parted after violent quarrels, and to whom he returned each time, celebrating feasts of reconciliation.

For the sake of the 'text' to be used afterwards, another biographical puzzle has to be mentioned: an 'intimate' physical affliction which, according to some of his letters, worried him with regard to his plans to get married (he never did). He was twenty-three at the time. The exact nature of the complaint is unknown; but as surgery appears to have cured him, it was probably a case of phimosis and the operation nothing more serious than circumcision.

Now the particular literary occasion of the long withheld text: In 1810, one year before his death, Kleist published in his own journal, *Berliner Abendblätter*, an essay, or an essay-story, 'On the Marionette Theatre'. During the century and a half that has passed since its first unspectacular and scarcely noticed publication (among contemporaneous writers E. T. A. Hoffmann recognized its importance), it has received an amount of attention quite disproportionate to its slender volume. Rilke called it, in the manner of many other illustrious judges, a masterpiece and used its thought and imagery in the fourth of his *Duino Elegies*. Its thought and its imagery indeed make for the great distinction of the essay and account for its fascination; in the concreteness of its 'parables' (*anschaulich* is the word Goethe would have used to describe this quality) the essay succeeds in unwittingly condensing a whole chapter in the history of aesthetics – and not only aesthetics.

This is to say that the 'story', a dialogue between the narrator and the premier dancer of the city's opera, rests on a wholly *intellectual* plot. The initial question posed by the narrator and interlocutor is: What kind of pleasure or instruction can the celebrated dancer possibly derive from watching the performances of a marionette theatre where the narrator had frequently observed him among the onlookers? This opening leads to a discourse on the spontaneity of a human being's expressive gesture and its corruption through consciousness and self-consciousness. The dancer maintains that he may learn much from the movements of the marionettes for these are ruled by the interaction of two *natural* forces: their own gravity and the mover's counteraction. Thus the marionettes need the ground only as the momentary support for their graceful leaps into the air, an all but unattainable ideal for the dancer. Would not the principal ballerina of the company give anything to be eighty pounds lighter or else to be pulled up by such a force from above in performing her entrechats and pirouettes? Or look at the young man dancing the part of Paris: 'As he offers Venus the apple, his soul – it is terrible to watch – seems to reside in his elbow.' Or observe the dancer who acts Daphne: when in her flight from Apollo she turns to see how close he is, twisting her body in as mannered a way as 'a nymph from the school of Bernini', 'her soul sits in the vertebrae of the small of the back'. For at these moments, the dancer's self-consciousness destroys any naturalness of bearing, and affectation assumes the place of gracefulness: 'Affectation takes over when the soul . . . has removed itself from the gravitational centre of the movement.' This can never happen to the marionette: it has no soul except the animation it receives from its mover who, on his part, is limited in his actions by the laws of mechanics; and the marionette, *lacking* soul and therefore consciousness, is immune from the most damaging effect of self-consciousness, affectation. This is the reason why no human being will ever equal the puppets' gracefulness, and reason enough for the dancer to watch them so intently.

What is particularly intriguing about Kleist's story is that its starting point is different from that of the customary Romantic worship of the natural grace of those unselfconscious beings, children and animals. Kleist, in contrast, starts with an artifice – the puppet, the marionette – to exemplify the simplicity and beauty inherent in the workings of natural laws, a simplicity and beauty only too easily destroyed by human consciousness. But although Kleist begins on an unusual note – the 'Romanticism', as it were, of mechanics – the child and the animal follow suit, providing striking examples of their superior gracefulness or, in the case of the animal, even of an instinctual perception unembarrassed by self-consciousness and thus triumphant over the contrivances of artful men.

The role of the child within the Romantic syndrome Kleist assigns to one who is no longer quite a child but a youth of very great charm. Yet he is old enough – sixteen – for this charm (*Anmut*) to be dramatically undone by vanity and self-consciousness. Kleist's narrator, inspired if not entirely convinced by the dancer's disquisition, tells the story of how the youth deplorably lost his natural grace. The youth and his companion, the narrator, bathed together and as the boy caught his own reflection in a mirror while drying himself, he exclaimed that in the position he had unwittingly assumed, he looked exactly like the *Spinario*, the famous Greek sculpture of a youth extracting a thorn from his foot. The narrator, 'be it in order to test the resilience of the boy's charm, or not to indulge too much his vanity', denied the claim (although he too had observed the 'classical' similarity). Thus he provoked the youth to attempt a repetition of the little spectacle. But however much the young bather tried, he did not succeed. Consciously he was unable to accomplish what had occurred unintentionally. His movements became more and more awkward and even comical. Still worse, this scene was only the first in a steady process of deterioration. He began to spend hours in front of the mirror, and within a year he had sadly lost all his charm.

If the child of Kleist's story is not quite a child and ends as a self-conscious, vain and mannered person, the hero of the anecdote with which the dancer reciprocates is indeed an animal, if a rather unusual one. Still, what it may lack in immediate plausibility, it gains in making Kleist's point; it even serves as a memorable exemplar of the poet's art, rare among German writers: the art of grotesque inventions that are capable of floating for quite a while above and between the comic and the serious before landing with scintillating effect in one domain or the other. In this instance it is a bear whose acquaintance the dancer makes while visiting the estate of a Russian aristocrat, owner of the beast. The dancer, who is also an excellent fencer, had just easily defeated the son of his host and was challenged afterwards to try his skill against the paws of the bear. *This* match he lost without having made a single hit. The bear not only parried all his attacks but did what no fencer could possibly accomplish: he remained completely unresponsive whenever his opponent feigned a motion – 'He stood there, gazing into my eyes as if he were able to read my soul in them, with his paws raised to meet my rapier's thrusts, and whenever these were not meant seriously, he would not stir.' No human consciousness could equal the infallibility of the animal's intuitive perception.

The force of Kleist's story 'On the Marionette Theatre' – we are still not ready to cite our 'text' – derives from roots sunk into the soil of the past. It is a novel variation on a theme the first author of which may well be Plato. For according to Plato the human mind has been in the dark ever since it lost its place in the community of Truth, in the realm, that is, of the Ideas, the eternal and eternally perfect forms, those now unattainable models which man in his exile is able to see and recognize only as shadows or imperfect copies. And this Platonic parable of the damage suffered by man's soul and consciousness is not unlike the Fall as it is narrated in Genesis. The Fall was the consequence and punishment of man's free will that for the first time had asserted itself against the universal God and rejoiced in a consciousness and pleasure entirely its own – tragically its own; for man had to forsake the in-dwelling in the supreme intelligence and thus the harmony between himself and Being as such. The reward for this betrayal was the embarrassment and shame of self-consciousness, the hard labour of maintaining himself in his state of separation, and, soon to follow, the murderous misdeeds of the self-will named Cain. Better to have no mind than a mind thus deprived and impoverished and cruel.

Ever since, it would seem, man has striven to transcend this 'unhappy consciousness' – to use Hegel's phrase; and it was indeed Hegel who built the most imposing and, in the opinion of many, most forbidding philosophical edifice to comfort the mind by giving it the means of understanding its trials and at the same time the prospect of a happy ending. The human mind's alienation from the supreme Intelligence, the pain of its constantly coming up against an opaque reality that will not yield to its desire to comprehend it – all this 'negativity' will, by dialectical leaps and bounds, issue in an ultimate reconciliation between mind and world: Mind will be World, World will be Mind. Marx, of course, took this happy consummation out of, as it were, the hands of Mind and entrusted it to those whom the inimical world has caused the greatest suffering. The most maltreated heirs of Adam's curse and labour, the most alienated of men, the proletariat, will create, or re-create, a harmonious order through revolutionary acts sanctioned by the dialectical laws of history. In the post-revolutionary end the bear will have found his match in a fencer-dancer whose skill will be entirely at one with the spontaneity of his perception. There will be a consciousness no longer encumbered by a world that insists upon its essential otherness. What we have learned to call 'history' will come to an end, paradise will be regained, and what his unhappy, imperfect consciousness has taken away from man, will be given back to him by the perfected Mind.

This is how Kleist finishes his story: If man succeeds in *infinitely* expanding his consciousness, natural grace will return to him. Grace was at its purest in the figure that was entirely unconscious; yet now it will abundantly emerge again in an existence partaking of infinite Mind. The two ends of the circular world meet: the marionette and the godlike being are, each in its own way, equals in gracefulness. Does this mean, the narrator asks the dancer, 'that we have to eat once again of the Tree of Knowledge in order to fall back into the state of innocence?' And the answer he receives is 'Indeed, this will be the last chapter of the history of the world.'

2

Countless are the designs of thought and imagination that have been inspired, before his time and afterwards, by the identical plot enacted on Kleist's marionette stage. What comes first to mind is Schiller's celebrated thesis 'On Spontaneous and Reflective Poetry' ('Über naive und sentimentalische Dichtung') and its less famous companion piece, Friedrich Schlegel's 'On the Study of Greek Poetry'. Goethe's *Novelle* would have to be remembered as would his *Elective Affinities*, the *locus classicus* of the deadly collision between nature and the arrangements of human consciousness; and certainly one must cite Wordsworth's ode 'Intimations of Immortality', with its apotheosis of the Child, the child not yet distracted by self-consciousness from its unconscious 'originality'

(originality in the sense of the child's closeness to the origins of life, to the Romantics' fountainhead of Being: Nature, or the heaven that 'lies about us in our infancy'). After Kleist, we might turn to Wagner's child-hero Siegfried, the fearless, naive 'pure fool' who wrests power from the deceitful dwarfs and the terrible dragon; Siegfried, the utterly unselfconscious youth who was meant to supersede the gods when their master, Wotan, had lost his will to rule, profoundly inhibited as he was by his 'knowing'. And where there is Wagner, there is Nietzsche, the author, for instance, of Zarathustra's first oration and parable, where the ascending journey of Mind reaches its goal with the Child in its innocence and unreflective creativity. And was not Freud's therapeutic method founded upon the conviction of the mind's deficiency, its pathological refusal to come to terms with the impulses from within, indeed with the unconscious 'memories' rejected and suppressed by our consciousness? Was not the utopian goal of his campaign, or at least its inherent tendency, the conquest of the unconscious through the perfect integration of the conscious mind: 'Where *Id* was, there shall *Ego* be' (even if this would mean, as Hegel said, the end of art: for art is inconceivable without the dark, fertile soil of the unconscious).

Finally, there are Rilke's *Duino Elegies* with their pervasive theme of the human consciousness that, corrupt as it is through hiding from itself its fatal defectiveness, functions as an insurmountable barrier between man and the Angel, the poet's symbolic figure standing for the fullness of Being in the *fullness* of consciousness. And with the Fourth Elegy Rilke has paid elegiac homage to Nietzsche's Child-*Übermensch*, and certainly to Kleist's Marionette Theatre. Regardless of whether he knew it or not, Yeats too joined in. The last stanza of his poem 'Among School Children', perhaps the most beautiful verse he ever wrote, celebrates that unity of Being and Doing, of a consciousness that has become entirely Nature, of substance and performance, the loss of which is the occasion of Rilke's elegiac Duino poems as well as of Kleist's reflections on the Marionette Theatre:

> O chestnut tree, great-rooted blossomer,
> Are you the leaf, the blossom or the bole?
> O body swayed to music, O brightening glance,
> How can we know the dancer from the dance?

3

I know I have taken a very long time to get to the 'text' that I intended to make the basis of my discourse. It now almost seems that I shall have to end with it. In any case, I have found it necessary to acquaint you, however sketchily, with the poetic and intellectual rank of Heinrich von Kleist, with the lineage of thought that issues in his story of the marionette theatre, in order to shock you with the inappropriateness of my chosen 'text'.* I even confess my reluctance to quote it now after having invited you to share my reading of Kleist's essay-story. The difference in manner is too wide, the gulf too precipitous. Still, I have to keep my promise and give you the 'text' at last. It is, I assure you, a representative section of the article and permeated by the spirit of the whole. After referring in the most direct, not to say brutal, manner to Kleist's 'intimate' medical problem, the author says that *this* was

probably the deepest source of his pre-occupation with mind-body fragmentation, paralysis of function, and loss of grace and beauty. The portrait of a fencer suddenly incapable of 'thrusting' is a thinly disguised expression of a fear of sexual impotence. Kleist's depiction of the puppet's legs as 'nothing but pendula', his notion of a dancer who has his 'soul' in his 'elbow', and the portrait of an adolescent suddenly unable to move his leg into a desired position all express symbolically the situation of sexual impotence. (The image of a dancer with his soul in the 'small of his back' in addition suggests a feminine sexual identification and anal penetration fantasies.) All suggest a sexualized hyper-awareness, a feeling of deadness in, and lack of control over, a body part which is not fully integrated with the self . . .

As this, and much else that is worse, is its own parody, involuntarily satirizing many psychoanalytical interpretations of literature, among which it conducts itself more boisterously than subtler analytical findings, yet in obedience to the same method, I shall not give offence by emphasizing the emphatic nonsense, or laugh at the laughable, or demonstrate the author's ignorant or wilful disregard of the 'analysed' work's quality and meaning, its

* Margret Schaefer, 'Kleist's "About the Puppet Theater" and the Narcissism of the Artist', *American Imago* 32, no. 4 (Winter 1975): 365–88.

roots in a tradition that begins, if not farther back, with Plato and the Old Testament. The dancer in the story knows this tradition: 'It seems', he says reproachfully to his interrogator, 'that you have not given much attention to the third chapter of Genesis,' the chapter recording the Fall. So far as the assertions of my 'text' are concerned, I shall only repeat that nobody knows for certain what Kleist's medical problem was, but it was surgically solved, as may be deduced from his letters, ten years before he wrote 'On the Marionette Theatre'. I also must add that the fencer of the anecdote is by no means 'incapable of thrusting', but thrust as he may, and by thrusting having easily conquered a human partner, he cannot prevail against the bear's intuitive perceptiveness; that the puppet's legs, viewed from the angle of physics, simply *are* pendulae; that the ballet-Paris's awkward moment when he looks as if 'his soul dwelled in his elbow', denies to a sane mind any sexual interpretation; that Daphne, pursued by Apollo, is determined to escape him; and that the 'adolescent' did indeed move his leg into the 'desired position' before self-consciousness interfered, and not only his leg but his whole body, so that he resembled the sculpture of the *Spinario*.

To remain for a while with that author's psychoanalytical pre-occupation – and I certainly would not have jeopardized my case by using that 'text' if I were not as certain as I am that it merely exaggerates and caricatures *the method itself*, even if others may employ it with greater restraint – there is no doubt that self-consciousness may inhibit the performance of any physical function; and this applies, of course, in equal measure to artistic displays. Indeed, it is an essential part of the performing artist's schooling to learn how to be oblivious of the gaze of onlookers, or at least to appear to be so in the subtlest and most effective of pretences. His immersion in what he does must be such as – one would think – only the loneliest of solitudes could afford, and at the same time he has to sense the presence of his public not as an embarrassment but as if it were his most private inspiration. This successful inter-play between the 'knowing unconscious' and the artistic intelli-gence that is as much guided by the unconscious as it controls it, is a miniature model of what Kleist had in mind when he makes his dancer speak of a paradise that we may enter again after the human consciousness has come to the end of its journeying around

the world, an idea not unrelated to Hegel's more systematic and
more radical secular eschatology.

Certainly, there are passages in Freud's writings that suggest his
being content with a less aggressive attack upon the unconscious
than 'where *Id* was, there shall *Ego* be' suggests, content indeed
with the kind of collaboration between the two spheres that
does occur in the performing virtuoso, whether he be a dancer,
an actor, a fiddler or a tightrope walker. When Freud writes about
the creations of genius, he admits – not consistently, it is true –
how difficult it is for psychoanalysis to come to grips with them.
He is also aware of the hurdles in the path of the analyst when he
attempts to examine the creator's mind by means of his works,
as if these were simply spontaneous, unformed utterances made on
the doctor's couch (and even there the 'spontaneity' is, after all,
'unnatural', contrived, *mise en scène*). Such insights by Freud
decisively modify the pugnacious utopia of the conscious *Ego*
victoriously invading and brightly illuminating all the secret
hiding places of the unconscious *Id*. Notwithstanding Freud's own
occasional attempts to interpret the psyche of artists psycho-
analytically from their biographies and productions – Leonardo da
Vinci is a case in point – he knows that in art the relationship
between the dark promptings of intuition and their ordering in the
daylight of discrimination, between 'Libido' and 'sublimation',
is too complex ever to be completely unravelled. Did he also know
that the utopian conquest of the *Id* by the *Ego* would spell the death
of the imagination and thus of art? This was *Hegel's* conclusion:
Mind's ever-progressing illumination of the human world, he
believed, was bound to reduce the sphere and power of the
Imagination and finally rob it of its confidence to contribute anything important to the spiritual and intellectual household of man:
'Art is, and will remain, a thing of the past', or, as Thomas Mann
puts it in *Doctor Faustus*: 'Illusion and play – these essentials
of art – have art's own conscience against them today. Art tends
to stop being illusion and play – and thus stops being itself. It
would like to become the consciousness of knowing: knowledge.'
For at this stage of the world's history the artistic imagination
was bound to look upon itself as a kind of atavism. Its out-of-
date cultivation, necessarily lacking seriousness, could only
weaken the energies of the *rational* mind engaged in fulfilling

its all-important functions as the sole executive organ of Truth. I doubt if Freud was even aware of the closeness of his theoretical and therapeutic enterprise to Hegel's burial of art; if he had been, it would have dismayed the man who in 1912 visited the Roman church S. Pietro in Vincoli day after day to contemplate the Moses of Michelangelo.

Rilke, to be sure, suspected that psychoanalytical enlightenment might lessen or even destroy the creative impulse: he refused to undergo treatment lest he cease to be a poet. Thomas Mann had similar misgivings. There was even a time when he called psychology 'the cheapest and meanest' manner of 'knowing', for there is 'nothing on earth, no belief, no feeling, no passion, which could not be reduced to worthlessness by psychological analysis'. But this was ten years before he made the discovery that Freud's 'demythologizing' might, on the one hand, weaken the hold that disreputable political myth-mongerers had on German minds and, on the other hand, focus his own ironical mind more firmly on the problem that fascinated him for a long time: the relationship between myth and psychology. And who would not gladly forgo the blessings of art if the sacrifice had spared the world such curses as Hitler?

But to return to our 'text': Although it is impossible to take it too seriously, the *method* that it unwittingly parodies must disquiet any mind setting out to gain a more thorough understanding of art and literature than is dispensed in most laboratories of academic instruction. For this method instantly raises the question of *what* it is that it explains, what it is that *can* be explained by the method even in its subtlest applications. In our case, Kleist's neurosis? But the diagnostic data at our disposal are far too scant to allow for any reliable findings. Yet even if these were entirely dependable, what would be gained by such an analysis of the psyche behind the story? A better understanding of the sickness of similar 'patients'? This indeed would be putting the cart before the horse; for it is from the presumed understanding of presumably similar 'patients', from the direct examination of their complaints and symptoms, that the psychoanalytical reading of Kleist's work would derive. And assuming that even this topsy-turvy procedure did yield some 'understanding', what kind of understanding would this be? Surely, not the kind of understanding that I have tried to share with you by the sketch of the Kleistean theme's historical ancestry and its later development; surely not the kind of understanding that might deepen and enrich the reader's appreciation of Kleist's literary art, the artistry of his phrasing, the persuasiveness of his incidents, the conclusiveness of his examples? And what else is left to be understood? The meaning of the story *intended by the author?* But this is transparently clear to any intelligent reader. At this point, alas, the question emerges, urgent and inescapable: What is meant by 'meaning', or What is understood by 'understanding'? Whole epochs in the history of the human mind differ by the implied or explicit answers to that question which, in its ultimate form, is tantamount to the question about the meaning of life – the question that no longer dares to show its face.

4

Every kind of understanding depends on our ability to relate a given phenomenon to a wider field of intellectual or imaginative familiarity. Whether lightning is understood as a bolt hurled by Jupiter or as the 'natural' result of electrical charges in the atmosphere, either explanation depends for its efficacy upon a general agreement about the nature of the world. Therefore, the authors of these two explanations are, if they could argue one with the other, unlikely to discover that these are by no means logically incompatible. There is no *reason* why the discoverer of the natural process should not simply have found out an invisible god's electrical ways of making thunderbolts and thus have acquired the power to outwit him by constructing lightning-rods. Yet it is an *empirical* fact that experts in electricity hardly ever believe in gods. Why? Because radically different 'explanations' do not merely explain differently; they reflect vastly divergent senses of plausibility. What is plausible in different epochs of history – why this explanation rather than that, why now one 'understanding' of lightning and then another receive the questioning mind's relieved assent, 'Ah, yes, this *is* it! *Now* I understand' – is likely to be the most fundamental problem of intellectual history.

Whatever the lasting validity of psychoanalysis may prove to be, it had its birthday *in history*. I mean this not only in the obvious sense of bibliographical dates but in the sense that this theory of the psyche would not have been invented had it not been for souls fashioned by a particular historical epoch, souls ready finally to respond with 'Ah, yes, this *is* it!' when confronted with the new doctrine about themselves. For there is no constant psyche. If it were not susceptible to change, there could not be as radical a therapeutic procedure as that offered by psychoanalysis: its very starting point is the changeability of psychic conditions. Indeed, it is possible to say that the mind cannot acquire any knowledge of the soul that the soul itself is not prepared to suggest; and once it has made itself known to the mind, it is no longer the same soul. Goethe and Schiller meant something similar when in their *Votivtafeln* they wrote:

Spricht die Seele, so spricht, ach, schon die *Seele* nicht mehr.

In other words, as soon as the soul begins to express itself through language, to articulate its pleasures, woes, confusions or anxieties, it is no longer the same soul. Is this not the *therapeutic* pride of psychoanalysis? It is, in any case, its crucial *theoretical* problem, at least as crucial as that facing the physical sciences after the discovery of the Uncertainty Principle: in some spheres of observation, it is observation itself that changes the phenomena observed; thus observation merely fortifies our ignorance concerning the state of the phenomenon before we observed it. It is impossible to learn anything about the nature of darkness by throwing light on it. It is not for nothing that the Tree of Knowledge marks the end of the divine monotony of Paradise and the beginning of one of the greatest variables in the world: human history.

To read the seventeenth-century documents reporting the demoniacal possession of a painter and then Freud's interpretation, in 1923, of that artist's neurosis is to enter, in quick succession, two vastly different domains of plausibility – and thus two vastly different souls. For the sense of plausibility is, of course, nothing extraneous to mind and soul; it is an essential characteristic of the inner being. The painter in question had called on the Devil to free him of so severe a state of melancholia that it prevented him from painting. As the day approached when, according to the pact written in blood, he had to surrender his soul to Satan, he was more and more cruelly plagued by demons. Yet he was finally saved through repentance, prayer and the intercession of the Holy Virgin of Mariazell, an Austrian place of pilgrimage. Had he been able to read Freud's analysis of the neurosis that, according to psychoanalytical theory, gave rise to those elaborate fantasies, he would have stared at them in blank incomprehension and certainly not have been persuaded to pay for analysis rather than pray for deliverance – not that he necessarily lacked intelligence, his soul was simply domiciled in another region of understanding. Indeed, the wicked demons may even today gain a measure of imaginative and intellectual respectability in comparison with the strenuous guess-work of the psychoanalyst, guessing over the distance of centuries.

Is there any compelling reason not to believe that it was the Devil who enticed the unhappy artist – any reason, that is, apart from our unbelief? For may not the Devil, who is not only a distinguished theologian but also a great psychologist (perhaps the 'first psychologist of Europe', a title Nietzsche once claimed for himself), know the ins and outs of psychic mechanisms well enough to use them for his purposes? If these questions may appear to be wanting in seriousness, they may still be accepted as expressions of serious doubts concerning the justification of *any* psychology conducting itself as if its object or patient, the human soul, were exempt from the moulding forces of history. Two centuries make no observable difference to anatomy or physiology: the bones and glands of the human body remain the same in form, location or function, at least during so short a span of time as measured on the scale of evolution. This is not true of the psyche. Freud himself may well have been prompted by an uneasiness about this to venture into his particular kind of speculative anthropology. Was it his desire to demonstrate permanence where there is, in truth, ceaseless change? But why, to assert the applicability of the same method, go back as far as Moses or those first religious neurotics that guiltily raised their fathers, murdered or castrated by them, to the rank of divinities? The difference is forbidding enough between the brooding psyche of a Victorian adolescent and today's lad, who without hindrance or scruples, leaves his father's house with a guitar under one arm and a girl under the other. No doubt, the spread of psychoanalysis has contributed to the change. If so, it has helped to bring about a soul different from the soul that Freud analysed.

Or *is* there fundamental sameness where there *appears* to be unending fluctuation? True, the human soul seems to have been in need of salvation at all times, for Time itself oppresses the soul that is conscious of death while it desires eternal life; at all times it is possessed by a mysterious, empirically inexplicable longing for perfection while it has to suffer unavoidable inadequacies within and without; at all times it needs love in abundance and finds it merely as a little island in an ocean of indifference; at all times its will, at the urging of its very nature, is condemned to willing infinitely more than it can ever obtain in a world ruled by the *principium individuationis* and inhabited by innumerable other individualized wills willing the same totality of satisfactions. And yet at all times it possesses nonetheless that priceless little share in the idea of universal humanity that allows us intelligently to comprehend and enjoy the gifts of past epochs, the Charioteer of Delphi, the Song of Solomon, the sonnets of Shakespeare, the music of Bach and Haydn and Mozart – at least to comprehend it all without our being able to re-create the spirit of those creations. But we have to be grateful for even this passive participation that saves our humanistic confessions from being entirely sham; and the first expression of our gratitude should be our abstaining from illegitimate intimacies with those other souls. It is one of the depressing results of popularized psychoanalysis that every unruly boy swears by the name of Oedipus.

For although there are these intimations of identity, there is also constant mutability. If this were not so, the panorama of cultures and mores would not be as varied as it is. It is unimaginable that the totems of savages, the pyramids of Egypt, the temples of the Acropolis, the cathedral of Chartres, the Sears Tower and that of Babel are all the creations of identical souls. What Homer, in making his poetry, knows or comes to know about his heroes is not less 'true' or less 'realistic' than Stendhal's very different grasp of his heroic-unheroic characters; but if Achilles or Odysseus have problems, these are so profoundly other than Julien Sorel's that it would be sheer obtuseness of the imagination or obstinacy of the indoctrinated mind to assume that their souls would yield their secrets to the same psychology. It is, at least, with regard to such *historical* myopia that Karl Kraus's satirical aphorism applies: 'Ein guter Psycholog ist imstande, dich ohne weiteres in seine Lage zu versetzen' – 'A good psychologist will with ease put you in his place.' And *historically* one century and a half – the time that separates us from Kleist – may be as decisive as the years that separate Homer from Stendhal. We need only read, side by side, the balcony scene from *Romeo and Juliet* and the pages of *Le Rouge et le Noir* that describe the embarrassments of Julien Sorel and Mathilde de la Mole after his nocturnal climb into her bedroom – a comparative reading much to be recommended – in order to realize that it would be sheer idiocy to apply the same 'psychology' to loves so greatly different. Psychoanalysis would, alas, accomplish much too much in the case of Romeo and Juliet, and much too little in that of Julien and Mathilde. Too much in the first case: for it would destroy Shakespeare's poetry by treating it as if it were a mere decoration of sexual circumstances and not the very substance of those impassioned souls; and too little in the other: for it would merely befog with jargon Stendhal's superbly intelligent comprehension of souls made after the anticipated images upon which rests Freud's theory without his quite realizing it; souls, that is, which confusedly *feel* according to what were articles of *faith* at the height of a bygone age (the value, for instance, of premarital virginity) but no longer *believe* in what has degenerated into mere social convention. This is why Mathilde, the radically 'emancipated' woman, experiences during that night of love-making none of the bliss, 'so much extolled in novels', but only 'misery and shame'. Stendhal knew that neuroses flourished in the lacunae between the old sensibilities and the new 'ideologies' of freedom and unbelief.

Still, there are some unquiet puddles left behind by the flood that has washed away many a Victorianism; and our 'text' is a caricature of 'explaining' poets and poems, artists and their work, by making Victorian taboos into principles of understanding. It is in such a puddle that the author of the 'text' discovers 'the deepest source' of Kleist's 'pre-occupation with mind-body fragmentation', that is, the deepest source of his masterly story 'On the Marionette Theatre'. '*Deepest* source'? 'Understanding' and 'Ah, yes, this *is* it!' can hardly assume a more narrowly particularized character. It is the genitalization of a whole chapter of intellectual

history and a free-for-all to guess the maladies of its other contributors from Plato to the present. Or will it be said that sexual
taboos were still intact and strong in Kleist's days, and that much
support for the psychoanalytical method can be gained by seeking
hidden meanings which the poet's language unwittingly reveals in
metaphorical disguises, meanings too offensive for the sensibilities
of his time or his own consciousness openly to accept? In this event
the poet's novella *Die Marquise von O.* or, even better, his drama
Penthesilea would have to be made into mandatory reading. When
Kleist sent his *Penthesilea* to Goethe, he expressed in the
accompanying letter the hope that it might be performed, but at
the same time his doubts that it would be. Only a theatre of the
future, he said, will be ready for such a performance; at present
considerations of taste and delicacy would make it impossible. In
the future? Goethe asked, and compared him to a Jew waiting for
the Messiah or a Christian expecting the New Jerusalem. Yet that
future arrived with a vengeance although Kleist's insights into the
pathology of sex, the intertwining of the sublime with the
degrading, the impulse of love with the rage of destruction would
have been as shocking on the Weimar stage as Freud's initially
were on the intellectual scene of his time. Kleist in analysis?
There would have been very little for him to learn.

5

A final word about the heuristic ambitions of such analyses, the
value they possess as guides to understanding a work of art or
even as 'scientific' tools; in other words, and once again, about the
limits of science and 'science'. We may be as sure as we are about
the connections between brain and thought, glands and feelings,
nerves and sense perceptions, libido and sublimation, or, to pass
on to another field of theorizing, hunger and revolution, economy
and ideology. Yet what will probably forever remain in the dark is
the metamorphosis, the mysterious qualitative transformation, of
what is physiological, biological, chemical, biochemical, electro-
physical, libidinous, economical, measurable, into the immeasur-
able life of the mind. That someone like old Karamazov, a 'real'
one, should have four sons as different as Dmitri, Ivan, Alyosha
and Smerdyakov, may present a problem for genetics; it may,

although it is unlikely ever to be solved. But no such understanding will ever understand, and no such explanation ever
explain, the emergence of an imagination able to imagine,
comprehend, create and communicate in words the intellectual,
passionate, religious, sublime or mean natures of this imaginary
father and his imaginary sons (and of a host of other characters
besides). It is mysterious enough that the same soil should produce
tastes – mind you *tastes* – as different as those of cabbages and
raspberries; that the same nervous impulses should be translated
into the sights – mind you, the *sights* of a beloved face or a hellish
nightmare painted by Bosch; and indeed that anatomically and
physiologically identical 'systems' should compose the music of
Mozart, the poetry of Goethe – and the oratory of Hitler. Should
not such mysteries suffice to make even the most intrepid
interpreter or analyst shy away from accounting, for instance, with
socio-economic configurations for nine symphonies, or indeed
with presumed sexual impediments for master essays?

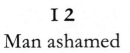

12
Man ashamed

'"Like a dog!" he said: it was as if the shame of it must outlive him.' This is the last sentence of Kafka's *Trial*, concluding the description of Joseph K.'s execution. The English rendering of the sentence is not and cannot be the equivalent of the original. For in the English vocabulary the one word 'shame' has to do duty for two German words: *Scham* and *Schande* (as it would have to do for the French *pudeur* and *honte*). Interestingly enough, this linguistic deficit of the English language would hardly embarrass a translator of *The Trial* if Kafka had written that '*die Schande*', the shame of it, the ignominy of this manner of dying, would live on after Joseph K.'s execution. But Kafka chose to write '*Scham*', a term much more startling in the context than '*Schande*' would have been, the disgrace which, quite understandably, persuaded the translators to add 'of it': the shame of it. In Kafka's German, the shame in *Scham* is left to itself and survives on its own as a grammatical absolute. This is as important as it is extraordinary. It would be easy enough for the shame that is in *Schande* to outlive the victim: as the disgrace he had brought on his and his family's name. This is not so with *Scham*. The shame that is in *Scham* must be *felt* by the person or it is merely an expletive. Yet in that last sentence of *The Trial* the heartbeat of shame is so intense that it seems to acquire a life independent of him who feels it. The inner state assumes bodily form after the manner that rapacity does in the fable's wolf or cunning in the fox, but without any allegorical metamorphosis.

It is a pity that the difference is lost in English. For this liberation of shame from its imprisonment in inwardness, and thus in psychology, is as characteristic of Kafka's art and moral sensibility as is the emancipation of guilt in *The Trial*. In his world both guilt and shame belong to the category of those phenomena, the *Urphänomene*, of which Goethe, in a playful and paradoxical mood, once said that they are effects without causes: 'People find it so difficult to discover the causes because these are so simple that they are hidden from sight.' Of course, this was meant as a joke at the expense of Immanuel Kant; for what is so simple and hidden is not at all a cause in any ordinary sense; and the phenomenon, if there has to be a 'because', is what it is because it is engraved in the metaphysical matrix of human being. Guilt and shame are such phenomena. Man would not be man without them. This does not mean that the *contents* or *expressions* of those essential *forms* of experience are as fixed as the *mould* itself. Far from it; they vary historically as well as individually. There were, among the many surprises that the exploration of exotic territories used to hold for anthropologists, the tribal women who obviously felt that they were quite adequately clad in their dark skins, but showed all the signs of being ashamed after missionaries had persuaded them to put on loincloths; then they tried to cover them with their hands and even hide in bamboo thickets. Their shame had been aroused by those sexual pennants that drew, they believed, immodest attention to what was decently unemphasized before.

But we need not travel in order to encounter such changes in the fortunes of shame. The passage of time, even of a few decades, is enough; and the changeability of the historical panorama of shame becomes particularly conspicuous when we read a description of his own landscape by one of the chief engineers of its transformation. Sigmund Freud, in his study of Leonardo da Vinci, observes with obvious disapproval that the sexual organs have for so long been regarded as *pudenda*, objects of shame, that, 'if one makes a broad survey of the sexual life of our time . . ., one is tempted to say that only with reluctance does the majority of those alive today obey the command to propagate their kind; they feel that their dignity as human beings suffers and is degraded in the process'. Although the desire actually to propagate the kind may not have much increased since then, yet the words 'our time' and 'today', sound very odd to a contemporary of suburban wife-switchers, group-sex purveyors, Masters-and-Johnson gymnasiums, and an entertainment industry in which more and more exhibitionists cater to more and more voyeurs.

But despite all the obvious changes in the mores of talk, conduct and feeling, the association of sex and shame has always been of such intimacy as perhaps only sex can engender; and there is, and has been at all times, something stridently hysterical, hopeless and desperate in the attempts to bring about their dissociation and to render sex shameproof. Indeed, it is only because of the moral bravado and impure excitement in daring displays masked as pure matter-of-factness, and because of the unnatural vibrato in what pretends to be the voice of nature, that the ceaseless public preoccupation with sex has not yet become the bore to all that it already is to the few, indeed so boring a bore that it might be looked upon as a device against overpopulation: before long the mere suggestion of sex might instantly put to sleep the potential propagators of the race. As it is, no such remedial effects are to be expected because at least a modicum of the shocks of shamelessness, even if they are administered with the monotonous regularity of a clockwork, is safeguarded by the imprint of shame on human sexuality – a mark that appears to be indelible although it may at times be reduced to extreme pallor.

In looking askance at the alliance between sex and shame, Freud seems to suspect that, far from being rooted in human nature itself, it results from some dark conspiracy. Perhaps a clan of cunningly clever priests has secured its power over mankind by casting the spell of guilt and shame on man's strongest impulses and has succeeded in 'conditioning' human responses by an insistence continued, as Freud puts it, for a 'long series of generations'. If so, the 'long series' could hardly be longer, and if ever it did 'originate', this must have happened in times immemorial. The question, therefore, is not when it began – an unanswerable question – but rather how it could be maintained through all those ages and societies, many of them ignorant of the customs of the others, unless the readiness to feel the inner rhyme of sex and shame was as deeply ingrained in the human psyche as the sexual instinct itself (and if there is nothing that deserves to be called human psyche – there being merely a random number of possibilities of feeling and thinking, indefinitely variable throughout time – then Freud and every form of psychology have never had a proper subject matter and employment). What remains outside the scope of this discussion is the kind of 'obscene' humour in literature, the 'pornography', so robust and unnervous that only the sheerest prudery can judge it pornographic, the comic-satirical audacity that is unashamed but not shameless. Yet such works are as rare as the vigour that brings them forth – the abundant strength, for instance, of Aristophanes or Rabelais or sometimes Goethe and Balzac. Even more 'outside' stays the incomparably more problematical, manifestly post-Puritan and post-Victorian 'phallic realism' and superstitious shame-exorcism of James Joyce and D. H. Lawrence.

Of course, Freud intermittently acknowledged the 'naturalness' of shame. He did so when he wrote the *Three Essays on Sexuality*. True, when Freud speaks there of shame, he calls it, a little shame-facedly, a 'mental force' that 'like the claims of aesthetic and moral ideals' is meant 'to impede the course of the sexual instinct'. While he amazes once again by his steadfastness, not to say stubbornness, in viewing the world *sub specie sexus*, so that all ethical and artistic achievements, say the Nicomachean Ethics, or the Categorical Imperative, or the saintliness of St Francis, or the murals of the Sistine Chapel, or the music of Mozart, would appear to owe their existence to 'dams' built to 'restrict' the flow of sexuality, he yet acknowledges that shame is *meant* to do this, determined as it is within the 'organic' constitution of man and 'fixed by heredity'. Education, he holds in this context, may merely help to articulate feelings of shame more clearly; it cannot possibly create them.

Certainly, Adam and Eve, for all we know, enjoyed very little positive education unless we regard the instruction Eve received from the subtle serpent as the beginning of pedagogy. It did, after all, lead to the first men's knowing what they did not know before: shame. Having accepted the evil creature's evil teaching and eaten from the Tree of Knowledge, 'they knew that they were naked, and they sewed fig leaves together, and made themselves aprons'. In this great and brief prologue to human existence Adam, after the fatal misdeed, hides from God 'among the trees of the Garden', for 'I was afraid', he says, 'because I was naked'; and with the Lord questioning him – 'Who told thee that thou wast naked? Hast thou eaten of the tree, whereof I commanded thee that thou shouldst not eat?' – there begins the history of the human race. Its beginning is shame; and as even God is not omniscient enough to leave off asking questions, and as He receives no answer, we seem to behold, in beholding shame, the kind of phenomenon of which Goethe says that it is 'an effect without a cause', at least without a sufficient cause, and are ready to believe, again with Goethe, that if, after all, there is a cause, it is hidden from sight somewhere amongst the trees of the garden.

This superb mythological history that, like no other history, has abundantly inspired the art and thought of centuries with its imaginative power, makes shame, together with guilt, the first concomitant of individuation. For as long as Adam and Eve were not ashamed of their nakedness, they were not individuals either, and this despite the poem's speaking of them as man and wife, as Adam and Eve. But *were* they Adam and Eve, man and woman, before 'Adam knew Eve his wife'? Is it not of the essence of man and woman that they desire 'to know' each other? The language of individuation – and there is no other; only music, as Schopenhauer believed, reaches beyond it – oversteps the limits of precise sense when it speaks of states of being that transcend the sphere of individualized existences, of a life before this life or a life hereafter, of life in Eden or life in the promised Land: of the limited bliss of all-oneness: 'The wolf . . . shall dwell with the lamb, and the leopard shall lie down with the kid; and the calf and the young lion and the fatling together; and a little child shall lead them.' Thus speaks Isaiah in his prophetic ecstasy; but what the ecstasy of poetry extols is the surpassing harmony of a world *without* ravenous wolves and anxious lambs, *without* predatory leopards and defenceless kids; and this is as much as to say: a world without wolves or lambs, without leopards or kids. For the wolf who would not feed on lambs is no wolf, the lamb that is no prey to wolves is no lamb. Such a world is a world before or beyond the *principium individuationis*, a world without individual beings. 'And they were both naked . . . and were not ashamed.' This must have been, *pace* Milton's poetic licence, before they were Adam and Eve. As soon as they were, they were ashamed. For the price of individuation is shame.

It may be said that Jehovah, despite His not minding the nakedness of His children before their lapse, was an exceptionally austere and puritanical deity; and there is, by the way, a charming version of the opening scene in Paradise – it is by the notoriously unpuritanical Boccaccio, the first story in his book of cautionary tales about the fall of illustrious personages from the heights of life, *De Casibus Virorum Illustrium* – where the initial bliss of Adam and Eve, 'great and incomparable as it was', is yet enhanced by their having received from the angels delightfully purple clothes which, adorned with gold and jewels, covered their bodies in never diminishing splendour. But far from being prudish, this characteristic Renaissance invention merely renders more poignant the shameful poverty of the post-lapsarian fig leaf apron. Prudery or not, surely the ancient Greeks, makers and worshippers of the most exquisite nudes, were no puritans. Yet it was they who raised the shame to the status of a goddess: Hesiod, their great didactic poet who lived in the eighth century B.C., deified her. Her name was *Aidós.** Yet even long before her acquiring divine status, *aidós* was most highly esteemed as the source of dignity, decency and good manners. Any offence committed against her called forth *Nemesis*, her avenger. Altogether, *aidós* was one of the soul's virtuous possessions which distinguish human beings from animals. She makes as frequent an appearance in Greek literature, above all in Homer, as she is central to the ethics of classical antiquity. Small wonder that every context in which *aidós* appears has been examined by scholars in search for its many nuances; and it is indeed fascinating and rewarding to watch the procession of meanings attendant upon a word that, on the one hand, denotes sexual shame (to the point of its giving the name, sometimes, to what in Latin is *pudenda*, the organs of sex) and, on the other, a disposition of the psyche, the faculty of being ashamed, the negation of which leads to extreme states of inhumanity: for instance to that terrible brutality for which Apollo, in the twenty-fourth book of the *Iliad* upbraids Achilles: like a beast, like a lion, did he behave – that is, *'without aidós'* – when he maltreated the dead Hector. Or else the absence of *aidós* accounts, in the ninth book of the *Odyssey*, for the monster Polyphemus's monstrosity that manifests itself most abominably in his incomprehension of Odysseus's plea to show *aidós*, reverence, respect for the gods, by obeying the laws of hospitality.

Reverence, piety, respect for the individual person, in short: humanity – in *aidós* it is all linked to shame, and not too surprisingly so if we think of the moral reach even in modern usage of its negative: shamelessness. Is there not in the word 'shameless' the utmost of moral opprobrium an adjective can carry? How firmly the law of *aidós* was fixed in Greek minds, and what catas-

---

* For this discussion of *aidós* I am indebted to C. E. v. Erffa's treatise, under the same title, in the supplement volume X X X, 2 of *Philologus*, Leipzig, Dieterich, 1937; also to Richard Harder, *Kleine Schriften*, Munich, C. H. Beck, 1960, 208ff.; and above all to the late Wolfgang Schadewaldt, Professor Emeritus of Classical Greek in the University of Tübingen, who kindly drew my attention to the literature on the subject.

trophes ensued upon its violation, can be seen from a story told by Herodotus. The story is about Candaules, king of the Lydians, his beautiful queen, and his friend and confidant Gyges. Not content with the intimate delights of his marriage, Candaules boasts of them and even insists upon displaying his wife's naked charms to Gyges who is reluctant at first to become party to what he knows to be an outrage, but is finally persuaded to hide in the queen's bed-chamber. She discovers the deceit and is beside herself with the fury of *aidós* having been shamelessly betrayed: Gyges, she demands, must either kill himself or her husband. In the following night Gyges murders the king and assumes his throne as well as his widow.

The story's offerings to the simple moralizer, or the manufacturer of lascivious farce, or the explorer of psychological sophistications, have proved almost as irresistible as those of the celebrated triangle of Amphitryon, Alcmene and Zeus. Thus it is not surprising the later authors, each very different from the others, have put the motif to their own good or not so good uses: Cicero, Hans Sachs, Lafontaine, Gautier, Gide, and above all the German dramatist Friedrich Hebbel in his tragedy *Gyges and His Ring*. He amalgamated it with the tale, told by Plato in the second book of the *Republic*, of an ancestor of Gyges, a shepherd who, searching a cave that an earthquake had torn open in a place where his flock used to graze, found a ring that turned out to possess the magical power of rendering its wearer invisible. Hebbel's Gyges, then, is an invisible voyeur, but not, alas, an inaudible one; and when, amazed by the allurements revealed to him, he utters a loud sigh, the queen, of course, cannot help suspecting the presence of an intruder. From this moment onward she insists upon the tragic solution. Gyges, who in Hebbel's version of the story falls desperately in love with her during those fatal moments, is enticed to murder Candaules, his friend, by her promise that she would marry him; but upon receiving the news of the king's death, she commits suicide.

Hebbel's drama is a failure; not because of his introducing the magic ring, and not only because the age in which he lived seemed to obstruct the writing, out of season, of heroic verse tragedies, but because he fitfully tried to make the story comply with his favourite and all but compulsively pursued Hegelian scheme: the clash of two epochs with their antagonistic moral sensibilities. But instead of historically revaluing the fable, as was obviously his intention, Hebbel merely succeeded in confusing and obscuring Herodotus's simple meaning: *Nemesis* revenging maltreated *Aidós*. From the beginning of Hebbel's play, where Candaules' despite the anxieties of his faithful servant, discards the traditional insignia of his regal office, to the end, or almost the end, where he realizes that he is being punished for having disturbed the slumber of the world – 'Nur rühre nimmer an den Schlaf der Welt' – hints abound of his being a premature innovator, a would-be avant-garde reformer tragically frustrated by the sleepily conservative resistance of his estate. In this perspective the magic ring would almost have the function of an advanced technical device making possible what was unfeasible before. The flaw, of course, is that fairy-tale furnishings do not easily fit the house of progress, nor are triangular bedroom arrangements the appropriate harbingers of noble reforms. Moreover, those Hegelian notions are contradicted, in the very heart of the drama, by the poet himself, who cannot help sympathizing with the queen's terrible if old-fashioned indignation. Of course, if this were not so, there could not be as much as the semblance of true tragedy; but what decides the matter is the fact that *her* feelings alone possess profundity. Dramatically, *aidós* wins over the playwright's Hegelian designs; and this cannot be otherwise, for shame cannot be done away with by the machinations of history if human nature is to have any definite attributes at all. Herodotus, calling the caprice of Candaules unhealthy, sick, took *aidós* to be such a quality.

So did Homer. In our historical minds we are quite prepared to find that many Victorian novels may serve as lexica of genteel manners, or that even in a comedy by Shakespeare a young woman, beside herself with jealousy, should address another:

> Have you no modesty, no maiden shame,
> No touch of bashefulness? . . .*

But we might not take it for granted that in a great and representative poetic work, created long before Christ, possibly three

* *A Midsummer Night's Dream* III, ii, 285f.

thousand years ago, modesty, maiden shame, and much more than a touch of bashfulness would emerge as the signs of good conduct. Yet the book Nausicaa, the sixth of Homer's *Odyssey*, is pervaded by the lyrical tenderness of these virtues. The following is a charming example. Athene, the goddess 'of the shining eyes', had appeared in a dream to Nausicaa, the royal princess of the Phaeacians, announcing the approach of her marriage and admonishing her to prepare the wedding feast by having all the household's clothes and linen washed in the mouth of a nearby river. With this, the goddess planned to help the ship-wrecked and exhausted Odysseus, who was asleep in an olive thicket on the river's bank. It is one of those roundabout strata-gems adopted by the Homeric deities to direct the lives of their protegées, indeed to raise accident to the rank of destiny: Nausicaa was meant to discover Odysseus and take him to the palace of her father, King Alcinous; and as, in obedience to Athene, she now begs him to let her have a wagon for the washing expedition, she gives, elaborating Homerically, many a reason for it, avoiding the real one. She was too ashamed to mention the promised wedding.

Everything then proceeds as planned by Athene: Odysseus awakes from the noise made by Nausicaa's party of girls and creeps out 'from under the bushes, after breaking off with his great hand a leafy bough from the thicket to conceal his naked man-hood'. Even so, it is only under the constraint of necessity that he appears before the women in his nakedness. 'Begrimed with salty mud', as he is, 'he makes a gruesome sight and sends them scuttling in every direction'. Only Nausicaa remains, 'emboldened by Athene, who helped her not to tremble'. Would she, Odysseus implores her, direct him to the town and give him some clothing, and be it only the wrapper in which she brought the linen? Scolding them for their timidity, Nausicaa calls out to the girls to return and asks them to let the divinely ordained kindness towards distressed strangers prevail over fear and shyness. Yet when, at Nausicaa's instruction, they lead him down to the river to wash him, Odysseus bids them to go back again and leave him to bathe by himself, for he is ashamed, he says, to be naked in their presence. Even the Greeks in the age of Homer regarded it as natural that the human body, in the presence of others, should be clothed; even they did not look upon clothes as the cover of nudity, but rather on nudity as being without clothes.

Pausanias, who in the second century A.D. collected what he found of stories from the Greek past and, traveller that he was, described the Greek lands, tells in his *Description of Greece* how the newly wed Odysseus and Penelope departed from the kingdom of Sparta, where her father, Icarius, much wanted them to settle down. He even pursued them after they had left and once more tried to persuade them, but in vain; and as he put before his daughter the choice of either returning with him or following her husband, she did not answer. She merely wrapped herself in her mantle and veiled her face. This was enough for Icarius to know that he had lost her to Odysseus, but instead of being angry, he erected in the place where he had caught up with them a statue in honour of the goddess *Aidós*. A little like Nausicaa in the *Odyssey*, Penelope was silenced by shame when she would have had to speak of her marriage and to hurt her father by the confession that she loved Odysseus more than him. Shame, respect and consideration mingle in her veiling herself.

This gesture contains the whole meaning of *aidós* and, moreover, reveals the link that exists between this warrant of humaneness and the awe felt in the face of the holy. For the holy too demands that man should cover himself; and even in his most 'positivistic' book, *Human, All-too-Human*, Nietzsche said that shame is everywhere where there is 'mystery', and never mind the inverted commas which the mood of this work forced upon what, after all, *is* mysterious. There were times when he meditated upon the conjunction of shame and mystery without those marks punctuating embarrassment. Some years before, at the time of *The Birth of Tragedy*, he entered in his notebook the entirely Schopenhauerian observation that shame seems to occur where man feels that 'he is nothing but a tool in the hands of a will infinitely greater than is his own within his separate individuality', and some years later, at the time of *Zarathustra*, shame for him has become the alpha and omega of the history of man and man himself 'the animal with red cheeks', his having acquired them because there were so many occasions for him to blush. Shame is now 'the fiend that attached himself to man when he desired to be more than an animal' – fiend, that is, to the animal in him.

For the Greeks, then, *aidós* was the warrant of humaneness, and shame an aspect of *aidós*; and Nietzsche is surely right in regarding shame as so essentially human that no humanity is thinkable without it. This, of course, and once more, does not mean that the *manners* of shame are always the same. Like all manners, they belong to the stuff of history. Not all women in all historical epochs would, like Nausicaa, be ashamed to speak to their fathers of their approaching weddings, or, like Penelope, of their great love for their husbands (or, as is the case with Shakespeare's Cordelia, for their fathers); and indeed the propensity for shame is so malleable that propaganda might one day succeed, as Nietzsche remarked, in evoking shocks of indecency at the mention of toothbrushes. But what *is* meant, is the very capacity for experiencing shame, the design of shame inscribed in the human soul. If this is a *sine qua non* of humanity, it follows that the campaigns of shamelessness, although they may be waged in the name of liberating ideologies, consciously or unconsciously have as their end the crippling of humaneness.

Ideology. One of the most intriguing dilemmas known (or, rather, only half-known) to the human psyche, and much aggravated in modern history, is that between the notions which the mind conceives and the ideas which the soul has, as it were, of itself and by itself; between the beliefs uttered in the outer trafficking of opinions and those to which unteachably the psyche clings; between, in brief, ideology and substance. Where these are at loggerheads, authenticity is brought into question, and surely the questioning of authenticity has been one of the intellectual obsessions of the age from Rousseau to the Existentialists. It would be impossible to present the major literary and speculative enterprises of the nineteenth and twentieth centuries without giving due weight to 'the problem of authenticity'. Merely to mention Constant's *Adolphe*, or Flaubert's *Madame Bovary*, or most of Henry James's novels, or André Gide's *Les Faux-monnayeurs*, or Thomas Mann's *Felix Krull*, or Freud's '*Id*' believing hardly a word the '*Ego*' says, or Heidegger's beings without Being, or Sartre's *mauvaise foi* is to feel all around the tentacles of the unauthentic octopus.

Perhaps it is Dostoevsky's Raskolnikov who is the most impressive character among the many who live, cheat, kill, struggle or repent in the expanses stretching between the persuasions of the intellect and the unpersuaded nature of the soul; but Stendhal's *Le Rouge et le Noir* contains the wittiest account of an episode enacted in that place. The scene is the bedroom of Mathilde de la Mole, the intelligent, cynical, sentimental, proud daughter of Julien Sorel's aristocratic employer. They fall in love with each other, if so simple a phrase is permissible where everything is complexity. Her love has chosen the interesting upstart partly from contempt for the mediocrity of her own 'Restoration' class. One night he climbs up to her window as she had asked him to do, not as much because she desired his amorous visit as in order to test his ardour and courage. Now, as he is in her room, it is less from passion – 'passion', she reflects, 'is after all only a model that is imitated rather than realized' – than from a 'sense of duty', a perversely programmatic duty, that she becomes his mistress: 'The poor boy was very brave, and I should make him happy, or I lack character.' Of course, Stendhal, the observer of the profundities and antics of sexual love, author of *De l'amour*, would know that there was 'no spontaneity in her throughout the night', and instead of 'that happiness of which she had read in novels', she found only 'misery and shame'.

She has done her duty by the 'poor boy' as well as by her intellectual convictions: by the contempt, above all, in which she holds the conventions of her society. Is it in spite or because of this that now she feels nothing but misery and shame? Neuroses are made of such misunderstandings between the tenets of the mind and the endowments of the psyche, with the intelligence eventually looking in helpless bewilderment at its being refuted by the soul. The final outcome may well be a hysterical intelligence and a soul not enlightened but darkened and diminished. Shame is not to be cheated by ideological opinions disguised as superior judgments. On the other hand: had Mathilde de la Mole been less of an ideologue and more of a woman passionately desiring Julien Sorel, that night would not have left her just miserable and ashamed; she would have come to know that the only conqueror of shame is the passion of love, the pleasures of which even feed on the soul's shy opposition to the conquest. This is why the transports of love would be unknown in a world without shame: Eros would not have taken delight in a shameless Psyche.

'Dans le véritable amour c'est l'âme qui enveloppe le corps': In true love it is the soul that envelops the body. It was probably the seventeenth-century French quietist Madame Guyon who wrote the sentence which Nietzsche called 'das züchtigste Wort', the chastest word, he had ever heard. It is unlikely that he knew its perfect foil, Shakespeare's sonnet about the sexual act:

> The expense of spirit in a waste of shame
> Is lust in action . . .

It is not chaste, although it is outraged chastity that so bitterly denounces the shame of lust. But then, it is not about love.*

Max Scheler's fragmentary essay on 'Shame and Feelings of Shame', written as early as 1913 and only posthumously published, contains in all its unchecked meandering much that is illuminating; for instance, the observation that in shame ' "the spirit" and "the flesh", the eternal and the temporal, essence and existence, meet in a strange, and dark manner'. Even in 1913 'the spirit' and 'the flesh' demanded quotation marks and received them; and indeed, those classical opposites have long since been discarded, together with 'mind' and 'body', 'body' and 'soul', although the philosophical resources of the age have proved insufficient for their satisfactory replacement. Be this as it may, the ancient meaning of those opposites can hardly be recaptured in times that have reversed St Mark's 'The spirit truly is ready, but the flesh is weak' by emboldening the flesh to be strong and ready at almost any time and leaving the enfeebled spirit to its own or its analyst's devices. But if there is still a chance of comprehending – directly and without the fuss of historical examination – what was meant by those great dualities, it is through the experience of shame. For in the first place, if not also the last, man is capable of being ashamed of almost anything that is nature about him, nature's nature, as it were, not human nature; of anything that shows him to be enslaved by laws and necessities impervious to his own will, and be it only the law of gravitation that, conspiring against his

---

* It was a student of mine who once, perhaps unwittingly, succeeded in turning the Freudian wheel full circle. I was a visiting teacher in an East Coast university and, insufficiently aware yet of the epidemic of psychological indigestion that had befallen the region, I expressed incredulity when he told me that more than half my class was undergoing psychoanalytical treatment. 'What is wrong with them?', I asked. His answer was: 'They all suffer from repressed chastity.'

upright dignity, brings him to fall on a slippery pavement. In such a moment he prefers not to have onlookers all around him.

Goethe even hated to be reminded of man's closeness to animal nature by the histrionics of apes. His beloved Ottilie, in *Effective Affinities*, calls them nasty creatures, humiliating to watch, and wonders how anyone can overcome this revulsion to the extent of drawing or painting them. Goethe was far from being a puritan; yet in those sublime verse passages celebrating, at the conclusion of *Faust II*, the salvation and transfiguration of Faust's soul, the angels that carry him bodily to heaven gently complain that, purified though he is, there still attaches to him 'ein Erdenrest zu tragen peinlich', a remnant of earthiness 'painful to bear' – painful in its lingering impurity. Moreover, the aversion to displaying that dependence on nature which man shares with animals may even include the need for nourishment. It was certainly hunger and digestion that Nietzsche had in mind when he said that 'the belly is the reason why man does not find it too easy to take himself for a god'. Also, man's natural need for nourishment shows very clearly that he has only two means of defence against the superior power of nature: concealment or ritualization; and there is no culture in which this necessity is not humanized and dignified by custom and etiquette, from simple table manners to the elaborate rituals of banqueting. Yet, while the giving-in of the hungry to the compulsion of nature is, if it is rewarded with food, entirely pleasurable, the defeat of the dying is terrible. The terror of death and its potential shame, arising from this defeat, were in better seasons of the human spirit mitigated or even altogether banished by the hope of redemption and resurrection or else the celebrations of the tragic. This is not so in the present epoch, which is quick in forgetfulness, obtuse to damnation, and so far as tragedy is concerned, it has sold all entrance tickets to the past. The rhetoric of the tragic may still survive in a somewhat debauched and dishevelled state, but in the new psychological surroundings cannot disguise the shame of death, not to mention its many near or distant relations: the unease that meets advancing age, the deceptions practised to conceal it, death's terrible postponement by means of medical techniques that prolong not as much living as dying, and the sad embarrassment of funerals.

Man ashamed

Death, terrible to say, has joined the class of *pudenda* just as if dramatically to make up for the losses inflicted elsewhere on Shame by shamelessness. Not to have succeeded in abolishing death is vaguely suspected to be the collective failure of science and progress. Nonetheless there must always have been, where death was, also an element of shame, productive of the exorbitant ceremonial ritualizations that have surrounded it in all traditions. Indeed, this is what death has in common with marriage, the festivities of the wedding, of that sexual event which Nausicaa was too bashful to mention in speaking to her father. Death too, and much more so, does not invite outspokenness, as can be seen from the abundance of euphemisms its terror and shame have provoked, euphemisms often shameless themselves in their obvious motivation. The shame of a death that is not attended by ritual is even the theme of one of the great tragedies of classical antiquity: of Sophocles' *Antigone*. For she – and, for that matter, all the other personages involved – are destroyed by the insult Antigone's pieties suffer when the king decrees that her brother, his enemy who was killed in battle, should be denied burial and inhumanly be seen to suffer what all animal nature suffers in death: the body's decomposition, helped by devouring beasts.

For all to see. Like language, love, or civilization itself, shame would be unthinkable if man had been designed to live entirely by himself, although even in this hypothetical condition he may choose God as his 'Other'. Despite this, it would be wrong to assume that shame is entirely a 'social phenomenon'. For in the last analysis, man is, when he is ashamed, ashamed of himself and his own nature, even if it is in the sight or knowledge of others that he is shocked into the most poignant awareness of his shameful condition. When Sartre was still a philosopher (and had not yet abandoned himself to a political fanaticism reinforced by lack of political wisdom) be knew this: shame, he wrote in *Being and Nothing*, makes a man recognize that he *is* as the other sees him. And certainly, what does gaze at him through the eyes of another person, even if the other person is a stranger, is he himself.

In the fourth book of Nietzsche's *Zarathustra* there occurs one of the strangest meetings the prophet has in the course of his strange perambulations. It is in the valley of death that he comes upon 'the ugliest man', a pitiably disfigured creature, and

231

as he sees him, Zarathustra is overcome by 'a profound sense of shame' and, 'blushing right up to his white hair', he averts his eyes and makes haste to leave the terrible sight behind. But it is his blushing by which 'the ugliest man knows him: That is how I recognized you as Zarathustra'. By his betraying shame, he is recognized as the 'higher being', and the ugliest man shouts after him: 'Guess my riddle, ... the riddle that I am ... who am I?' and what is meant by 'the revenge taken on the witness'? Zarathustra stops and solves the riddle: '*You are the murderer of God*', he says, and now 'let me go. You could not *bear* him who saw *you* – who always saw you through and through, you ugliest man! You took revenge on this witness!' Yes, says the ugliest man, 'he *had* to die: ... he saw man's ... concealed disgrace and ugliness. His pity knew no shame: he crawled into my dirtiest nooks ... He always saw *me*: on such a witness I wanted to have revenge or not live myself. The god who saw everything, ... this god had to die. Man cannot bear it that such a witness should live.'

This is Nietzsche–Zarathustra's last and most disguised proclamation of the *Übermensch*. God, the witness, is being killed by 'the ugliest man' so that there should be no need any more for shame. Is the ugliest man then really no longer ashamed, not even in the face of Zarathustra, who blushes for him? If such questions are to be rendered illegitimate, man himself would have to be left behind, for 'the ugliest man' is nothing but a superlatively ungainly name for man himself: the utopian *Übermensch*, the most beautiful human or superhuman being, would have to take his place. Only he would know of nothing to be ashamed of and thus, paradoxically, not mind being seen by God. Yet if the *Übermensch* is an unattainable goal, the ugliest man, surely, has made a mistake. He would have had to kill shame, not God, in order to forget what it is like to feel ashamed. For shame is not 'another': it is he himself who sees himself through the eyes of God – and despises himself. Zarathustra knows this. As he moves on, he muses: 'None have I found yet who despises himself so deeply. That too is a kind of height.' – It is, despite the Wagnerian *mise en scène*, a profound story. Had the ugliest man succeeded in doing what he really desired to do and destroyed shame, he would have abolished man. For man, to reverse the last sentence of *The Trial*, would not outlive his ability to be ashamed.

13

Theodor Fontane

the extraordinary education of a Prussian apothecary

I T is not far from the estuary of the Rhône, in the region – roughly
–between Toulouse and Montpellier, where the Western border of
the Gascogne meets the foothills of the Cévennes. This relatively small
part of the earth was the homeland of my ancestors, both from my father's
and from my mother's side. They lived in neighbouring districts, and
because two profoundly different kinds of people exist within this narrow
space, it surely is not surprising that *mes ancêtres* reflect these differences.
They persisted in my parents despite the fact that their families, long
since, had transplanted themselves into the Mark Brandenburg. My
father was a big, impressive Gascognian, full of *bonhomie*, fantasies and
humour, a *causeur*, fond of telling stories and, when he was completely
at ease, tall stories – 'Gasconnades'. My mother, on the other hand, was
a child of the Southern Cévennes, a slender, delicate woman with black
hair, eyes like coal, energetic, selfless, a strong character, and of so
passionate a nature that my father used to say of her: 'If she had stayed
where she came from, the wars of the Cévennes would rage to this very
day.'

By the 'wars of the Cévennes' Fontane *père* meant the uprisings,
in 1638, of the Huguenots (although his wife was far from being
a religious fanatic). The son's *Years of my Childhood (Meine Kinder-
jahre*), from which this passage comes, appeared in 1894, when
he was seventy-five years old. Fontane rightly called it 'an autobiographical *novel*' for his ancestors were to a large extent Germans
after Jacques François Fontaine, a Calvinist who manufactured
stockings in Nîmes, left France in 1694 and settled in Germany.

Theodor Fontane's grandfather was the first who officially
dropped the *i* in 'Fontaine'. He had a successful career at the courts
of the Prussian king Friedrich Wilhelm II and Queen Luise. A
contemporary court diarist wrote of him, 'A Herr Fontane, painter
by trade, has become Cabinet secretary to the Queen; he paints
badly, but speaks French well.' His grandson, born in 1819, would
no longer enjoy such linguistic distinction. He was to become
a very good writer, but his French was poor. True, his father,
son of the bad painter and his second wife, a Westphalian woman,
was christened Louis Henri, but as the beloved amateur teacher
of his son, who had inherited but hardly ever used 'Henri' as his
first Christian name, he must have badly neglected French in his

rather improvised syllabus. Although the family pronounced their name without sounding the *e*, the French nasal pronunciation was heard only 'on Sundays and holidays', as Theodor's son Friedrich (who became his father's publisher) once remarked.

It seemed advisable to give this sketchy account of Fontane's genealogy because much, far too much, has been made – in explaining his artistry or, in accordance with political fashion, in justifying his being neglected – of his 'purely' French descent. The fact is that there is nothing 'pure' in his family history. At the same time it is very strange that the most 'Gallic' among the German writers of the late nineteenth century had such tenuous links not only with the French language, but also with French literature. It would be useless to seek a place for him in a literary mode fashioned by Stendhal, Balzac, and Flaubert; and this is not a matter of comparative importance but of essential difference. The truth is that Germany's first modern 'realist' novelist before Thomas Mann (first not in time – well, yes, there were Freytag and Spielhagen and Gutzkow before him – but in rank) would read the books of his French predecessors or contemporaries, if he read them at all, in German translations, and this despite his father's veneration of Napoleon. Old Fontane's love of the heroic and the adventurous was altogether excessive. In his apothecary's existence it took the form of gambling and led to his bourgeois Waterloo: he lost his pharmacy in Swinemünde by the Baltic sea (where he had moved from Neuruppin in the Mark Brandenburg, birthplace of his son Theodor) and finally also lost his wife, who left him because she could not bear the perpetual threat of financial ruin.

Indeed, one of the most dramatic lessons in history that young Henri Theodor received from his father, and later described with belletristic artistry and humorous affection, would take the form of a scene in which the father played the part of a flank man in a Napoleonic military detachment while the boy was the commanding officer. 'Latour d'Auvergne', the son would call out, and father, standing to attention, would answer in his basso profundo voice, 'Il n'est pas ici.' 'Où est-il donc?' 'Il est mort sur le champ d'honneur.' This was how Latour's comrades, by daily repeating the scene, honoured the memory of the man whom Napoleon designated 'le premier grenadier de France'. Theodor

Fontane would never forget such pedagogy, neither its subjects nor its methods, and would come to detest the dry pedantry of orthodox school instruction. In the most moving chapter of *Years of my Childhood* – an insertion of a much later episode, his last visit at his father's solitary house in the country – the old man would talk about his school days in Neuruppin: 'I was embarrassed sometimes how much more I knew than the teachers, except of course Horace and the irregular verbs. There was, for instance, old Starke. His hobbyhorse was Aristotle; and what Aristotle had long since forgotten, Starke knew. But what *really* mattered, *that* he didn't know. Our schools teach us the wrong things. Nobody will convince me that this isn't so. People don't learn what they ought to learn.'

Napoleon and Latour notwithstanding, old Fontane's heroes were not necessarily French. At least one was Prussian. In another passage of *Years of my Childhood* – this time a true childhood memory – Fontane describes his father's living room in Swinemünde. The sofa was its most important piece of furniture – at least to the apothecary himself, who would lie down on it for his prolonged after-lunch naps (a habit that no doubt contributed to the failure of the pharmacy). Above the sofa there hung a much-treasured heirloom: an engraving with the caption 'Frédéric le Grand retournant à Sanssouci après les manoeuvres de Potsdam, accompagné de ses généraux'. It was reportedly a very sound sleep that was guarded by so dependable a warrior; and young Fontane stood before this picture again and again, gazing intently into the eyes of the Prussian king, and did so 'with a premonition, perhaps, that he would become my own favourite hero'.

Napoleon and Frédéric le Grand (in the king's preferred writing of his name), France and Prussia, 'Fontaine' and Brandenburg: there is nothing unusual in this combination – however surprising it may seem in other contexts. In the 'French Colony' in Prussia – the Fontanes belonged to it – it was commonplace. This French Colony – the most important concentration in Germany of the Calvinist French expatriates, the Huguenots – came into being in 1685 when Friedrich Wilhelm, the Grand Elector of Brandenburg, opened his country to the French refugees who fled after Louis XIV had revoked the religiously tolerant Edict of Nantes of 1598. They were even treated in a privileged way and developed into a state within the state, culturally and economically prosperous and politically loyal. Fontane, who joked that every third Berliner was a Frenchman, described the members of the Colony as puritanically stiff, earnest and ambitious – more Prussian than the Prussians. He might have said it of himself. He certainly used every puritanical cliché when he gave his exceedingly negative impressions of his first visit to 'lascivious' Paris, and called Prussia his true home in a poem he wrote in 1885 to celebrate the two-hundredth birthday of the French Colony. He was sixty-six then and his novelistic masterpieces, *Effi Briest* and *Der Stechlin* were still to be written. This is what makes it so difficult to write a well-proportioned biography of Fontane. For what he said of his father may well be said of him: 'What he was in the end, was his real self.'

Before his late liberation as a writer, Fontane's professional career was varied and most insecure. In consequence, he postponed for five years marrying the woman to whom he had become engaged in 1845, and often reproached himself for making her life so uncomfortable. What, then, was his profession? To begin with, he followed in his father's footsteps and was apprenticed to several apothecaries. But he knew this could not be for life. In his spare time, illicitly extended now and then, he wrote, rehearsing many genres; poetry, story, epic, journalism. His early fictional writings brought him the attention of some of the literary celebrities in Berlin (none of them destined to attain to the rank in German literary history that is now justly and safely assigned to him), and he was invited to join a literary circle, whimsically called 'The Tunnel above the Spree' (the Spree is the river that flows through Berlin). There the young apothecary recited his first ballads, which faithfully accepted as their model the creations of the German masters of the genre: Bürger and Schiller and Goethe. He earned much applause from 'The Tunnel' and through its members came to know many literary personalities even outside the club.

In 1844 he was invited by a friend, wealthier than he, to join him on a trip to England. During these two weeks in London he was in a state of perpetual enchantment and never quite 'recovered' from it. Not even the mounting criticism of England's social conditions, an indignation widespread and culminating a

year later in Friedrich Engel's book about the wretchedness of
the English proletariat, damped his enthusiasm for the country
in which he breathed the air of the great world and of political
freedom. Although he was to say on one occasion that the Frenchman in him was responsible for his style, the *Plauderton*, the
causerie, the conversational lightness, no French writer had any
strong influence on him, certainly none that would be comparable
to the impression made by Shakespeare, Scott, Thackeray,
Dickens, or Byron – leaving aside the role that in later years the
ballads of Scotland and the history and landscapes of England
and 'beyond the Tweed' would play in forming his imagination,
a role almost as important as that of the Mark Brandenburg.

He would visit England again; indeed in 1855 it seemed that
he might settle there permanently. He had terminated, six years
before, his uncongenial and tedious activities as a pharmacist and,
to finance his married life, accepted in 1850 a position in the
'Literary Cabinet', the central agency for controlling the press set
up within the Prussian Ministry of the Interior. He obtained this
highly 'reactionary' appointment (he later referred to it as having
sold himself) despite the fact that, as the Berlin correspondent
of the liberal *Dresdner Zeitung*, he supplied the Saxon newspaper
with 'horror stories' of the lawless police regime that had replaced
the rule of the honest and law-abiding Prussian army. When the
editor rejected one of his articles in praise of the old Prussian
militarism, Fontane, rather than continue 'to please those *par force*
democrats', made his peace with that arbitrary police government
by joining its censorship 'cabinet'.

If we remember that he had played the revolutionary on the
Berlin barricades in March 1848 – a somewhat confused role that
he himself described with considerable *vis comica*: how he tried
single-handedly and in vain to break into a church ('Protestant
churches are always locked') in order to ring the bells and thus
rouse the masses ('All great events begin with the ringing of bells');
and how later that day he seized a gun from the stage properties
of an undefended theatre (it was probably used 'fifteen years before
in the popular comedy *Seven Girls in Uniform*') and filled it with
so much powder that it became blocked rather than loaded; and
how in the midst of the turmoil his father arrived and the two
went to drink coffee in a peaceful garden restaurant – if we

remember all this, without omitting the less facetious journalistic contributions he made at the time to the revolutionary cause, we can appreciate that he earned the reputation of an *unsicherer Kantonist*, a politically unreliable character. But his love of Prussia – the 'good Prussia' – was unshakable, and so was his admiration of England despite the sobering effect that the years spent in the country (from September 1855 until January 1859) had upon his initial enthusiasm. There too he moved in official business: as the founder and director of a German–English Press Office, a Prussian propaganda centre. It lasted only six months, but Fontane stayed in England as the foreign correspondent of a variety of German newspapers.

Years of uncertainty, restlessness, and failure followed upon his return to Berlin in 1859; yet he gradually emerged as a literary figure. He began to write his *Wanderungen durch die Mark Branden-burg* in the belief that this austere part of the German lands with its richly aristocratic history had not yet found its 'singer'. The 'song' was to become longer and longer, until in 1882 it filled four volumes. What he later said of the style in which he undertook those 'walks' applies to many more of his writings – as it does to the works of his Austrian counterpart Adalbert Stifter: 'It was my proud intention to describe the seemingly most insignificant things with the most detailed precision and thus to raise them to a certain artistic level, indeed to make them *interesting* by means of the kind of simplicity and transparency that appears to be easy but is most difficult to achieve.' During the years following his return from London, he also published the journalistic exploits of his 'travelsome' time in Britain, *From England* and *Beyond the Tweed*, but he could still not afford to become a 'free writer', a vocation he described as ranking in respectability next to that of 'travelling showman'; and so eventually, in 1860, he joined the staff of the arch-conservative Berlin *Kreuzzeitung*, a journal that Nietzsche regarded as representing the 'German spirit' at its most hideous.

Yet Fontane later justified this alliance by saying that 'all serious people who show dependability, constancy, character, and (which is all right with me) a little fanaticism and obstinacy – that all such people are conservatives; the rest is nothing but quicksand'. Before long, however, his own conservatism ceased to be dependable. He felt 'chained' to the *Kreuzzeitung*, and in a letter to his wife – it made her apprehensive of yet another spell of economic instability – called the newspaper intolerably 'brutal', masking with Christian rhetoric its own 'inhumanity'. Indeed, he left the *Kreuzzeitung* in 1870 to become the drama critic of the more liberal *Vossische Zeitung*. In this new function he, the descendant of French Protestants, courageously rejected a play by the firmly established and all but unassailable Karl Gutzkow on account of his crude anti-Catholicism. And although, in his very first review, he had written approvingly of the patriotic demonstrations with which an audience, eager for the war against France, responded to the national liberation oratory of Schiller's *Wilhelm Tell*, he later praised a decidedly 'unpatriotic' play that caused one of the most notorious scandals of the Berlin theatre: Gerhart Hauptmann's *Before Sunrise* (*Vor Sonnenaufgang*). Thus the critic Fontane helped to inaugurate the naturalist revolution in German drama.

During the war against France, Fontane's work as a critic, hardly begun, was interrupted by his short but eventful trip, as a reporter, to the French theatre of war, where he was arrested in October 1870. He was suspected of being a Prussian spy, but was soon released at the intervention, it is said, of Bismarck himself. In December of the same year he was back in his seat in the Berlin theatre. *Prisoner of War* (*Kriegsgefangen*) is the literary product of his martial adventure. It is free of any chauvinism, so much so that it became the first book of Fontane's that was translated into French. But he was still not simply a man of literature. Only after a brief and uncongenial appointment as First Secretary of the Berlin Academy of Arts did he decide that he could no longer play any part in the 'totally confused machinery' of the state or its more or less official representations and, to the rancorous dismay of his wife, at last hazarded the career of an independent writer.

'The novel', he said in the autumn of that decisive year, 'is my only solace in these disconsolate days ... Working at it, I know for sure that I cannot be anything else but a writer.' The historical novel in question, a work of long gestation, was hardly received as promising a novelist of genius. *Before the Storm* (*Vor dem Sturm*) was its title, its subject an episode from the uprising of Prussia against Napoleon in 1812–13, and its sentiments were 'religious,

moral, and patriotic'. The author himself said so. Who would have
expected such unambiguously pious attachments from the loyal
son of a Napoleon-besotted father or from a writer who, after
his 'prostitution' in the service of the Prussian 'Literary Cabinet'
and the 'religious, moral, and patriotic' *Kreuzzeitung*, had at last
asserted his freedom? But he also described the theme of the novel
as something more subtle and important: 'A great idea, a great
moment, breaks into very simple human conditions.' The delineations of 'simple human conditions' did not meet with universal
applause. One influential critic found it all rather silly. Dramatic
tension, he asked? Perhaps; but only if one is prepared patiently
to wait for resolutions brought about by an outing in a coach
or by setting the table or by going to bed.

Certainly, such 'simplicities' may be too simple, but the theme
itself, just as the historical subject, is reminiscent of *War and Peace*,
and although clashes between the commonplace and 'the great
moment' are not new in the literature of the nineteenth century,
this theme is, by virtue of his temperament and artistic disposition,
Fontane's very own, just as it was Chekhov's; and there *is* something Chekhovian in this citizen of the Mark Brandenburg, son
of the apothecary from Neuruppin and Swinemünde. (As the incongruity between spectacular deeds and mediocre doers, between
the heroic measure of the suffering and the unheroic character
of the sufferers, it has become one of the most terrible themes
of our age.)

After *Before the Storm* there were to be many novels and novellas:
eighteen, to be exact. Among the novellas his artistically most
accomplished work is *Irretrievable (Unwiederbringlich)*. When the
first novel of his newly won freedom appeared in 1878, Fontane
was fifty-nine; at the time of *Irretrievable*, seventy-three – and his
greatest works were still to come. This may be unique in the
history of literature. Tolstoy was ten years younger than Fontane,
but *Before the Storm* was published ten years after *War and Peace*,
not to count the years by which *Anna Karenina* is older than
Fontane's novel of adultery *Effi Briest*. The latter appeared in the
same year as *The Poggenpuhl Family (Die Poggenpuhls)*: in 1896, when
Fontane was seventy-seven. It seems both incredible that *Effi
Briest* was written by so old a man and clear that Fontane could
not possibly have written it when he was younger. For in his

younger days he was given to uttering firm convictions and having
'opinions', different ones at different times. He held no beliefs
for any length of time, and sometimes not even the same beliefs
at the same moment. It has justly been said of him that there is
no political advocate in the warring world of politics who could
not support his advocacy with one or other of the many contradictory utterances of Fontane's.

'The bourgeois is terrible', he would say, and would praise the
proletariat for being incomparably more genuine, more vital, and
more truthful. It accords with this – but far less with his wholly
admiring poem on Bismarck that is inscribed on the tomb of the
'Iron Chancellor' only half admired by him – that he called Gerhart
Hauptmann's most revolutionary drama, *The Weavers* (*Die Weber*),
a 'splendid achievement' that would inaugurate 'a new epoch' in
German literature. But he is offended by the crass social criticism
of Turgenev and Zola, objecting to their 'naturalism' because it
is 'too pessimistic'. But since he himself, the 'realist', is pessimistic
enough, or at least extremely sceptical with regard to 'human
nature', one cannot help suspecting that what he means by the
pessimism of the 'naturalists' is their tendency to look upon the
good manners of style as a violation of truth, the truth that comes
to light through 'revolutions' in art as well as in politics. And
revolutions, he writes, 'are usually initiated by the rabble, by
adventurers, or by madmen'. Yet instantly he exclaims, 'But what
would have become of us without revolutions!' This is the same
Fontane who earlier pronounced that there could not be *any* social
order without the masses being kept down by fear or religion,
by the regimen of powerful governments, secular or ecclesiastical:
'Any attempt to do without the great overlords of the world',
he concluded, 'can safely be regarded as having failed once and
for all.'

In other words, Fontane was a born novelist, even if this birth
took place late in his life. What, then, did the art of the novel
and his advancing years teach him that he had not learned as a
journalist, as an author of travelogues, or even as a maker of poems
and ballads? He himself rather naively believed that it was respect
for what *is* rather than a hankering for what ought to be, the
almost passive readiness to let life speak for itself rather than tell
it how it should behave, to allow every character – no, not the

right to his own deeds and convictions, but the unquestionable privilege of his existence. Fontane discovered that he was a novelist – and with some of his works he was a great novelist – when after years of uncomfortably upholding contradictory 'ideologies', he arrived at the exact point at which Turgenev confessed that he felt always lost when challenged to say what he 'in his own person' felt or believed about this or that without being given the chance of shifting the responsibility to the exchanges, the dialogue, of imaginary characters: 'As for myself, it has always seemed to me that I might just as well, and with equal right, maintain the opposite of what I was saying.' This is – almost word for word – what one of Fontane's most impressive and lovable creations, Dubslav von Stechlin in *Der Stechlin*, says after having ventured a definite opinion: 'And if I had said the opposite, it would be equally right' – which does not prevent the old man from being obstinately and delightfully sure about certain principles of morality. Still, it was Keats who said that 'the poetical Character has no character. It has as much delight in conceiving an Iago as an Imogen. What shocks the virtuous philosopher delights the chameleon Poet.' The 'chameleon' in the poet certainly did shock, for instance, Kierkegaard and – in one of the greatest inner dramas of literary history – Tolstoy.

Dubslav's words are Fontane's own: 'And if I had said the opposite, it would be equally right.' To be sure, this would be incongruous and even perverse when uttered by the critic sitting in judgment of performances in the theatre, or by the maker of moral or political decisions; yet it is 'dubiously', 'dialectically', 'metaphysically' true in the mouth of one who is about to become a very considerable novelist. Is this the *Erkenntnis*, the knowledge, that Fontane meant when he quoted Goethe's belief that the work of the *good* poet or writer reflects not some vague and partial intuition, but the measure of his knowing insight? Is this what made the critic into a novelist, into a writer who said of his art that it was 'psychography and criticism' and, coming from the dark ground of creativity, was ordered, pruned and trimmed in the sobering light of day? Very likely. It was the *Erkenntnis*, Turgenev's insight, that the truth of a novel, of any work of art, is far beyond the truths of convictions and opinions. These are at all times mere fragments within the ultimate justification of

the whole – or indeed its senselessness. ('Was soll der Unsinn'
– 'What on earth is it all about?' – was what Fontane's soul every
so often muttered to itself.)

In *Effi Briest* it is certainly Fontane himself speaking – or at
least the part of himself that is ineradicably 'Prussian' – when
Instetten, Effi Briest's husband, in making up his mind to
challenge his wife's lover to a duel, insists on the necessity of
the social order being protected by the power of established
morality. Yes, Fontane himself – or what is left of his self once
it has withdrawn, leaving the stage to the interplay of opposing
natures and convictions. But has this self ever really and literally
withdrawn? Or is speaking like this only an aesthetic *façon de parler*?
Is not most literature critique, critique of life? And if so, who
is the critic? Most of Fontane's works are certainly a critique of
the moral ideas and social institutions of the epoch, to the same
degree that they *reflect* their increasing instability. This much he
has in common with Ibsen, Zola, Shaw (or rather, they with him)
or even with Schnitzler (how much of Fontane's most 'modern'
book, *Schach von Wuthenow*, is there in the early Schnitzler!). Yet
there is an important difference. For while Fontane's sympathy
and affection lie with tradition, he knows of its historical fragility
and its ethical dubiousness. Is this pure 'and' correct? Should it
not be 'and *therefore* . . .'? The question would be almost senseless
when speaking of Zola or Shaw. For them, what is historically
outlived, is morally objectionable; and insofar as this is so, it is
to the detriment of their artistic rank. This was certainly not so
– or not simply so – in the case of Fontane. Hence his social
criticism is far less vigorous than theirs. Again and again, it is
as if the critic stood still for a while before leaving behind the
old, just as someone departing from an accustomed place might,
however many things he disliked there, turn round with tears in
his eyes as he glimpses it for the last time.

Therefore, with Fontane, it is an extreme victory of the
novelist's art when he who speaks the author's mind (or speaks
what was the author's mind just before he wrote it) is at the same
time denied the reader's sympathies; when the author deflects the
flow of the reader's emotions away from the man the author deems
to be in the right (or did so before the novel took shape). It is
what happened to Tolstoy – in a much more acute distress of

the spirit – when his imagination and affection compelled him to leave to God the judgment that he himself, in his novel, had intended to pass on Anna Karenina's sin. In both cases this rout of moral righteousness at the hands of the affectionate imagination is even in excess of that artistic objectivity – the objectivity of ·Nature herself – as it has been stated with grim brilliance by Schopenhauer: 'Nature', he said, 'does not do as bad writers do when they show a knave or a fool and set about it so full of clumsy purpose that behind every such figure we see the writer himself disavowing their minds and words, and warning us with a raised finger: "This is a knave, this is a fool: do not listen to what he says!"' Fontane, in his engagingly modest ways, goes beyond this. *Do* listen to Instetten's words, he seems to say, but *don't like him.* (Thomas Mann, who in more than one way is much indebted to Fontane, accomplished the same in *The Magic Mountain* with his famous pair of antagonists: Naphta, who is nearly always right and nearly always objectionable, and Settembrini, who, by comparison, is shallow and nearly always likable.)

In the sixteenth chapter of Fontane's *Years of my Childhood*, during that excursion into the future that tells of the son's last visit to his father, there occurs a scene that is not only, like the whole chapter, deeply moving but, in its apparently perfunctory way, allows us a glimpse of the novelist's moral problem. The old man, chatting away, suddenly comes upon 'the thing' that must have caused him continual moral uneasiness: his professional and financial failure, his fatal passion for gambling, his inability to support his family:

'Please, Father, let's not talk about it. Don't you know that it is now all the same to us?'
'Maybe to you, but not to your mother.'
'She has put up with it.'
'Put up with it. You see, my boy, that's her way of accusing me, and of course the old woman is right. That is what I tell myself day after day . . .'
'You take it too much to heart, Father. It's harder for you than for us.'
'Possibly, possibly. And it would be even harder if I didn't also tell myself: It's the circumstances that make the man.'
'I remember your saying this even when we were still children. And it is certainly right.'

'Yes, right it is ... But it doesn't quite put one's mind at ease. A little, but not entirely.'

'A little, but not entirely.' The human world as character and circumstance: this is the universe of the novelist, the definition of his art. At the height of his power it was Fontane's ambition that everything presented in his writing should emerge with that 'naturalness and necessity' that Schopenhauer demanded of great literature. Fontane even went one step further: *one* step; the next might lead into the territory of the amoral. It was his intention that differences between 'big' and 'small' or 'good' and 'bad' were not to be endowed with particular emphasis. What mattered was 'objective reality', 'the circumstances'. Fontane spoke with Stifter's voice when in a letter he confessed that he did not think highly of such differences: he treats with the same affection every particle of 'reality', and says even more: 'If it so happens that I come upon something really great, I don't make many words about it. Greatness speaks for itself. It needs no artistic support to make an effect.' Although this aesthetic mood is appealing, it is nonsensical – as appealing and nonsensical as Stifter's much-quoted assertion (it was polemically aimed at the dramatist Hebbel and his Hegelian themes of historical grandeur) that the eruption of a volcano is not 'greater' than a milk pan boiling over; for both are expressions of the same natural law. There would be no classical literature – no Iliad, no Odyssey, no Oedipus, no Lear and no Faust – if poets had heeded the implied prescription. Rather were they inclined to obey Nietzsche's injunction that of great things they ought to speak greatly (even if one wishes for more moderation when it comes to the Zarathustra tone of Nietzsche himself).

But what Fontane very probably had in mind is that beloved – and utopian – principle of 'equal poetic justice' for *all* things, the principle of realism itself. In this declared – but happily never practised, indeed impracticable – radicalism, Fontane went so far as to question the reputation that a celebrated realist writer of the epoch, Gottfried Keller, enjoyed as a 'stylist'. Of course, he admitted, the Swiss writer did have 'style' in the sense that he was unable to write a line that would not instantly be recognized as his. Yet Fontane meant 'style' in a different sense. For he wanted to believe that the style of a work was true only if it was 'objective', that is, the more the object itself appeared to say what it was without its identity being veiled by peculiarities or idiosyncrasies of the author's manner. If this were so, indeed if this could possibly be achieved by *any* style, Fontane himself would be the arch-sinner. It has even been said – by an admirer of Fontane's – that his last novel, *Der Stechlin* (he was seventy-six when he began to write it), is so riotous in old-age 'sinning', and the 'method', the 'style', the 'Fontane tone' so omnipresent that the contours of individual characters are hopelessly blurred, so that one might easily exchange many roles without affecting the organization – or disorganization – of the work. This is not true. For the characters of the novel are far from indistinguishable; their characteristics are merely subdued for the sake of their harmonization.

The musical allusion is not out of place. The 'instruments' for which *Der Stechlin* has been written are those of a chamber orchestra. No doubt, louder, more 'characteristic' effects can be produced by trombones and kettledrums, but this is not to say that to finer ears the viola d'amore has no distinct personality whose voice could not be distinguished from the sound of the fiddle. One year before his death in 1898, Fontane described the novel to his publisher as 'uneventful': 'In the end an old man dies and two young people marry – this is about all that happens on five hundred pages.' What mattered to him, was the *Mache*, the way the novel is made. Fontane even placed an admiring exclamation mark behind the words: 'die Mache!' Indeed, it is the indefinable quality of its 'manufacture', the love, the verbal music, the very mind and humour of wisdom that transmute the lazy 'circumstances' into a dynamic order that carries within itself a whole ensemble of aesthetic and ethical discriminations. The 'circumstances' that, according to Fontane *père*, were to be blamed for everything – a belief that, as he confessed, would yet not allow the morally troubled soul to feel at ease ('a little, but not entirely') – are wholly freed of their overcrowded 'factual' causality and have ample room for guilt and redemption in the art of the mature artist.

'Der Stechlin' is the name of a little lake in a wooded corner of Fontane's native Mark Brandenburg. It is mysteriously joined to 'the other world' outside, as Fontane puts it in that letter, and in all its smallness reflects the great events from beyond the woods of the province. 'When in Iceland or on Java a mountain spits fire and the earth trembles, the Stechlin bubbles up and forms funnels and whirlpools.' In truth, the lake and the people living by its shore are capable of subtler responses; for put like this, the lake's symbolic role would be too obvious. Fontane's description was meant for the publisher. To the reader the superb book insinuates itself by the most discreet persuasiveness and sympathy. The sympathy is above all for the main character: Dubslav von Stechlin, a Prussian aristocrat. Although the aristocracy in Fontane's novels is by no means immune from his ironically critical and even satirical treatment – the ever more tenuous and often vacuous idea of honour, catastrophically upheld by this declining class, is one of his recurring *motifs* – it is yet true to say that he never ceased to be fond of what he regarded as the aristocratic virtues, the cast of mind elsewhere associated with 'the gentleman'. It certainly reflects upon the unhappy history of modern Germany that the grand swan song by a burgher writer for the Prussian nobility, *Der Stechlin*, is separated by only a few years from the novel of the decline and fall of the German burgherdom, Thomas Mann's *Buddenbrooks*.

'This is about all that happens on five hundred pages.' What Fontane said in 1897 about *Der Stechlin* he could not possibly have said about a novel the very old writer for more than a decade dreamed of writing, and for which he made many notes and studied documents. It was to be called *The Like-dealers* (*Die Like-deeler*) and would have gone far back into history, much, much farther than *Before the Storm*. Indeed, it would have been set in times in which the writer's imaginative engagement was bound to be stronger than his inclination to acquire the historical erudition necessary for depicting them: namely, in the early fifteenth century, among pirates of noble character and revolutionary intentions, not unlike the *Robbers* of the young Schiller, communist distributors of the treasures conquered in audacious feats of seafaring. They were the terror of the Baltic and the North Sea under the leadership of Klaus Störtebeker, and their end was a mass execution in Hamburg. Indeed, this story would have called for a more voluminous instrumentation than *Der Stechlin* and, as a great historical 'phantasmagory', could not have been played by a chamber orchestra of words: the trombones and kettledrums would probably have come into their own. This, at least, is what the plan suggests. But it suggests even more: the ambition of an old man to recapture the emotions of youth as he evoked them in *Years of My Childhood*.

There he describes how, during the boy's time in and near Swinemünde, he would seek out the cave where Störtebeker and his pirates reportedly used to hide, and how the child, lying in its deepest recess, would be overcome by sublime feelings while the leaves of the beech trees outside rustled in the wind and the sea sounded in his ears just as it did in Klaus Störtebeker's all those centuries ago. The sagacity and realistic irony of the aged writer had taken all this away; where there was the fabled bravery of Störtebeker and his men, there was now the prudence of the knowing and detached observer, and the sober magic of the 'Fontane tone' had smoothed the waves. Would he succeed in writing the masterpiece – 'It does not matter whether it will ever be finished', he said – that would be the synthesis of his youthful enthusiasm for Nordic ballads with the measured rhythms of his present narrative style, between 'the old gods', as he wrote, and his mundane scepticism. It was not to be. His last word was not Klaus Störtebeker but Dubslav von Stechlin, an ending hardly to be regretted.

14

The little world of Wilhelm Busch

W ITH the publication in 1865 of *Max und Moritz*, Wilhelm
Busch's career was made, his fame established, and his artistic

Max und Moritz

destiny sealed. He was thirty three years old at the time, had given
up hoping that he would become known to the world as a painter
and resigned himself to earning his livelihood as a verse-maker
and cartoonist. It was an immensely productive resignation, and
what it produced was a variation of genius – genius, it is true,
within the limitations of the genre, but genius none the less; the
power to speak with perfect fluency and felicity in two idioms,
verse and drawing, and to accomplish in both what no linguistic
translator can ever achieve, namely, so close a correspondence
between the two that the memory of the reader and viewer is
prone to run them into one. Remembering, for instance, the following drawing and line from *Abenteuer eines Junggesellen* (A Bachelor's Adventures 1875) he feels sure that, if a picture were able to
make itself heard, it would say exactly what, according to the
caption, Debisch, the indignant father, exclaims in bidding his
naughty son to leave the room, a sentencing followed by the
declaration of Debisch's pedagogical wisdom: corporal punishment touches surfaces only, but the condemnations the mind pronounces penetrate to the depth of the soul.

> Das ist Debisch sein Prinzip:
> Oberflächlich ist der Hieb.
> Nur des Geistes Kraft allein
> Schneidet in die Seele ein.

253

'Pfui, mein Sohn, entferne dich!'

The rhyme of 'Hieb', on 'Prinzip' is as shattering as might have been the beating, forgone for the sake of the lofty principle.

Many of Busch's caricatures and verses seem not to come to a halt at the boundaries of the genre, but cross them with elegant ease and the verve of high irony, making inroads into regions where profundities are domiciled:

> Die Lehre von der Wiederkehr
> Ist zweifelhaften Sinns.
> Es fragt sich sehr, ob man nachher
> Noch sagen kann: Ich bin's.

This comes from his posthumous poems, published in 1909 under the title *Schein und Sein* (Appearance and Reality – the notorious metaphysical contrast of which German has made a graceful rhymed accord, distinguishing the grave opposites by no more than an initial fuller sibilant). The doctrine of resurrection, the lines say, is wide open to doubt; for it is highly questionable whether afterwards one will still be able to say: 'It's me.' The *principium individuationis* and the defeat it suffers at the hands of death has never been put with such epigrammatic and ironical succinctness, with that offhand lightness that mocks, and at the same time wittily states, problems of solemn antiquity, as do also the two lines:

> Denn hinderlich, wie überall,
> Ist hier der eigne Todesfall

– a verse that, in the context of the story, speaks of death as if it did no more than get in the way of one's carrying out plans made only the day before. Busch excels in such rhymed aphorisms that approach the depths in a spirit of seeming frivolity but still preserve the echoes of the deep.

A lifetime, almost half a century, lies between *Schein und Sein* and the early book about the misdeeds of the two little rogues, *Max und Moritz*. Despite its having been surpassed by his later works, it has remained Wilhelm Busch's most popular work. To this day some of its verses come as readily to German minds and tongues as certain proverbial utterances of Friedrich von Schiller and, like Schiller's, they appear to have jumped into literature as fully armed quotations. There is, first and above all, the

immortal Widow Bolte whose darling chickens are being cunningly undone by Max and Moritz: the rascals cause them to get entangled in a wicked arrangement of string and morsels of bread. Swallowing them, the birds choke to death in the branches of an apple tree to which they have risen in panicky flight. When the unfortunate woman discovers them hanging there, she intones a dirge worthy of a great Romantic grief. Thus she bids her eyes profusely to shed tears at this rude awakening from her life's most cherished dream – until the chicken pathos is comically twisted in the last of the four lines where the dream ends, suspended as it was from the apple tree and joined to it by the simplest rhyme:

'Hängt an diesem Apfelbaum!!' And, as life reclaims its rights and Widow Bolte resolves to put the outrageous frustration of her love to some use and fry the chickens, we see her descend into the cellar, not suspecting that Max and Moritz would meanwhile angle the birds from the frying-pan through the chimney. On the contrary, confidently looking forward to her tragic dinner, she fetches from down there her favourite vegetable, sauerkraut, of which she is fondest when it is warmed up once more:

Dass sie von dem Sauerkohle
Eine Portion sich hole,
Wofür sie besonders schwärmt,
Wenn er wieder aufgewärmt. –

Warmed-up pickled cabbage as the inspiration of the arch-Romantic indulgence of the sentiments that the German verb 'schwärmen' conveys, is an early example of Busch's gift of creating satire by means of calculated linguistic incongruities. It is a method that, with increasing virtuosity, is maintained throughout his works.

The enormous success of *Max und Moritz* had international repercussions. True, its many translations – among them, owing to the exertions of witty and scholarly men, practical jokers of higher learning, into Latin and even Old English – cannot possibly be expected to live up to the original, firmly anchored as it is in the German language itself. (A talent equal to the task would emerge, as will be seen, much later.) But the American comic-strip industry owes to Busch's two rogues one of its most profitable inventions which, of course, would not and could not claim artistically to rival the achievements of the German master.

Indeed, it is to be doubted whether without the effect his work had on New World graphic journalism, there would have been an ambitious exhibition such as the American Institute of Graphic Arts arranged in 1942, 'The Comic Strip, its History and Significance', that earnestly traced the genesis of this unearnest entertainment as far back as the year 3000 B.C.: to cave drawings discovered in Spain. But it was very much A.D. when the first William Randolph Hearst came to know *Max und Moritz* and asked the nineteen-year-old Rudolph Dirks to produce something in that vein for his *New York Journal*. This is how, in 1897, the Katzenjammer Kids were born – they were to inhabit the imaginations of American children even beyond the life-span of Hearst's chosen artist.

In the autumn of 1858, during one of his not infrequent bouts of Munich-Schwabing bohemianism and seven years before he was commissioned to produce *Max und Moritz*, Wilhelm Busch, at the age of twenty-six, met Caspar Braun, the publisher of *Fliegende Blätter*, the journal that was for Germany what *Punch* has been for England. It was then that the young painter, rather diffident and weak in purpose, turned caricaturist. For Braun instantly recognized his gifts and invited him to become his contributor. It was the first time that Busch was paid for drawing cartoons and caricatures, an activity that until then he had looked upon as hardly more than a trifling diversion from his serious but as yet unfulfilled vocation. True, he was close to despairing of it at the time and had even toyed with the idea of becoming a bee-keeper in Brazil.

His sporadic spells between 1851 and 1854 as a student of art, first in Düsseldorf, then in Antwerp and finally in Munich, had ended in disillusionment or, in Belgium, in a serious illness. Yet the Netherlands taught him the only enduring lesson in painting, not in the classrooms of the Antwerp Royal Academy, but in churches and galleries. When much later, in 1886, at the pinnacle of his success as the author of comic stories, drawn and versified, he wrote a short autobiographical sketch 'Regarding Myself', he remembered his first encounter with the paintings of Rubens, Brouwer, Teniers and Frans Hals. (He should have added Brueghel, for some of his drawings, though never his paintings, put the viewer in mind of Brueghel's portrayal of mankind as a race of inveterate bumpkins.) Of those painters he said that they won his love and admiration by virtue of their 'divine lightness of touch' and 'the innocence of a clear conscience that need not conceal anything'. He would even forgive them, he added, for what they did to him; their mastery, he believed in retrospect, persuaded him that he would never be able to make a living as a painter. Yet paint he did – without ever displaying what he accomplished. Long after his death there were, of course, exhibitions of the paintings that had survived his destructive discontent. Most of them are too loyal to the example of Frans Hals to be capable of an independent existence, but there are a few, as Paul Klee noted in his diary, that deserve a place in a respectable gallery, particularly some showing men in red jackets. (Klee singles them out as one might the men with red hats, the singular red spots in the paintings of Corot.)

Apropos of red jackets: in 'Regarding Myself', Busch speaks very affectionately of the couple Jan and Mie – 'she fat and he thin' – in whose little Antwerp house he lodged. When he fell ill with typhoid fever, they nursed him back to health and gave him as he departed, 'a warm red jacket and three oranges' for the return journey to the place where he was born in 1832 and where his father was a grocer of modest means: Wiedensahl, a village in what was at the time the Kingdom of Hanover and is now the *Land* Lower Saxony in the Federal Republic of Germany.

To Wiedensahl he returned again and again; and if it was not Wiedensahl, it was other country places, not too far removed, geographically or in character, from his birthplace. As his reputation increased, he made many acquaintances and even close friends among contemporary celebrities: the painters Franz von Lenbach and Friedrich August von Kaulbach, the architect Lorenz Gedon, the playwright Paul Lindau and the Bayreuth conductor Hermann Levi who was, next to his childhood companion, Erich Bachmann, the most intimate friend of his mature years. Levi had the singular distinction of being addressed in letters by the reticent Busch as 'dearest friend', or once, in fun, as 'Mein lieber Spektakelmacher' – 'My dear noise-maker'. Through him he also met Richard Wagner and Cosima. But despite the pleasure such metropolitan company gave him, he spent most of his later bachelor years in the seclusion of the countryside, in the houses of relatives, mostly in parsonages. Even in his very early years, between 1841 and 1844, he lived away from his parents in the parsonage of his maternal uncle Georg Kleine, a knowledgable and intellectually lively man, who undoubtedly was his most important educator. And it was in the parsonage of a nephew in Mechtshausen, near the Harz mountains, that he died in January 1908.

There was a time – the time of Wilhelm Busch – when Protestant parsonages had a big share in the making of German cultural history, although this was hardly ever a matter of the sons' continuing traditional pieties. More often than not it was, on the contrary, their loss of faith that released vital energies of the mind. Nietzsche is, of course, the most conspicuous apostate among them. Wilhelm Busch, who was to all intents and purposes the son of Pastor Kleine, emerged with a more conventional freedom from faith, a lighter burden of unbelief. Had it not been for his genius, he might well have been a typical patriot of the Bismarck era. He was, for instance, quite capable of gloating, in a tasteless series of drawings, over the miseries Paris suffered after the military débâcle of France in 1871, and displayed all the sentiments required of a partisan in Bismarck's *Kulturkampf* against the Catholic Church, that belated Prussian Counter-Counter-Reformation and feeble, much belated epilogue to the Thirty Years War. Echoes of its raucous anticlerical battle-cries reverberate through Busch's *St. Antony in Padua* (1870), unhappily disturb one's amused contemplation of much that is exquisite and exquisitely funny in *Die fromme Helene* (Pious Helen – 1872), as is, for instance, Uncle Nolte's philistine triumph, at the end, over those who became victims of their own wickedness. The good, he is convinced, is merely the evil that one is lucky enough to miss; and so he contentedly rubs his hands, immensely pleased because, thank goodness, he is not like those – not, that is, like the hell-bound evildoers.

As can be seen, the poet–draughtsman's genius remained fundamentally unaffected by the partisan's mean opinions, and pious Helen's Uncle Nolte emerges as the perfect caricature of the German petit bourgeois, the *Kleinbürger*, most probably, like his author himself, a warrior in the *Kulturkampf*. None the less, there were occasions when Herr Busch, obedient citizen of Bismarck's

new Reich, forced his genius into the service of his political senti-ments. Thus he yielded to the urging of his business-minded publisher Bassermann to exploit the blasphemy stir and censor-ship scandal caused by *Fromme Helene*, and followed it up with something even more blatantly – and certainly more cheaply – anti-Catholic. The outcome was Busch's crudest and unfunniest work, *Pater Filuzius*.

In his later and mellower years he regretted such excesses and disliked to be reminded of them. When his first biographer, one Eduard Daelen, who lacked the talent for his enterprise and any tact in his devotion, dwelt emphatically on Busch's 'anti-ultramon-tanism', he rebuked him in a letter from Wiedensahl (July 1886) for his 'aggressive and impassioned tone of voice' that, although he himself was no friend of 'the Romans', jars on his temperate character. Or he wrote (in September of the same year) to Franz von Lenbach: 'It seems impossible to make people understand that I have done all my things from a reckless desire to please myself – except a few "hunger products" and the tendentious trifle *Filuzius*.' Yet he never tried to apologize for the – sometimes exceedingly – intemperate exercise of anti-Semitism in the earlier works. Although there is no trace of it in his later masterpiece, *Balduin Bählamm* (1883), the 'epic' of an aspiring poet's frustrations and the funniest version of the celebrated conflict between Art and Life, or *Maler Klecksel* (1884), the 'education' of a painter, it recurs in *Eduard's Traum* (Edward's Dream – 1891), a work by which its author set great store, perhaps just because it differs so much from his other productions: it is in prose and un-accompanied by pictures. It certainly does not lack interest, and this not only because its opening sentence seems to mock, in anticipation, Freud's interpretative earnestness while at the same time it accepts the notion of sleep's disarming the *Superego* (or what afterwards was to acquire this name): 'Some people are unfortunately fond of telling their dreams although these are hardly more than dubious entertainments the mind arranges in its servants' quarters after the master of the house has gone to bed . . .'

Thus it also employs at the outset the rather advanced literary device of that radical irony which pretends to bring into question the worth of the whole story. In this case it is not so much a story as it is a sequence of dream fragments and above all the occasion for ironical or sarcastic demonstrations of the impurity of human motives, the deceptions of love and the wickedness of man's purposes. And having just deplored the readiness of people to communicate what they dream, the author makes Edward, the dreamer himself, tell his dream – despite his being 'otherwise quite a good fellow'. Well, the good fellow is sometimes also anti-Semitic in a conventionally silly manner, even though that passage of the dream is immediately followed by a much longer account of the disreputable transactions taking place in the house of a professed anti-Semite.

Of course, it is impossible today to speak of anti-Semitism without at once being assailed by the paralysing thought of Auschwitz; and indeed Auschwitz might never have been, had the unspeakable outrage not been preceded by the speakable and, alas, spoken attitudes of mind shared by Wilhelm Busch and countless other Germans, eminent and ordinary, not to forget such emancipated German Jews as, among others, Heine, Marx, Otto Weiniger, and Karl Kraus. Yet it would be a great mistake to bring 'in principle' their anti-Semitism or that of Wilhelm Busch (or of his favourite philosopher, 'the great and grim' Schopenhauer whose pessimism has invaded, in comic metamorphosis, many of Busch's misanthropic verses) into too close a connection with the mindless and yet systematic malefactions of the later mass executioners. For this link is more tenuous and problematical than necessarily appears to a generation intensely mindful of the holocaust. But there has been a great deal of anti-Semitism, 'theoretical' and practical, in other Western nations, without the abysmal German consequences ('Nietzsche and the Ideology of Fascism' raises similar questions – and he was the very opposite of a consistent anti-Semite). The anti-Semitism of a man who, like Wilhelm Busch, educated himself by reading Homer, the Bible, the *Confessions* of St Augustine, Shakespeare and Dickens (did he feel confirmed in his anti-Semitism by the last two?) cannot possibly be like Julius Streicher's, even if a few of his caricatured Jews might have found a place in *Der Stürmer*.

One whose suspicions of mankind expresses itself in verses like

> Wie schad, o Mensch, dass dir das Gute
> Im Grunde so zuwider ist –

(What a pity that the good is at bottom so contrary to human nature), or who answers a journal's question about his preferred occupation by saying: 'To let the mind travel to those boundaries where the incomprehensible begins'; or who ironically knows how 'refreshing and edifying it is to observe the grievances and follies of other people' and 'to laugh even about oneself' because this affords the special pleasure of believing 'that one is cleverer than oneself'; or who, having watched with horror country children present at the slaughtering of a pig, writes in a letter: 'Death, cruelty, lust – they are all one in the expression of their faces'; or who accounts for the attraction the art of drawing has for him with the temporary absolution it grants him from the sins and oppressions of the world, projected as these are into the disembodied contours of creatures 'who, particularly if they are not beautiful, can be made to put up with a lot before it begins to hurt their maker' – such a sage and artist cannot simply be a precursor of the apocalyptic thugs with unlimited executive power.

Wilhelm Busch once said of himself that he was a rationalist and freethinker during the day, but saw ghosts at night. The Jews of his anti-Semitism, just as those of many intellectual anti-Semites before Hitler, were more like Busch's nocturnal spectres than presences in the light of day. In the light of day they were the playwright Paul Lindau or, above all, the 'dear Spektakelmacher' Hermann Levi. Indeed, a revealing analysis of this kind of anti-Semitism could be made on the basis of the friendship of the two and their exchanges of letters, many of which refer in a jocular or not-so-jocular vein to the 'Jewish problem'; on Levi's being a chosen conductor of the anti-Semitic Richard and Cosima

Wagner; on the passages about Hermann Levi in the correspondence between Cosima and H. S. Chamberlain; and, *mutatis mutandis*, on Levi's once asking Busch in a letter written after they had together visited an old abbey: 'Why, in that crypt, did you not throw me into its baptismal font and thus liberate me?'

Of course, such an analysis would not solve the problem rendered insoluble by its endlessly twisted and intertwined roots in religion, irrational anxieties, racial antipathies, economic history, tribal customs, commercial competitiveness and casts of mind; but it would help in the teaching of differences (to quote *King Lear* – I, iv l. 86 and Wittgenstein) – the perception of differences as the only intellectual defence against the 'terrible simplificateurs'. No doubt, every form of collective 'anti' is a wicked, if often irrepressible, habit of the mind; but, as is the case with every other disposition of the intellectual character, there are degrees of wickedness, and even the transition from one degree to the next, let alone the last, is a more complex matter than the simplifiers can see. If this were not so, Doomsday would be upon us every other week.

Balduin Bählamm, untroubled by such problematical intrusions, is Busch's grand petit-bourgeois odyssey of the 'thwarted poet'. Here the unity of verse and drawing is as perfect as the discord that is its theme: the persistent clash between the 'higher striving' of the human spirit and the meanness and petty frustrations he unavoidably encounters in the world he bodily inhabits; and as the spirit and the world of Balduin are as unheroic as can be, the traditionally tragic opposition turns to comedy or superior farce. The tone is set by the dishevelled little sprite of the title-page: his wings are rudely tied together at which he is shedding an incongruously big tear:

In the age of prose

The hilarious overture follows: the juxtapositions of the beatitude
of the inspired poet and the dingy miseries of every day:

> Wie wohl ist dem, der dann und wann
> Sich etwas Schönes dichten kann!
>
> Der Mensch, durchtrieben und gescheit,
> Bemerkte schon seit alter Zeit,
> Dass ihm hienieden allerlei
> Verdriesslich und zuwider sei.
> Die Freude flieht auf allen Wegen;
> Der Ärger kommt uns gern entgegen.
> Gar mancher schleicht betrübt umher;
> Sein Knopfloch ist so öd und leer.
> Für manchen hat ein Mädchen Reiz,
> Nur bleibt die Liebe seinerseits.
> Doch gibt's noch mehr Verdriesslichkeiten.
> Zum Beispiel lässt sich nicht bestreiten:
> Die Sorge, wie man Nahrung findet,
> Is häufig nicht so unbegründet.
> Kommt einer dann und fragt: 'Wie geht's?'
> Steht man gewöhnlich oder stets
> Geweissermassen peinlich da,
> Indem man spricht: 'Nun, so lala!'
> Und nur der Heuchler lacht vergnüglich
> Und gibt zur Antwort: 'Ei, vorzüglich!'
> Im Durchschnitt ist man kummervoll
> Und weiss nicht, was man machen soll –
> Nicht so der Dichter . . .

> I envy people who can pen
> A pretty poem now and then.
>
> Congenitally shrewd and clever,
> man recognizes, now as ever,
> That much contrariness and woe
> Besets him daily here below.
> Joy is capricious and elusive.
> Annoyance blatant and obtrusive.
> One goes about all glum and dank,
> His buttonhole so void and blank;
> Another feels that life is blighted
> Because his love is unrequited.
> Perplexities dog every stride;
> And one that cannot be denied,
> The worry how to make ends meet,

Keeps us forever on our feet.
A hearty 'How are you' will quickly
Make most of us feel somewhat sickly;
We manage but a feeble glow
And mumble 'Oh, so-so, you know . . .'
Avoid the lying hypocrite
Who yodels 'Splendid! Very fit!'
For by and large, we spend our days
In vague discomfort and malaise.
Not so the bard . . .*

'Not so the bard' – his way of transcending the 'discomfort and malaise' of life is now, in a splendidly sustained metaphor, likened to the labour expended by the farmer's wife in making butter from the 'fatty element'. 'Worried' by her forceful treatment,

It squelches, squooshes, gulps and goops,
leaps up and down in tortured loops,
Until the substance, tickled sick,
Disintegrates in thin and thick.
When finally the great moment comes, she lifts
With tender fingers from the mould
The cake of butter, plump and gold.

This is a successful paraphrase of the incomparable and untranslatable two German lines, rhymed by means of a dialect form, phonetically rendered:

Und sieh, in frohen Händen hält se
Die wohlgeratne Butterwälze

– whereupon follows the explosive 'Just so the poet'. He too labours with the force and devotion of the farmer's wife and, having 'squeezed and sweated something out', he then

. . . eyes with pleasure and respect
The product of his intellect.

* The translation comes, as do all the following, from Walter W. Arndt's very successful rendering of *Balduin Bählamm* – renamed 'Clement Dove, the Poet Thwarted' – in his *The Genius of Wilhelm Busch*, University of California Press, 1982. This anthology contains also Arndt's English translations of most other works quoted in this essay, which was written before the publication of *The Genius of Wilhelm Busch*. Arndt's rendering of *Balduin Bählamm* was, through the kindness of the translator, available to this author because it had previously appeared in a bilingual edition, long out of print: Sigbert Mohn Verlag, Gütersloh 1967.

Balduin – the name is irresistibly comic and suggestive of ineffectual gentleness, as is Bählamm, 'lamm' meaning 'lamb' and 'bah' being the vocal utterance of the animal, Balduin Bählamm (or Clement Dove, as Arndt has ingeniously christened him in English) is never to reach that happy consummation although he knows what he wants:

Ein guter Mensch, der Bählamm hiess
Und Schreiber war, durchschaute dies.
Nicht, dass es ihm an Nahrung fehlt.
Er hat ein Amt, er ist vermählt.
Und nicht bloss dieses ist und hat er;
Er ist bereits auch viermal Vater.
Und dennoch zwingt ihn tiefes Sehnen,
Sein Glück noch weiter auszudehnen.
Er möchte dichten, möchte singen,
Er möchte was zuwege bringen
Zur Freude sich und jedermannes;
Er fühlt, er muss, und also kann es.

A gentle clerk named Clement Dove
Was well aware of the above.
Not that he feels deprived or harried.
He has a job, and he is married.
Four healthy children, too, all told,
Are his to cherish and to hold.
And yet he feels, for all his bliss,
That deep down something is amiss.
He yearns to write, to speak with tongues,
He wants to blossom forth in songs
That strike a chord in every man.
He feels he must, and therefore can.

Whether, having left his office, his wife and his obstreperous

children to seek the peace of the countryside, he is distracted from his poetic intent by the charms of a village maid leading a goat; or whether he seeks relief from the painful consequences of his little escapade – a toothache induced by the cold water of the pond into which he is thrown, à la Falstaff, by an alliance of goat, girl and boyfriend (Busch is the Homer of the unmitigated calamity toothaches were before aspirin and modern dentistry); both the drawings and the text that in unison create and narrate these scenes, possess the wit and assured mastery that prove the artist's initiation into the folly, pretence and vanity of human ambitions. The old theme is not merely stated in words and pictures; at least in his most successful works it has shaped the rhythm of his verse, the shocking naturalness of his rhymes and every curvature of his drawings. These show, for instance, the aspiring poet, who has finally returned with empty sheets of paper, dreaming of his heavenward flight, obstructed by the hostile goat from above, and from down below by the anxious family that

Frau Bählamm ruft als er erwacht:
'Heraus, mein Schatz! Es ist schon acht!'

His lady's voice at ten past eight:
'Wake up my pet! It's getting late!'

sends him back to the world of their mundane needs and his mundane office.

In his early years, Wilhelm Busch read Kant. As he remembers in *Myself about Myself*, written when he was sixty-two, he had a rather difficult time with the *Critique of Pure Reason*. But it left him, he writes, with a passion for exploring the secret recesses of the mind 'where there are so many hiding places'. It is this passion that his art communicates, and his disciplined rummaging in hidden attics that endows his work with a quality not to be acquired in the more readily accessible parts of the house.